WITHDRAWN

Antitrust and Regulation

Antitrust and Regulation

Edited by

Ronald E. Grieson
University of California
at Santa Cruz

Lexington Books
D.C. Heath and Company/Lexington, Massachusetts/Toronto

Library of Congress Cataloging-in-Publication Data
Main entry under title:

Antitrust and regulation.

   Based on papers presented at a conference held at the
University of California, Santa Cruz, in Oct. 1984.
   Includes bibliographies and index.
   1.   Antitrust law—Economic aspects—United States—
Congresses.   2.   Competition, Unfair—United States—
Congresses.   3.   Industry and state—United States—
Congresses.   I.   Grieson, Ronald E.
HD2783.A58   1986   338.8'0973   85-13115
ISBN 0-669-09301-7 (alk. paper)

Published simultaneously in Canada
Printed in the United States of America
Casebound International Standard Book Number: 0-669-09301-7
Library of Congress Catalog Card Number: 85-13115

The paper used in this publication meets the minimum requirements of
American National Standard for Information Sciences—Permanence of
Paper for Printed Library Materials, ANSI Z39.48-1984.

The last numbers on the right below indicate the number and date of printing.

10 9 8 7 6 5 4 3 2 1

95 94 93 92 91 90 89 88 87 86

Contents

Figures and Tables

Tables

Acknowledgments

Much of this book resulted from the conference on Antitrust and Regulation held at the University of California, Santa Cruz, in October, 1984. The conference was funded by the Seminar in Applied Economics/Public Finance of the University of California, Santa Cruz. I thank my colleagues for their participation, Janice Robinson for her editorial help, and Chancellor Robert L. Sinsheimer for his support of the seminar.

Ronald E. Grieson

Introduction

Ronald E. Grieson

The highly important issues of regulation and antitrust have recently come to the fore in economics. New research, both theoretical and applied, has brought into question the benefits and costs of many of the methods or goals: Are regulatory or antitrust actions (antitrust itself can be thought of as another form of regulation) efficient with regard to the economy as a whole? And do these actions maximize or increase consumer benefits even at the greater expense of producers? Or do they merely benefit one group of producers or consumers at the expense of others and therefore society as a whole? These modern views have become rather widespread and extend to many policymakers and the courts, who have been increasingly inclined to question many of the traditional goals or means of regulation and antitrust.

Though the vast majority of chapters in the volume are devoted to analyses of specific areas, issues and cases, it should be pointed out that based upon this type of modern critical analyses, some economists, including some whose works are in this volume, have come to tentative general conclusions with regard to regulation and antitrust. Almost all economists working in the area would support the recent deregulations in transportation and energy, and almost the same number would support the deregulations in financial services, telecommunications, etc. There exists, however, wider diversity of views with respect to antitrust. Some would reject almost all economic regulation, antitrust or otherwise. Some take the interest group theory of regulation (extended in this volume to include antitrust) that says that in a political/bureaucratic framework, regulation and antitrust are going to become methods of inefficient and perhaps ineffective redistribution of income or property rights to a particular group. Another view holds that the simplified means of antitrust become goals in themselves that do more damage than good, implicitly, that antitrust cannot be refined given the complexities of the world and sophisticated economic analysis needed to apply antitrust to increase efficiency. Such views are generally pessimistic and would tend to the conclusion that economic regulation or antitrust might best be abandoned.

Of course, many would support the redistribution accomplished by regulation and antitrust even at the sacrifice of some economic inefficiency. This support would be more general if the policies successfully redistribute to consumers and foster competition even if the harm to producers is greater and therefore the policy is socially inefficient. Conversely, this support would decrease if the protection or redistribution were to individual inefficient competitors or firms and thus anticompetitive, or if it were largely ineffective.

Many also take the view that economic research and the proliferation and acceptance of economic knowledge and methods by regulators, the Justice Department, agencies, bureaucrats, government officials, lawyers and the courts can make antitrust policy and the areas where regulation is appropriate both more efficient and cost-effective. Those who take this view are also critical of much in antitrust and the remaining economic regulation. The goals of these individuals would be regulation at Ramsey-type efficient price discrimination to cover fixed costs where regulation is justified by truly pervasive economies of scale or natural monopoly or Pigouvian, marginal social cost, pricing if possible. In antitrust, this view would favor an antitrust policy that took full cognizance of the increased cost entailed in increasing the number of competitors where economies of scale (or indivisibilities) are present and the economic complexities of any particular situation. These complexities would include market failure and externalities and the attempts of firms to handle them in addition to the effects of international competition and competitors. The old simple rules and ratios that had no *a priori* theoretical support but were only supported by partial correlations, are almost universally criticized by economists. While almost all economists would support the above type of regulatory and antitrust policies, even those who are most supportive of the institutions would acknowledge a very flawed record to date. Thus the terms "the antitrust paradox" or "the antitrust dilemma" have been coined.

There has been a growing academic and judicial consensus on the need to examine many aspects of regulation of antitrust. In fact, the Supreme Court has liberalized or altered its holdings on a broad spectrum of antitrust issues. The federal courts have begun to look for results that increase overall economic efficiency or at least serve consumer interests. There is similarly less tolerance of protecting small or inefficient producers at the expense of large or efficient producers or consumers in general. In like fashion, outright bans are being replaced by a growing application of the rule of reason and an interest in enhancing the ability of firms to compete more effectively.

Two chapters in this volume are studies of the issue of regulation and/or antitrust as broad categories. Nonetheless, they and all of the other chapters are studies of important theoretical and/or measurement issues in actual or generic cases. Given that the works in this volume are original (frontier) research, areas such as airline and truck regulation that have been considered settled by economists for quite a while are not taken up. The important and controversial issues of financial (regarding mortgages, etc.) and telecommunications (specifically A.T.&T. breakup, etc.) deregulation are not yet settled and are therefore dealt with, as are the possible benefits of a recent Federal Trade Commission mandatory disclosure rule for used cars. Among the issues examined here are: the potential benefits and losses involved in the real world use of antitrust versus its alternatives; the interest group theory of antitrust and the effects of bureaucracies; verticle manufacturer–distributor restraints in general, especially resale price maintenance; competition and collusion in the corrugated container industry and the recent antitrust suites; voter participation and choice in government limiting referenda; world competition and its effects on mergers; the effects of capital adjustment costs (during growth and contraction) on monopoly power and regulated firms; the "contestability" or ultra free entry theory and its applications; and the effects of input monopolies and the verticle integration of them to final product markets. The detailed specific analyses are of significant interest not only in themselves but in appraising the broader questions.

1

Antitrust and Its Alternatives: A Compleat Guide to the Welfare Tradeoffs

Donald Dewey

> To see what is in front of one's nose needs a constant struggle.
> —attributed to George Orwell

An Uncertain Foundation

Most economists believe that the tools of price theory can be used to throw light on the welfare effects of antitrust rules that restrict freedom of contract. We could hardly believe otherwise and retain our self-respect. However, most economists also seem to believe that, when these tools are properly employed, it will be found that at least some antitrust rules serve to increase economic welfare. This conviction survives despite the fact that over the last thirty-five years many of the arguments long used to justify antitrust rules have been discredited and no new ones have been advanced.[1] True, many of the economists and lawyers who most closely follow antitrust in action now view it with a mixture of exasperation, regret, and even outright contempt. But for almost every critic a spark of hope remains. According to an argument much favored by economists, what is needed is the correct understanding and use of price theory—especially by federal judges. For their part, lawyers have proved to be surprisingly receptive to this argument, probably because they have concluded that in the strange and often unpredictable world of antitrust they need all the help they can get.

Possibly a psychiatrist well versed in economics and American history could offer some interesting insights into the need of American economists to

For their generous (and often exacting) attention to earlier drafts of this paper I would like to thank my colleagues Bruce Bassett, Nicholas Economides, and William Vickrey.

believe at least in the possibility of doing good through antitrust. They might, for example, be able to throw some light on why we jeopardize our professional standing with colleagues by appearing to speak approvingly of either big business or big government. Still, it is not necessary to call in psychiatry to make a *prima facie* case that the faith in the economic possibilities of antitrust may have no very firm foundation. We can readily cite reasons for doubting that it is possible to devise a set of antitrust rules that creates more economic welfare than it destroys—even under the most favorable circumstances that can reasonably be imagined.

One reason has already been mentioned. In recent years economists have had far more success in using price theory to discredit antitrust rules than to justify them. Four others deserve mention here.

First, we have ancient ancestral warnings against trying to do good by imposing restrictions on freedom of contract. Adam Smith contemptuously likened the eighteenth-century forerunner of antitrust—laws against forestalling, engrossing, and, regrating—to laws against witchcraft.[2] And in the 1980s most American economists received the new Sherman Act with hostility or indifference.[3] Considering the enormous volume of writing on antitrust, it is surprising that no study has yet traced the steps by which American economists came to accept the policy and assist in its elevation to the status of sacred cow in American law and politics. My own suspicion is that this conversion was due more to the conclusion that antitrust was here to stay than to any enlightenment traceable to theoretical or empirical work.

Second, there is an unmistakable void in the very considerable literature on "welfare economics" that should give us pause. The possibilities of using taxes, subsidies, and marginal cost pricing to increase economic welfare are debated at great length in this literature. The possibility of using antitrust rules to advance this good cause is scarcely ever mentioned.[4]

Third, at least until recently, faith in the economic possibilities of antitrust has been a particularly American phenomenon. Thus, the English observer A.D. Neale, after his careful look at American antitrust, concluded that, while the policy was undoubtedly a political success in this country, it imposed economic costs that the British economy could not afford.[5] The disdain of Joseph Shumpeter for the policy—his long residence in this country not withstanding—is well known.[6]

Finally, we have the uncomfortable truth that the "naive" case for antitrust is too shoddy to be taken seriously. This is the case that explicitly or implicitly (1) equates a high concentration ratio and/or collusion in an industry with "monopoly power"; (2) assumes that measures that increase the number of viable firms and/or reduce collusion make an industry "more competitive"; and (3) assumes that an increase in competition must lead to an increase in economic welfare.

Look closely at this argument. Point (1) assumes a tie between industrial concentration and/or collusion that is a matter for empirical study. Point (2) assumes the truth of point (1) and, on this assumption, becomes a tautology. Point (3) again assumes that which must be proved. While economic welfare may be difficult to measure, in economic analysis the meaning of the term is unambiguous. So also is the test by which the impact of an antitrust rule on economic welfare is to be evaluated. There is no increase in economic welfare unless, as a result of the rule's use, people who gain would in principle be able fully to compensate those who lose and still be better off themselves.[7] The whole point of the exercise that follows is to try to assess the impact on economic welfare of several alternative ways of organizing the economy—one of which is antitrust.

Clearly there is no self-evident reason for presuming that whatever increases competition (however defined) must also increase economic welfare. Has not virtually every basic theory book published in the last forty years contained the diagrams taken from Joan Robinson[8] and Edward Chamberlin[9] that show how free entry in an imperfectly competitive market leads to the "wastes of excess capacity"? The Chicagoans have often complained that textbook treatments of imperfect competition are highly misleading. This is true enough. But the textbooks mislead not because they contain gross errors of logic, but because they fail to make clear what must be assumed before imperfect competition necessarily leads to excess capacity.[10]

In this chapter we shall take up the challenge implicit in much of the popular and professional literature on antitrust: to identify the conditions that must be met before antitrust is, on welfare grounds, preferable to its alternatives.[11] To respond to this challenge it is not necessary to believe that the maximization of economic welfare is the only proper goal of antitrust or that price theory is the only acceptable organon for estimating the welfare impact of antitrust rules. One need only believe that no antitrust rule should be allowed to escape the scrutiny of price theory (and the compensation test).

Four Policy Alternatives

Let us begin with fundamentals. Antitrust is good or bad only in relation to something else. The leading alternatives in their purest form—as Max Weber's ideal types[12]—are three: (1) regulated monopoly with marginal cost pricing (henceforth called regulation) that may require a subsidy; (2) laissez-faire leading to multiplant firms or cartels that practice limit pricing (henceforth called laissez-faire); and (3) totally unregulated monopoly completely protected by law or nature (henceforth called monopoly).

We shall take "ideal" antitrust (ideal only in the Weberian sense) to be a policy that has two main goals. First, it seeks the maximum number of viable firms in an industry that can be achieved without imposing a limit to internal growth of firms. This it does by banning mergers among viable firms in the industry[13] and outlawing predatory and exclusionary pricing. Second, ideal antitrust seeks to suppress collusion. In short, our "ideal" antitrust has goals virtually identical to those that the late Justice Douglas endeavored to embed in the law in his many antitrust opinions.

Some friends of antitrust would prefer to say that these two goals are not ends in themselves but merely the means by which economic welfare can be increased. I will not stop to quarrel with the value judgment that economic welfare ought to be the main concern of antitrust. No doubt many federal judges and most Federal Trade Commissioners believe that, in some rough and ready way, they promote this larger end by preserving viable firms and suppressing collusion. These considerations do not alter the fact that, in the routine administration of antitrust, the preservation of viable firms and the suppression of collusion are treated as ends in themselves—or, at any rate, as ends mandated by the policy that are now almost beyond question. Price-fixing agreements have long been illegal per se. Since *Brown Shoe* (1963),[14] mergers that are thought to reduce the number of "healthy" competitors might as well be. Admittedly, the Reagan administration has been somewhat softer on mergers than its predecessors; it remains to be seen whether this policy revision will be accepted by Congress or retained by future administrations.

In this exercise we are not concerned with what the goals of antitrust ought to be, nor will we try to discover what Congress "really" hoped to accomplish by the Sherman Act in 1890. Rather, relying on the venerable maxim that men must be presumed to intend the consequences of their acts, we infer the major goals of antitrust from its most obvious consequences.

Each of the above four organizational alternatives is, of course, dependent upon the observance of legal rules that have enforcement costs. In the first instance, however, we shall examine the comparative welfare merits of antitrust and its rivals on the premise that these costs are null.

A Method for Comparing Welfare Tradeoffs

The conventional models of monopoly, marginal cost pricing (with subsidies to decreasing-cost industries if necessary) and limit pricing, are well known and require no detailed description here.[15] But we need a model of "competition." When the number of firms that antitrust can sustain in the market is relatively small, the model of perfect competition is obviously inappropriate. The model of competition that we shall use to discern the impact on welfare of the market structure that antitrust presumably seeks to create is "Cournot with cost curves."[16]

This model is admirably suited to our purposes. It is totally free of collusion to restrict output and of pricing to intimidate rivals. Each firm, in selecting its rate of output, takes the outputs of all other firms in the industry as given. Some economists distrust the results of any analysis based upon the Cournot model because it assumes that each firm knows the industry demand function, and the outputs of all rival firms, but never learns from experience that any change in its own output will cause other firms to change their outputs.[17] While this criticism says the true and virtually obvious, it does not tell against the use of the Cournot model as a proxy, especially as its properties have been elaborated by William Vickrey.

Some years ago, in investigating the behavior of the firm under conditions of uncertainty, Vickrey obtained a quite remarkable result.[18] He considered the case in which sellers in an imperfectly competitive market begin production in near total ignorance. They do not know the demand for the product, nor do they even know of one another's existence. A seller's only means of gaining information is by varying output during some time period, tabulating the results, and constructing a statistical demand function. Vickrey assumed that a seller would use the derived demand function for a time and then vary output again to construct a new one. No information would be exchanged among sellers. It was Vickrey's achievement to show that, on these assumptions, the industry will converge to the same price and output as in a static Cournot equilibrium containing the same number of sellers. In view of this extension of the Cournot model to noncollusive pricing under conditions of uncertainty, it would be almost gratuitous to ask for a better proxy for the "competition" sought by real-world antitrust.

Models of imperfect competition may be indispensible in any analysis of the welfare effects of antitrust and its alternatives. Unhappily, such models are not easy to describe mathematically since the demand function of each firm changes every time another firm enters or leaves the industry. The Cournot model is no exception. To make the problem tractable, we shall resort to the diplomat's technique of best-case and worst-case analysis and to elementary probability theory. That is, we shall first estimate the maximum and minimum impacts on economic welfare of shifting to antitrust from "something else." We shall then assign a probability distribution to the possible welfare outcomes that lie within these upper and lower bounds. We do so with the aid of three additional assumptions.

Assumption 1. All firms in the industry have identical cost functions and hence are replicates of one another; any proposition about one firm applies to all firms.

Assumption 2. The industry's demand function is linear and can be written as $p = a - bx$ ($a > b > 0$) where p denotes price and x output.

Later on we shall consider the consequences of relaxing this assumption of linearity. For the present it will suffice to note that the principal requirement of a demand curve is that it describe a total revenue function that has a maximum. A linear demand curve satisfies this test. Since there is no obvious reason for prefering nonlinearity to linearity, we shall use the latter and so avoid the often excruciating algebraic complexities associated with operations involving nonlinear demand curves.

Assumption 3. At every output in the firm, marginal cost is either zero or infinity.

This last assumption—possibly rather strange on first meeting—immensely simplifies our analysis in two ways. (Indeed without it, a comparison of the economic consequences of antitrust with those of its alternatives would be impossible.)

First, assumption 3 means that we need concern ourselves with only two possible unit cost curves. The first is the rectangular hyperbola ZZ' in figure 1–1. With the aid of ZZ' in figure 1–1, we shall be able to measure the welfare impact of antitrust in the worst case, that is, under the most unfavorable conditions. The second unit cost curve is the fishhook curve in ZZ' in figure 1–2. This curve will allow us to measure the welfare impact of antitrust in the best case.[19]

Let us be clear that the unit cost curves ZZ' of figures 1–1 and 1–2 are "limit cases." Their usefulness in our analysis is not affected by the probability, amounting to a virtual certainty, that they are nowhere exactly reproduced in the real world. For our purposes it is enough that they establish the limits within which any real-world curve of unit cost must fall.

Used in conjunction with an industry demand curve that is linear, the assumption that at every output marginal cost in the firm is either zero or infinity makes possible the second essential simplification in our analysis. It allows us to identify the equilibrium demand function for the individual firm when the industry operates under antitrust.

The firm will not produce an output at which marginal cost is infinite; therefore, in n-firm equilibrium, each firm produces an output at which marginal cost is zero. And it is a property of the linear Cournot model that, when marginal cost is zero, each firm in n-firm equilibrium believes its demand function to be of the form $p = [2a/(n + 1)] - bx$.[20] For our purposes, an n-firm equilibrium exists when (1) with n firms, price is not less than unit cost, and (2) with $n + 1$ firms, price would be less than unit cost. Once we know the demand function for a firm in n-firm equilibrium under antitrust, we can make the computations necessary for a comparison of economic welfare merits of antitrust and its alternatives. For example, if under antitrust, each firm always produces where marginal cost is zero and its demand function is of the form $p = [2a/(n + 1] - bx$, then whatever the value taken by n, in n-firm equilibrium, price is always equal to $a/(n + 1)$.

Figure 1–1 depicts a set of equilibrium demand functions for various equilibrium n's on the assumption that marginal cost is zero. Thus AA' is the demand curve for each firm when $n = 1$. BB' is the equilibrium demand curve for each firm when $n = 2$, and so forth. A most convenient feature of

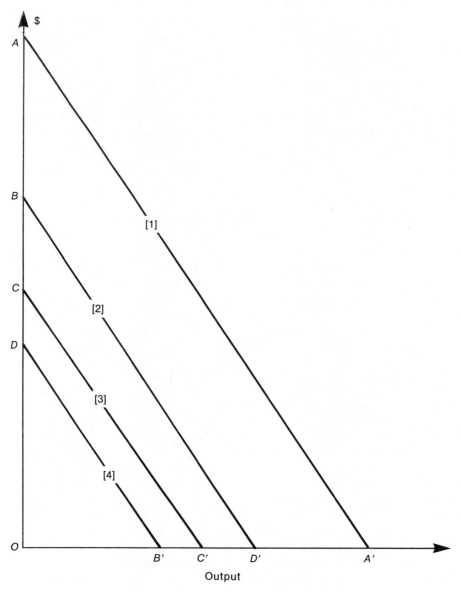

Figure 1–1. Demand Functions for Various N-Firm Equilibria

the Cournot model with a linear demand curve is, of course, that while the demand curve will change for each firm as *n* changes, the slope of the firm's demand curve does not change.

Antitrust in the Worst Case

The worst-case view of antitrust when the number of firms is four is given by figure 1–2. (Resort to geometry requires us to assign a numerical value to *n*, and *n* = 4 is as good as any.) *EG* (and *EG'*) is the industry demand curve. *BI* is its own demand curve as perceived by each of the four firms. The unit cost curve of each firm is *ZZ'*. Why does figure 1–2 depict the worst case of 4-firm equilibrium under antitrust? Simply because it shows the maximum amount of excess capacity waste that is consistent with 4-firm equilibrium.

A firm does not produce on the inelastic segment of its demand curve. Thus, in figure 1–2, *OJ* is greatest possible output per firm in 4-firm equilib-

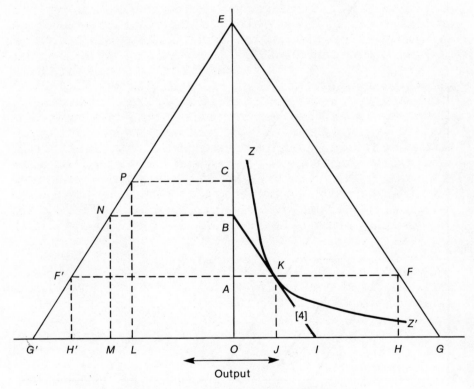

Figure 1–2. Antitrust: Worst Case

rium. The rectangular hyperbola ZZ' is the limit case of so-called "natural monopoly." Three of the four firms are redundant, and excess capacity waste is given by $JHFK$ in figure 1–2. If the production of industry output OH were any more wasteful, at least one firm would leave the industry.

And the welfare gain of antitrust in the worst case? If antitrust is here substituted for monopoly, price falls from OC to OA in figure 1–2; and industry output increases from OL to OH'. The additional output (which is LH') adds to economic welfare the area $H'F'PL$ in figure 1–2. However, the cost of this additional output is $JKFH;$ the reason is that the shift to antitrust has caused the entry of three more firms, each with the unit cost curve ZZ'. Thus, in the worst case, the *net* gain in economic welfare resulting from the substitution of antitrust for monopoly is the area $H'F'PL$ minus the area JKFH in figure 1–2. Close inspection of figure 1–2 will show what will be given a mathematical proof later: that the latter area exceeds the former. Hence, in the worst case, an antitrust action that replaces monopoly with 4-firm equilibrium leads to a net loss of economic welfare.

If antitrust is substituted for laissez-faire (with limit pricing), price falls from OB to OA in figure 1–2 and industry output increases from OM to OH'.[21] The additional output (which is MH') adds to economic welfare the area $H'F'NM$ in figure 1–2. The cost of this additional output is again the area $JKFH$. Close inspection of figure 1–2 will show that the area $JKFH$ is greater than the area $H'F'NM$, so that the substitution of 4-firm equilibrium under antitrust for laissez-faire causes a net reduction in economic welfare. This too will be given a formal proof later on.

Finally, in the worst case, let antitrust be substituted for ideal (subsidized) regulation. In figure 1–2, the substitution will cause price to rise from zero to OA and output to fall from OG' to OH'. This reduction in output will cause economic welfare to fall by the amount $G'F'H'$. However, because three more firms enter the industry under antitrust (each with the unit cost curve ZZ') total cost does not fall; it increases by the amount $JKFH$. Thus, in the worst case, the net loss of economic welfare when antitrust is substituted for ideal regulation is the sum of the areas $GF'H'$ and $JKFH$ in figure 1–2.

Our analysis shows that, if antitrust can create only four viable firms, then in the worst case it is the worst possible choice. Even monopoly is better. However, a close look at figure 1–2 will reveal that, while antitrust in the worst case always creates less economic welfare than regulation, antitrust even at its worst is an improvement on monopoly when n is great enough.

In figure 1–2 suppose the curve of unit cost ZZ' to move downward toward the origin. As this happens, additional firms enter, price falls, and the consumer surplus created by antitrust increases. At the same time, the industry's total cost decreases, and, as n goes to infinity, total cost goes to zero. Thus, there must exist a set of n's for which, even in the worst case, antitrust is preferable to monopoly. (We shall presently show that antitrust is always better than monopoly when $n > 6$.) From figure 1–2 it is not immediately clear whether antitrust is ever preferable to laissez-faire. We will consider this problem later. In worst-case analysis, regulation remains the best of the alternatives so long as n is a finite number.

Antitrust in the Best Case

Now consider the best-case view of antitrust when the equilibrium number of firms is four.[22] This view is given by figure 1–3. Once again, *EG* (and *EG'*) is the industry demand curve. Again, *BI* is the demand curve as perceived by each of the four firms. Now the unit cost curve is given by the fish-hook curve *ZZ'* in figure 1–3.

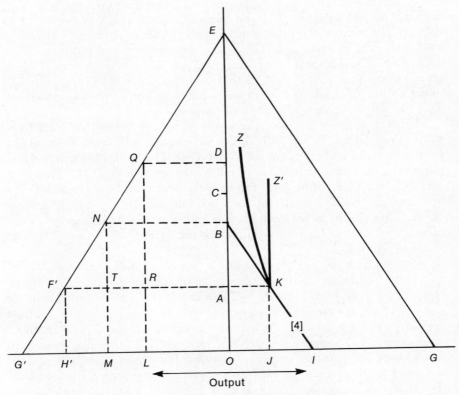

Figure 1–3. Antitrust: Best Case

In figure 1–3, price is *OA,* and output per firm is *OJ* under antitrust—the same as in figure 1–2. But in this best-case antitrust, there is no excess capacity waste; each of the four firms produces at the minimum point on its unit cost curve *ZZ'*. (*K* designates this minimum point.) One cannot improve upon perfection.

If the industry were organized as monopoly (either through a cartel or a multiplant firm), the monopolist's long-run marginal cost would approximate *OA* (or *JK*) in figure 1–3. For marginal cost is equal to *OA* for all multiples of output *OJ*. Under best-case antitrust, industry output is *OH'*. Under monopoly, industry output is *OH'/2*, or *OL,* and price is *OD.* The substitution of antitrust for monopoly now leads to additional output *LH'*. Thus the net gain in economic welfare from substituting antitrust for monopoly is here the triangle *F'QR* in figure 1–3. To repeat, best-case antitrust is best because its substitution for something else creates no excess capacity waste.

In figure 1–3, the substitution of antitrust for laissez-faire produces a net gain in economic welfare equal to the triangle *F'NT.* Note that in the best case, the welfare impact of antitrust is the same as that of regulation (with marginal cost pricing). In figure 1–3, *OA* approximates the long-run marginal cost to which regulators will presumably equate price, for *OA* remains minimum attainable unit cost as production units (firms or plants) are added or dropped.

In the best case (figure 1–3) where antitrust leads to no excess capacity waste, it is always preferable to both monopoly and laissez-faire. And here it is just as good as regulation leading to the same price and output.

Probable Tradeoffs

The economic import of figures 1–2 and 1–3 can now be generalized for *n*-firm equilibrium for any industry demand function of the form

$$p = a - bx \ (a > b > 0).$$

Suppose that we are given one additional bit of information: the equilibrium number of firms that will emerge when the industry operates under antitrust, that is, the value of *n.* It is now possible to make some quite specific statements about the net gain (or loss) in economic welfare when antitrust is substituted for one of its alternatives.

Assume that in this *n*-firm equilibrium we have the hyperbolic curve of unit cost (*ZZ'* in figure 1–2) that makes possible worst-case antitrust. We can easily reckon, for worst-case antitrust, all of the following: price, total output, total revenue, and excess capacity waste.

We can go further. Our information also allows us to reckon all of the above values for our three alternatives to worst-case antitrust: regulation (with marginal cost pricing), laissez-faire (with limit pricing), and monopoly. Let us be clear that the substitution of worst-case antitrust for these three alternatives does not affect the industry's demand curve or the unit cost curve of the individual production unit (plant or firm). Hence, any change in economic welfare resulting from the substitution can be imputed entirely to the change in legal rules. When the necessary algebraic operations have been performed, the results are those entered in table 1–1.

Similar calculations can be made for the industry on the assumption that each firm has the fishhook curve of unit cost (ZZ' in figure 1–2) that makes possible best-case antitrust. When they are made, the results are those entered in table 1–2.

From the information in tables 1–1 and 1–2, we can determine the net welfare gain (or loss) obtainable by substituting antitrust for each of its alternatives, first on worst-case assumptions and then on best-case assumptions. We use the notation set forth in table 1–3.

M_n denotes the net change in economic welfare that occurs when antitrust is substituted for monopoly (and n-firm equilibrium results). Suppose that we wish to find M_n—the value for M_n when this substitution is made in the worst case. This shift will cause industry output to increase, but it will also cause excess capacity to appear. Specifically, in the worst case, replacing monopoly with antitrust will cause output to increase from $a/2b$ to $na/b(n + 1)$. The increase in economic welfare from this additional output is given by:

$$\int_{a/2b}^{na/b(n + 1)} (a - bx)\,dx$$

Recall that the industry's demand function is $p = a - bx$ where p denotes price and x denotes output.

The cost of the additional output is given by:

$$(n - 1)a^2/b(n + 1)^2$$

Thus,

$$\text{Min}_n \int_{a/2b}^{na/b(n + 1)} (a - bx)\,dx - \frac{(n - 1)a^2}{b(n + 1)^2} \tag{1.1}$$

Integrating and simplifying, we get

$$\text{Min } M_n = \frac{a^2(n^2 - 6n + 5)}{8b(n + 1)^2} \tag{1.2}$$

Table 1–1
Antitrust: Worst Case

	Antitrust	Regulation (MC Pricing)	Laissez-faire (Limit Pricing)	Monopoly
Price	$\dfrac{a}{(n+1)}$	0	$\dfrac{2a}{(n+1)}$	$\dfrac{a}{2}$
Output	$\dfrac{na}{b(n+1)}$	$\dfrac{a}{b}$	$\dfrac{a(n-1)}{b(n+1)}$	$\dfrac{a}{2b}$
Total revenue	$\dfrac{na^2}{b(n+1)^2}$	0	$\dfrac{2a^2(n-1)}{b(n+1)^2}$	$\dfrac{a^2}{4b}$
Total cost	$\dfrac{na^2}{b(n+1)^2}$	$\dfrac{a^2}{b(n+1)^2}$	$\dfrac{a^2}{b(n+1)^2}$	$\dfrac{a^2}{b(n+1)^2}$
Excess capacity waste	$\dfrac{(n-1)a^2}{b(n+1)^2}$	0	0	0

Table 1–2
Antitrust: Best Case

	Antitrust	Regulation (MC Pricing)	Laissez-faire (Limit Pricing)	Monopoly
Price	$\dfrac{a}{(n+1)}$	$\dfrac{a}{(n+1)}$	$\dfrac{2a}{(n+1)}$	$\dfrac{a(n+2)}{2(n+1)}$
Output	$\dfrac{na}{b(n+1)}$	$\dfrac{na}{b(n+1)}$	$\dfrac{n-1}{b(n+1)}$	$\dfrac{na}{2b(n+1)}$
Total revenue	$\dfrac{na^2}{b(n+1)^2}$	$\dfrac{na^2}{b(n+1)^2}$	$\dfrac{2a^2(n-1)}{b(n+1)^2}$	$\dfrac{a^2 n(n+2)}{4b(n+1)^2}$
Total cost	$\dfrac{na^2}{b(n+1)^2}$	$\dfrac{na^2}{b(n+1)^2}$	$\dfrac{a^2(n-1)}{b(n+1)^2}$	$\dfrac{na^2}{2b(n+1)^2}$
Excess capacity waste	0	0	0	0

Table 1-3
Notation for Probable Tradeoffs

M_n = the net welfare change when antitrust replaces monopoly

L_n = the net welfare change when antitrust replaces laissez-faire

R_n = the next welfare change when antitrust replaces regulation

Max M_n = maximum value of M_n consistent with n-firm equilibrium

Min M_n = minimum value of M_n consistent with n-firm equilibrium

Max L_n = maximum value of L_n consistent with n-firm equilibrium

Min L_n = minimum value of L_n consistent with n-firm equilibrium

Max R_n = maximum value of R_n consistent with n-firm equilibrium

Min R_n = minimum value of R_n consistent with n-firm equilibrium

---

Using information tabulated in table 1-1, we can go on to find the values of Min L_n and Min R_n. Using the information tabulated in table 1-2, we can find the values of Max M_n, Max L_n, and Max R_n. The results are summarized in table 1-4. We note again that in best-case antitrust there is no excess capacity waste; hence, the maximum values for M_n, L_n, and R_n are equal to the changes in consumer surplus that result from antitrust replaces monopoly, laissez-faire, and regulation respectively.

As table 1-1 shows, when antitrust is substituted for something else, there is some uncertainty about the welfare effects. For example, when antitrust replaces monopoly and n-firm equilibrium results, the possible changes in economic welfare form a bounded set on the interval (Min M_n, Max M_n). When M_n closely approximates Max M_n, welfare is always increased by the substitution. When M_n closely approximates Min M_n, the story is different. As table 1-4 shows, in the worst case Min M_n takes a positive sign when $n \geq 6$ and a negative sign when $n \leq 4$.

Some uncertainty about welfare effects there may be. Nevertheless, we know the limit values of M_n. Therefore, we can estimate the probability that, when antitrust replaces monopoly and an n-firm equilibrium results, an increase in economic welfare also results.

Let k designate the number of possible welfare outcomes when antitrust replaces monopoly. Let us assume that the probability that any single outcome will occur is $1/k$; that is, we assume a uniform distribution of M_n over the interval (Min M_n, Max M_n). There is no economic reason not to assume this distribution. Anyway, as we shall presently see, our results would be affected very little by the choice of a different probability distribution.

We know that Max $M_n > 0$ for every n. So long as Min $M_n \geq 0$, there is no problem. Here ($Pr\ M_n \geq 0$) = 1. When Min $M_n \leq 0$, we have, with uniform distribution:

$$Pr\,(\,M_n \geq 0\,) = \text{Max } M_n / (\text{Max } M_n - \text{Min } M_n)$$

Table 1–4
Net Welfare Change When Antitrust Replaces Various Alternatives

	Regulation (MC Pricing)	Laissez-faire (Limit Pricing)	Monopoly
Best case	Max R_n	Max L_n	Max M_n
	0	$\dfrac{a^2}{2b(n+1)^2}$	$\dfrac{a^2n^2}{8b(n+1)^2}$
Worst case	Min R_n	Min L_n	Min M_n
	$\dfrac{-a^2(2n-1)}{2b(n+1)^2}$	$\dfrac{a^2(5-2n)}{2b(n+1)^2}$	$\dfrac{a^2(n^2=6n+5)}{8b(n+1)^2}$

When the terms on the right-hand side are replaced by values from table 1–2, equation 2 reduces to

$$Pr(M_n \geq 0) = n^2/(6n-5)$$

An analogous series of operation yields, for almost all values of n,

$$Pr(L_n \geq 0) = 1/2(n-2)$$

And, of course,

$$Pr(R_n > 0) = 0$$

The probability that the substitution of antitrust for something else will increase economic welfare (or at least not lower it) is given for various values of n in table 1–5.[23]

The meaning of table 1–5 is unmistakable: price theory can be more easily employed to discredit antitrust than to justify it. Is this conclusion really so surprising? The superiority of regulation (with marginal cost pricing) to antitrust has long been known. And the superiority of laissez-faire (with limit pricing) to antitrust has been strongly suggested by developments in the literature on limit pricing over the last twenty years.

Perhaps the most surprising result of our analysis is the quite respectable showing of the monopoly alternative when antitrust can create only two or three viable firms. Thus,

$$Pr(M_n \geq 0) = 0.571 \text{ when } n = 2 \text{ and}$$

$$Pr(M_n \geq 0) = 0.692 \text{ when } n = 3.$$

Table 1–5
Probability That Antitrust Equals or Betters Various Alternatives

Number of Firms: Antitrust:	Regulation (MC Pricing)	Laissez-faire (Limit Pricing)[a]	Monopoly
2	0.0	0.571	0.571
3	0.0	0.692	0.692
4	0.0	0.250	0.842
5	0.0	0.167	1.0
6	0.0	0.125	1.0
7	0.0	0.100	1.0
8	0.0	0.083	1.0
9	0.0	0.071	1.0
10	0.0	0.063	1.0
11	0.0	0.056	1.0
12	0.0	0.050	1.0

[a]for $n = 2$ and $n = 3$ limit price is monopoly price.

and these probabilities were computed on the assumption that the administrative cost of substituting antitrust for monopoly is null!

Table 1–5 confirms that regulation is always superior to antitrust.[24] The probability that the substitution of antitrust for laissez-faire will increase economic welfare is less than 0.3 for $n \geq 4$. As noted above, the probability that the substitution of antitrust for monopoly will increase economic welfare is 0.571 when $n = 2$, and 0.692 when $n = 3$. We do not get $Pr(M_n \geq 0) = 1$ until $n \geq 5$.

Note that in table 1–5 the probability that antitrust is "better" than monopoly increases as n increases over the interval $2 \leq n \leq 5$; whereas the probability that antitrust is better than laissez-faire decreases as n increases, provided that $n \geq 4$. The reason for this discrepancy is that the difference between monopoly price and n-firm equilibrium price under antitrust becomes greater as n increases; whereas the difference between n-firm equilibrium price and limit price becomes smaller as n increases. (See figures 1–2 and 1–3.) As n goes from 2 to 3, this difference increases under limit pricing. The reason for this is that, as noted in note 23, for $n = 2$ and $n = 3$, monopoly price is also limit price.

Antitrust the Worst Choice?

For some years this writer has argued that the absence of antitrust would produce not "monopoly," but limit pricing carried out by a multiplant firm or cartel. Multiplant firms and cartels that pool profits and assign output quotas are means by which production can be organized efficiently.[25] And if the efficient multiplant firm or cartel has no protection against the entry of new firms, its managers will presumably maximize profit by pricing to discourage entry. While this would seem to be "obviously" true, the idea of a limit price, though hardly new, must still fight for a place in price theory.[26] Economists now know, of course, that in the absence of a legal barrier to entry a high concentration ratio is unlikely to be associated with any close approximation to monopoly price. But as yet we find it difficult to discard the notion that we did so much to popularize: that a concentration ratio is a valid index of "monopoly power."[27] The courts, having no clear lead from price theory, have even fallen into the vulgar error of treating pricing to discourage entry as a monopolistic practice.

Without much trouble we could show that for any economic model that posits free entry of firms, the equilibrium concentration ratio is a function of the legal system and optimum firm size in relation to magnitude of demand. Likewise, without much trouble, we could show that the profit rates and concentration ratios are simultaneously determined and that one in no sense "causes" the other. (As mentioned in note 22, when competition is less than perfect, free entry does not necessarily produce an equilibrium with zero profit; here, free entry merely imposes an upper bound on the set of profit rates that is consistent with equilibrium.) In short, a high concentration ratio is not in any meaningful sense a "barrier to entry." It is merely evidence that, given the constraints of law, technology, and demand, the industry cannot support more firms.

The policy implications of table 1–5 are quite startling. Antitrust comes at a cost because it tends to create excess capacity. This it does by discouraging the price wars and mergers that would otherwise reduce the number of firms. This tendency to excess capacity is not inherent in any of the alternatives to antitrust. In fact, to the extent that the imperfect regulation and laissez-faire of the real world succeed in keeping down excess capacity, they may be preferable to antitrust even though they lead to prices that have drifted upward toward the monopoly level.

It is generally assumed that real-world regulation in particular is very far from ideal. Certainly this writer so believes. Unfortunately, the method usually chosen to carry out "deregulation"—relaxing entry controls while restricting mergers and discouraging cartels—is thoroughly suspect on welfare grounds. It is the perfect formula for creating excess capacity. Deregulation of air transportation has undoubtedly resulted in lower fares. Basic price theory leads us to believe that another result has been too many small planes flying too often.

A Pitfall Noted

The analysis of this chapter underscores another old truth often forgotten: the welfare consequences of substituting antitrust for monopoly and laissez-faire cannot be seen by looking only at what happens to prices, output, and profit rates. As tables 1–1 and 1–2 make clear, replacement of either system by antitrust always leads to lower prices and lower monopoly rent. Indeed, in our model, resort to antitrust completely eliminates monopoly rent no matter what happens to economic welfare. Clearly, consumer welfare, narrowly defined, is not the same thing as economic welfare.[28]

A Reassurance?

Our conclusions about the welfare effects of substituting antitrust for something else have been based upon the assumption that for an *n*-firm equilibrium these effects are uniformly distributed between a lower bound and an upper bound. These bounds (Min M_n, Max M_n and so forth) are the important constraints. Little would change if a different probability distribution were used. Whatever the distribution, ideal regulation is always better than antitrust (except at the limit of best-case antitrust, where it is equally good). The probability that antitrust is better than laissez-faire is almost always less than 0.3; and, provided that $n > 5$, antitrust is always better than monopoly. Suppose that a different probability distribution were assumed. The only result would be marginally to strengthen (or weaken) the case for replacing laissez-faire or monopoly with antitrust.

Economic Welfare and "Squandered Monopoly"

Lest we appear to do less than justice to the case for antitrust, one further calculation should be made. In recent years, Gordon Tullock, Richard Posner, and others have suggested that the welfare loss of monopoly can be much greater than the deadweight loss of any consumer surplus destroyed.[29] They point out that, if a monopoly rent is to be had, rational people will invest resources to create, appropriate, and protect it; and that, at the limit, monopoly can induce a waste of resources equal to the monopoly rent gained.

In a world of regulated industries with entry controls, regulators seldom revoke franchises already issued and rather routinely renew franchises at expiration. Therefore, it seems likely that the magnitude of this induced waste is much exaggerated by popularizers of the idea. For example, the value of resources devoted by owners of television stations to cosseting their licenses (legal fees, public-service broadcasts, and so forth) is surely far less than the monopoly rents created for them by government policy. Still, to the extent that monopoly induces a waste of resources, the case for antitrust over monopoly is strengthened. Indeed, it can be shown that at the limit, when all monopoly rent has been frittered away in resource waste, the substitution of antitrust will *always* increase economic welfare.

Let S_n designate the welfare gain to be gotten by shifting to antitrust from squandered monopoly, and Min S_n the minimum values that S_n can take. We show that antitrust is always better than squandered monopoly by proving the $Pr(S_n > 0) \geq 1$. To this end, we need only demonstrate that Min $S_n > 0$ for every n.

By definition, Min S_n is the sum of Min M_n and the monopolist's economic rent, that is, his total revenue minus his total cost. Using the information on worst-case antitrust provided by tables 1–1 and 1–4 we have:

$$\text{Min } S_n = \frac{a^2(n^2 - 6n + 5)}{8b(n + 1)^2} + \frac{a^2}{4b} - \frac{a^2}{b(n + 1)^2} \tag{1.3}$$

or

$$\text{Min } S_n = \frac{a^2(3n^2 + 2n - 1)}{8b(n + 1)^2} \tag{1.3a}$$

Thus, Min $S_n > 0$ for all values of n and economic welfare will always be increased by the substitution of antitrust for squandered monopoly.

Other Costs Noted

So far in assessing the welfare impacts of antitrust and its alternatives we have ignored the costs of implementing these policies. When these costs are put into the picture, price theorists must either step aside in favor of econometricians or speak in generalities. Speaking in generalities, it seems safe to assume that the cost of implementing antitrust must be greater than the comparable cost of laissez-faire. To go no further, the number of American lawyers who are presently making a living out of antitrust almost certainly exceeds by fivefold the combined total of practicing barristers and solicitors in Great Britain.

It is not so obvious how the cost of implementing antitrust compares with the cost of implementing monopoly or regulation aimed at marginal cost (or even average cost) pricing. Most economists, or at any rate most American economists, probably feel that the antitrust cost is lower. But we do not really know.

Antitrust and the Demand Function

To this point, our analysis has assumed that the industry's demand curve is linear. We chose to accept this restriction because a linear demand function greatly simplifies the algebra and because there was no obvious reason for not making use of this advantage. But let us be clear that the conclusion that "antitrust comes at a cost" does not depend upon anything so trivial as the exact slope of a demand curve. Our analysis could be conducted with any differentiable demand function that yields a total revenue maximum for some positive rate of output. Introducing nonlinear demand functions would deprive our analysis of much of its precision (and simplicity) without telling us anything new or interesting about the welfare tradeoffs of antitrust and its alternatives.

For the record, we can easily show that the more convex the demand curve, the greater the welfare gain to be had (or the smaller the welfare loss to be suffered) by soliciting antitrust for monopoly or laissez-faire. Likewise, the more concave the demand curve, the smaller the welfare gain to be had (or the greater the welfare loss to be suffered) from such substitutions.[30] There would seem to be no point in pursuing the implications of curvature in greater detail. It is doubtful that even the most fervent trustbuster would try to strengthen the case for antitrust by arguing that real-world demand curves are highly convex. Certainly there is no extant body of empirical or theoretical work that would support such a view.

Final Thoughts

How seriously should the above results be taken? The answer depends, of course, upon the role assigned to price theory and conventional welfare criteria in antitrust policy. If one believes that these are the only acceptable instruments for distinguishing good from bad in antitrust, the results would seem to be quite disturbing. Price theory and conventional welfare criteria can provide libertarians of the Von Mises school and market socialists of the Oskar Lange school with a great deal of intellectual ammunition and spiritual comfort. They can provide little of either to friends of antitrust.

If one does not require the case for antitrust to be grounded only in price theory and welfare economics, our results can be viewed as interesting, but without decisive significance for policy. As wise elders have often cautioned, economic progress is a much more important desideratum than efficient resource allocation.[31] Certainly it is a logical possibility that antitrust may create market structures that at the same time reduce economic welfare and raise the rate of economic progress. As yet, we have neither theoretical nor empirical work that allows us to estimate the likelihood that antitrust will have this result.[32] The most we can say is that no good evidence has been produced to show that antitrust reduces the rate of economic progress.

Still, suppose that one day the economic effects of antitrust will be revealed as totally perverse, that is, that antitrust will be found to reduce both economic welfare and the rate of economic progress. All of the so-called non-economic arguments for the policy will remain. (Small business builds character, economic decentralization improves political democracy, and so on.) It is, after all, a professional conceit to believe that the main object of antitrust is (or should be) an increase in that rarefied thing that economists have defined as economic welfare.

If the goals of antitrust are to be inferred from what judges and legislators do (forget what they say), it is clear that antitrust's paramount goal from 1890 onward has been the preservation and promotion of decentralized decision making, subject to two main constraints. Economic efficiency must not be jeopardized in any gross and obvious way, for example, by using divestiture to create firms with poor chances of survival. Established stockholder and employee interests must not be too rudely disturbed. For better or worse, great corporate size scares a great many people in this country.[33] "Monopoly power" divorced from great corporate size scares hardly anybody and, indeed, mostly goes unnoticed. In this country, the suspicion of centralized decision making extends far beyond the large corporation—to government, political parties, churches, universities, labor unions, and the money and credit system. Why this should be so is, of course, a subject much too vast for this chapter.

These concluding thoughts are not meant to depreciate the value of price theory in analyzing antitrust issues. Price theory provides the most powerful set of tools that we have for identifying and estimating tangible costs and benefits. As long as we are thinking straight, our willingness to sacrifice economic welfare to achieve other goals is necessarily affected by such calculations.

Will it greatly matter in Congress and the courts if economists conclude that the price theory of the textbooks provides virtually no support for antitrust? At first glance an affirmative answer would seem to be out of the question. No political leader with any hope of office or influence dares to speak against antitrust. Few American economists and even fewer American lawyers ever bother to consider what the American economy would be like without it, and the policy now has the respectability conferred by age and the support of an organized constituency in the large and prosperous Antitrust Bar. For the record, antitrust was born in the populist turbulence of the last century and gained its great 1911 victories without the benefit of price theory or price theorists.[34]

Still, as the recent movement toward deregulation in transportation and communications should remind us, ideas can matter in the long run. The movement is directly traceable to the discrediting of the Brandeis-Sharfman case for public utility regulation that began at the University of Chicago in the 1930s. The support belatedly given to antitrust by economists after 1900 did have one obvious and possibly important result: it conferred intellectual respectability. If this respectability is taken away, the ultimate consequence cannot be predicted. Presumably, the disenchantment of economists with antitrust will have some effect; even the most pessimistic of us cannot believe that his work counts for nothing in the forum. The only reasonable prophecy is that our loss of faith in antitrust will cause the alternatives—and not only those considered in this chapter—to be more closely examined. That could be a most interesting development.

Notes

1. M.A. Adelman, "The Measurement of Industrial Concentration," *Rev. Econ. Stat.* 33 (1951):269; D.T. Armentano, *Antitrust and Monopoly: Anatomy of a Policy Failure* (1982); Peter Asch and Joseph Seneca, "Is Collusion Profitable?" *Rev. Econ. Stat.* 58 (1976):1; William J. Baumol, James C. Panzer, and Robert D. Willig. *Contestable Markets and the Theory of Industry Structure* (1982); Robert H. Bork, *The Antitrust Paradox: A Policy at War With Itself* (1978); Ward S. Bowman, Jr., "Tying Arrangements and the Leverage Problem," *Yale L.J.* 67 (1957):19; Yale Brozen, *Concentration, Mergers, and Public Policy* (1982); Donald Dewey, "Information, Entry, and Welfare: The Case for Collusion," *Am. Econ. Rev.* 63 (1979):69; Kenneth G. Elzinga and William Breit, *The Antitrust Penalties: A Study in Law And Economics* (1976); John McGee, *In Defense of Industrial Concentration* (1971); John Moore and G. Warren Nutter, "A Theory of Competition," *J. Law Econ.* 19 (1976):39; Richard A. Posner, *Antitrust Law: An Economic Perspective* (1976); George B. Richardson, "The Theory of Restrictive Trade Practices," *Oxford Econ. Papers* 17 (1965):432; Joseph E. Stiglitz, "Potential Competition May Reduce Welfare," *Am. Econ. Rev.* 71 (1981):184; L.G. Telser, "Cutthroat Competition and the Long Purse," *J. Law Econ.* 9 (1966):259; B.S. Yamey, *The Economics of Resale Price Maintenance* (1954).

2. Adam Smith, *The Wealth of Nations* (Mod. Lib. ed. 1937), 501.

3. See, for example, William Letwin, "Congress and the Sherman Antitrust Law, 1887–1890," *U. Chicago Law Rev.* 23 (1956):221; or H.B. Thorelli, *The Federal Antitrust Policy* (1954), 108–27.

4. See, for example, I.M.D. Little, *A Critique of Welfare Economics* (2nd ed. 1957); or E.J. Mishan, *Welfare Economics: Five Introductory Essays* (2nd ed. 1969).

5. Alan D. Neale, *The Antitrust Laws of the United States of America* (2nd ed. 1970), 478–93.

6. See, for example, Joseph Schumpeter, *Capitalism, Socialism, and Democracy* (3rd ed. 1950), 87–106.

7. As usually formulated, an increase in economic welfare does not require that compensation actually be paid to losers—only that it could be paid out of the gains of the winners from a rule change. The compensation test seems originally to have been suggested as a way of getting policy makers to think twice about rule changes whose advocates promise economic benefits. John R. Hicks, "The Foundations of Welfare Economics," *Econ. J.* 49 (1939):696, 711–12.

8. Joan Robinson, *The Economics of Imperfect Competition* (1933).

9. Edward Chamberlin, *The Theory of Monopolistic Competition* (1933).

10. Harold Demsetz, "The Welfare and Empirical Implications of Monopolistic Competition," *Econ. J.* 74 (1964):622; Donald Dewey, *The Theory of Imperfect Competition: A Radical Reconstruction* (1969), 60–86.

11. For the pioneer effort to estimate antitrust tradeoffs, see Oliver Williamson, "Economies as an Antitrust Defense," *Am. Econ. Rev.* 58 (1968):18.

12. Max Weber, *The Theory of Social and Economic Organization,* trans. A.R. Henderson and Talcott Parsons (1947), 79–102.

13. That the concern of antitrust has long been not with the efficiency of firms, but with their viability is easily documented. Since International Shoe Co. v. FTC, 280 U.S. 291 (1930), a showing that a firm is likely to fail unless allowed to merge has been the only complete defense against the government's effort to prevent a merger that would otherwise violate Section 7 of the Clayton Act.

14. United States v. Brown Shoe Co., 370 U.S. 294 (1963).

15. On the details of limit pricing, see Donald Dewey, *Microeconomics: The Analysis of Prices and Markets* (1975), 141–54; Darius W. Gaskins, "Dynamic Limit Pricing: Optimal Pricing under Threat of Entry," *J. Econ. Theory* 3 (1971):306–22; and B.P. Pashigian, "Limit Price and the Market Share of the Leading Firm," *J. Ind. Econ.* 16 (1968):165–77.

16. In using the Cournot model with cost curves as a proxy for "competition," I also have the comfort of knowing that I am in highly respectable company. See William Novshek and Hugo Sonnenschein, "Cournot and Walras Equilibrium," *J. Econ. Theory* 19 (1978):223.

17. A.A. Cournot, *Recherches sur les principes mathématiques de la théorie des richesses* (1838); translated by N.T. Bacon as *Researches into the Mathematical Principles of the Theory of Wealth* (1897).

18. William S. Vickrey, *Microstatics* (1964), 304–9.

19. For evidence that some unit cost curves of the real world really do approximate the fishhook curve of figure 1–3, see William J. Eiteman and Glenn E. Guthrie, "The Shape of the Average Cost Curve," *Am. Econ. Rev.* 42 (1955), 832.

20. In Cournot equilibrium, when the aggregate demand function is of the form $p = a - bx$, the equilibrium demand function of a single seller is

$$p = \frac{(n + 1)m + 2(a - m)}{n + 1} - bx \tag{1.4}$$

where n denotes number of sellers and m denotes marginal cost (or marginal revenue).

When $m = 0$, equation (1.4) can be rewritten as

$$p = \frac{2a}{n + 1} - bx \qquad (1.4a)$$

21. In figures 1–2 and 1–3, let the price charged by a sole producer in the market be *OB* and his output *OM* (or *BN*). Here the "unused" portion of the industry demand curve *EG'* is the segment *NG'*. This gives the potential entrant the demand curve *BI*. Faced with this demand curve, the potential entrant can enter and break even by producing *OJ*. Therefore, assuming that the sole producer wishes to discourage entrants, he must charge a price that is below the upper limit *OB* and so put the demand curve for a potential entrant below *BI*.

22. To simplify the presentation, in figures 1–2 and 1–3 the unit cost curve *ZZ'* has been drawn tangent to the demand curve *BI* at point *K;* that is, our choice of geometry has ensured that the entry of the fourth firm exactly eliminates all monopoly rent (usually called profit). An *n*-firm equilibrium with positive profit for all firms is, of course, possible, provided that the aggregate profit is not great enough to draw an additional firm into the industry.

Let *s* denote total sales revenue per firm, *t* total cost per firm, and *r* the profit-sales ratio. Then $r = (s - t)/s$. It can be shown (though we will not stop to do so) that in *n*-firm equilibrium in a Cournot model, the maximum value that *r* can take must be less than $[1 - (n - 1)^2/(n + 2)^2]$. The technique for locating the upper bound for *r* in an oligopoly model that allows free entry is described and illustrated in Donald Dewey, "Industrial Concentration and the Rate of Profit: Some Neglected Theory," *J. Law Econ.* 19 (1976):67.

23. Note that in table 1–5, when $n = 2$ and $n = 3$, the substitution of antitrust for monopoly has the same likelihood of increasing welfare as the substitution of antitrust for laissez-faire. The reason is that, for $n = 2$, $a/2 < 2a/(n + 1)$ and, for $n = 3, a/2 = 2a/(n + 1)$. That is, when $n = 2$ and $n = 3$, monopoly price is limit price, since it is low enough to discourage entry.

24. In the construction of table 1–5, the R_n's consistent with *n*-firm equilibrium have been treated as an open set on the interval (Min R_n, Max R_n). Thus, Min R_n— the value of R_n in best-case antitrust—is not included in the set. Antitrust creates as much economic welfare as ideal regulation only at this best-case limit.

25. It is a simple, though not a popular, exercise in price theory to show that when an industry cannot support the number of firms needed for perfect competition, it will never be organized with maximum efficiency in the absence of a multiplant firm or cartel, for a necessary condition of maximum efficiency is that unit cost be minimized in all production units. When competition is less than perfect, this condition is achieved only with some form of command guidance. On cartel theory generally see Donald Dewey, *The Theory of Imperfect Competition: A Radical Reconstruction* (1969):41–59; Don Patinkin, "Multiplant Firms, Cartels, and Imperfect Competition," *Q. J. Econ.* 61 (1947);173–80; William Fellner, *Competition Among the Few* (1949):200–210.

The most famous of American cartel cases, Addyston Pipe & Steel Company, et al. v. United States, 175 U.S. 211 (1899) laid the basis for the per se rule against price fixing and has been almost universally praised over the years, even by Robert Bork and Richard Posner! However, a recent reconsideration of the case strongly suggests that the cartel of cast iron pipe producers condemned in this case served to increase economic welfare. George Bittlingmayer, "Price-Fixing and the Addyston Pipe Case," *Research in Law and Economics* 5 (1982):57.

26. Perfectly lucid descriptions of limit pricing appear as early as John B. Clark, *Essentials of Economic Theory* (1907):380–81; and Alfred Marshall, *Industry and Trade* (1920):397.

27. No originality can be claimed for the complaint. For an earlier and more detailed version, see Harold Demsetz, "Economics as a Guide to Antitrust Regulation," *J. Law Econ.* 19 (1976):371.

28. Robert Bork is a leading proponent of the view that the goal of antitrust ought to be consumer welfare, narrowly defined. He holds that an antitrust rule is acceptable only if price theory supports the presumption that it will increase output with an increase in output being, by definition, an increase in consumer welfare. *The Antitrust Paradox: A Policy at War with Itself* (1978):81–82. Under our "ideal" antitrust, only output-increasing rules would be in force; thus, such a rule would always increase consumer welfare, though as we have found, by creating excess capacity it might at the same time reduce economic welfare. Bork's output test is, I believe, perfectly defensible as a judicial rule of thumb since, for the present it is too much to expect that courts should be concerned with such a rarified thing as the economist's distinction between economic welfare and consumer welfare. A judicial focus on a simple output test would at least discourage such welfare-reducing monstrosities as Utah Pie Co. v. Continental Baking Co. 386 U.S. 685 (1967).

29. See, for example, Gordon Tullock, "The Welfare Cost of Tariffs, Monopolies, and Theft," *Western Econ. J.* 5 (1964):224, or Richard A. Posner, "The Social Cost of Monopoly and Regulation," *J. Pol. Econ.* 83 (1975):83.

30. Let S denote any set of continuous demand functions such that, for values of p^* and $x^*(p^* > 0, x^* > 0)$, [i] $\phi(x^*) = 0$, [ii] $\phi(0) = p^*$, and [iii] on the interval $(0, x^*)$ the sign of $\phi(x)$ does not change. Let marginal revenue be given by:

$$m = d[x\phi(x)]/dx.$$

Let the concavity of $\phi(x)$ be given by $e = \int_0^x \phi(x) - 1/2\, p^*x^*$.
Let $p = \phi_i(x) \in S$ and $p = \phi_j(x) \in S$.
Then for every $x(0 < x < x^*)$, if $e_i > e_j$, we have [i] $\phi_i(x) > \phi_j(x)$ and [ii] $m_i > m_j$.

A monopolist is presumed to equate marginal cost and marginal revenue. Therefore, for any given cost function, the more concave the industry demand curve, that is, the greater the value of e, the greater will be equilibrium output under monopoly; and the smaller will be the welfare gain (or the greater will be the welfare loss) obtainable by substituting antitrust for monopoly.

An analogous line of argument can be used to show that the more concave the demand curve, the smaller will be the welfare gain to be had (or the greater the welfare loss to be suffered) by substituting antitrust for laissez-faire.

31. Notably, John M. Clark, *Competition As A Dynamic Process* (1961), and Joseph Schumpeter, *Capitalism, Socialism, and Democracy* (3rd ed., 1950).

32. For an appraisal of the work on what we know (and suspect) about the tie between technological progress and market structure, see Morton I. Kamien and Nancy L. Schwartz, *Market Structure and Innovation* (1982).

33. Admittedly the recent breakup of the Bell System may inflict injuries on workers and investors that contradict the above generalizations. I think it fair to say that, if this result comes to pass, it can be attributed to management's miscalculation about its ability to compete in unregulated markets (and hence its willingness to accept the actual consent decree) than to the court's determination to destroy the monopoly rents of workers and stockholders. (In defense of the managers' decision to settle, lawyers will hasten to point out that they had to weigh the value of a consent decree that expressly provided some protection against private treble damage suits against the probability of an unfavorable ruling that would have given third parties a *prima facie* case against the Bell System. United States v. Western Electric Co., Inc., and American Telephone and Telegraph Co., 1982–82 Trade Cases 72,555 at 72,558). My own expectation is that if workers and stockholders ultimately suffer severe losses as a result of the Bell System dissolution, the country will not see a comparable adventure in trustbusting for many years.

34. Standard Oil Co. of New Jersey v. United States, 221 U.S. 1 (1911); United States v. American Tobacco Co. et. al., 221 U.S. 106 (1911).

2
Vertical Restraints in Manufacturer–Distributor Relations: Incidence and Economic Effects

Richard E. Caves

V ertical restraints in contractual relationships between manufacturers and distributors have always received a patchwork treatment under the antitrust laws. At times some of them (such as resale price maintenance) have been legal, while others (for example, tying agreements) close to illegal per se. When *Continental T.V.* v. *GTE Sylvania*[1] widened the application of the rule of reason to vertical restraints, it opened the door to a judicial reconsideration of the balance of social benefits and costs of most or all types of vertical restraints. At about the same time, advances in the economic understanding of contractual relationships made economists increasingly interested in this area. This coincidence of judicial and economic interest is fortunate. To assess the net economic consequences of a vertical restraint—the concern of public policy—we require an understanding of why the parties employ the vertical restraint in the first place, and what alternative they would grasp if it were banned or restricted. The economic analysis of contractural relationships can contribute a good deal to this background. Specifically, it can suggest

1. which transactional independences cause manufacturer and distributor to bind themselves to restrictive contracts;
2. whether vertical restraints constitute first-best or second-best arrangements, and what market failures ultimately underlie them;
3. how the various vertical restraints may be related to one another as complementary terms of mutually acceptable contracts; and
4. how these restraints may relate to the exercise of market power, the traditional concern of the antitrust laws.

An earlier version of this manuscript was prepared in conjunction with a Federal Trade Commission study of the effects of vertical restraints. I am indebted to Richard Schmalensee for suggestions.

This chapter offers an overview of the economic side of this discussion. Deductive ingenuity in devising models to explain vertical restraints has lately outrun empirical resourcefulness for testing competing explanations. If public policy is to apply a rule of reason to vertical restraints, it requires information on which explanations for vertical restraints actually carry the most empirical weight, and what tradeoffs the parties will choose to implement among vertical restraints following a change in the legality of any one of them. The data simply do not permit one to perform the ideal empirical investigation: an explanation of the incidence of vertical restraints as it varies among situations in which both the legality of the various restraints and the structural characteristics of the market are allowed to differ. However, past antitrust cases themselves and various other sources of empirical evidence allow very rough approximation to this design. The chapter therefore consists of two main sections. First, we will review the thrust of recent economic research on vertical restraints, stressing the interrelation among the various restraints and the relation of the new "contractual" explanations of them to the more traditional concern for market power as their possible source or consequence. Then we will search the available evidence on the incidence of vertical restraints for any discriminations it will support among competing explanations.

Modeling Vertical Restraints

Two traits mark contractual relations between manufacturers and distributors of their products in most situations where vertical restraints are present. Involving assorted mutual obligations going beyond the dealer's purchase and receipt of the transferred product, the relationships are complex. And they are durable, linking the parties by explicit and implicit obligations that extend over substantial periods of time. The contractual approach to vertical restraints stresses a variety of market failures that the parties can avert or mitigate through such agreements in comparison to spot transactions or contracts with less complete terms.

Externality and Free-riding

One class of market failure lies in externalities that arise when the policies of one party to the transaction create rents that are captured by another. Without contractual terms to compensate for the externality, the policy setter underprovides the policy in question. The externality can run in various directions—rents from one dealer's policies accruing either to other dealers or to the manufacturer, or rents from the manufacturer's policies accruing to the dealers.

The prototype source of this free-rider problem is the provision of pre-sales information to the prospective customer (Tesler 1960). The retail firm that provides information must set a markup that covers its cost; however, the customer has an incentive to absorb the information and then to decamp for the nearest discount store and purchase the same article at a price not incorporating its cost of provision. The example of pre-sales information, however, tends to understate the generality of this problem. As Porter (1976, chap. 3) pointed out, if the customer selects among competing brands on the basis of signals and incomplete information, many parameters influencing a brand's perceived qualities will be within the retailer's control. These include not only tailoring information to the customer's needs, but also providing an ambience that has a significant value as a quality signal, extending guarantees, and providing facilities for prompt after-sales service that cannot always be priced at its full cost, and so forth. When the retailer provides services to his own customers or to those who have bought the same brand from other retailers, the services' full contribution to the shared goodwill asset may exceed the revenue that he takes in. This is, incomplete contracts between dealer and ultimate customer expand the range of dealers' policies that create externalities, the benefits accruing partly to the manufacturer (when the customer cannot costlessly apportion the product's performance attributes between the manufacturer's and the dealer's inputs) and other dealers (when customers make repeated purchases of the product, but are mobile among dealers).

Porter showed that this problem of intangible assets and free-rider incentives particularly afflicts so-called nonconvenience goods—those commodities for which the final buyer shops comparatively and seeks auxiliary information and services from the retailer. The retailer's premises and the tone of his advertising themselves transmit a signal regarding the quality of the merchandise offered, and the costly signal of high quality creates goodwill for both the dealer and the merchandise offered. After-sales service may often be consumed jointly with the nonconvenience good itself, as well as auxiliary advice and information that contribute to a goodwill asset shared by dealer and manufacturer. For both nonconvenience and convenience goods, a franchise distribution system that cloaks the dealer in the identity of the manufacturer makes the dealer's premises themselves an advertisement for the good and conveys an advertising image even to those who do not patronize them. The neat gasoline station with the ubiquitous soft-drink vending machine is thus a billboard as well as a retail outlet.[2]

Second-best and First-best Restraints

The manufacturer encountering this free-rider problem can employ various strategies to resolve it. Potentially the most efficient approach is to pay the retailer directly for implementing the preferred policies, and indeed we observe many such payments as subsidies to retail advertising, below-cost provision of signs and displays, and the like. However, many services that the retailer provides to final buyers are difficult for the manufacturer to meter and verify. Information supplied to prospective customers and repairs carried out so as to raise the chances of a repeat purchase are heterogeneous and intangible services. Therefore, as Telser (1960) pointed out, the manufacturer's second-best strategy may be to elevate the retailer's profit on sales of his product above a level that would yield the retailer a normal rate of return when he follows policies that maximize his own profits. His inflated profit margin induces the retailer to increase the level of activities that raise the expected sales of the manufacturer's products, although perhaps not to the level that the manufacturer would choose if he were vertically integrated into retailing. Telser was concerned with resale price maintenance (RPM) as an instrument available to inflate the retailer's margin.

More recent research places these findings in perspective by showing what contractual restraints are required for the manufacturer to maximize his profits when his product is distributed through specialized dealers who can be recruited at a constant supply price. Mathewson and Winter (1983, 1984; also Bittlingmayer 1983) analyzed vertical restraints in a setting where the dealers serve spatially dispersed customers and thereby acquire localized market power. The manufacturer therefore seeks to avert not only any externalities among dealers due to free-riding, but also the vertical market distortions that result when the dealers as well as the manufacturer set prices above their respective marginal costs (the "chain of monopolies" problem). Apart from his wholesale price, the manufacturer needs to use some combination of instruments (franchise fees, resale price controls, minimum quantity requirements, territorial restrictions) to maximize profits from production and distribution taken together. Caves and Murphy (1976) noted that franchise systems in this spirit employ multiple-term contracts in their efforts to prevent free-riding and to maximize net revenue from franchisees serving diverse territories whose potential profit levels are hard to assess in advance.

Duration of Contracts

Recent theoretical contributions clarify the role of vertical restraints in pursuing first-best optima for the manufacturer, but they do not deal explicitly with the long-term character typical of contracts that involve vertical restraints. This durability has important but complex implications for the normative assessment of vertical restraints. Assume that manufacturer and dealer each must incur significant transaction costs if they break their agreement and seek to recontract with new partners. These transaction costs give the parties a shared interest in sustaining a satisfactory relationship that has consequences for the role of vertical restraints. On the one hand, a long-term relationship allows an intertemporal balancing of considerations that cannot be optimized individually on a short-run basis. The principle that a satisfactory relationship will be sustained potentially reduces the costs of negotiation and haggling per period of time, and makes it feasible for more complex arm's-length contracts to be reached and maintained. On the other hand, the shared quasi-rents are appropriable by opportunistic parties; a dealer, for example, can benefit from underproviding investments in shared intangibles, as long as it does not pay the manufacturer either to undertake an effective enforcement action or to cancel and seek a new dealer.[3]

Relation to Market Power

The appropriability of quasi-rents flags one issue of market power in manufacturer-dealer relations. In essence, a large-numbers bargaining situation prevailing before the parties commit to each other becomes a small-numbers situation when they come to divide a stream of quasi-rents. However, this is not the long-term problem of market power that has underlain the more traditional focus of antitrust policy toward vertical restraints. First, it is worth noting that a concern about market power in vertical relations cannot be put aside simply by referring to the large numbers of participating firms and generally easy entry that mark the distribution sector. For this purpose, national-market concentration associated with chain stores is probably less important than local concentration of specialized outlets, some types of which can be few in number even in large metropolitan areas. Porter (1976, 30–35) pointed out that local retail markets may be subject to entry barriers due to scale economies of the limited availability of specialized skills, and this pertains particularly to the nonconvenience goods that have been the principal site for several types of vertical restraints. Furthermore, some classes of retailers in the past were able to accrue some market power through the political route, even when economic structures did not favor them (Palamountain 1955).

The implications of bilateral market power have escaped reconciliation with the theoretical analyses of optimal contracts for the manufacturer (summarized above) because of the model-builders' seemingly innocent assumption that dealers are specialized to the contracting manufacturer, who can therefore be supposed to deal with a limitless supply of potential dealers. The assumption is appropriate for some franchise systems. However, most manufacturers distribute through multiproduct dealers and therefore can only choose among what may be a significantly more limited set of potential distributors. That fact warrants Porter's emphasis on concentration in some relevant markets for distributors' services; and it explains why manufacturers may not be able to manipulate contract terms freely with multiproduct distributors whose common costs and operating policies restrict the range of potentially acceptable terms, as do contracts offered by other manufacturers.

The contractual analysis of vertical restraints assumes that the manufacturer possesses such market power as product differentiation may yield, but that the distributor *ex ante* has none; what happens to the analysis if retailers enjoy market power? The theory of bilateral market power points to a shared interest of the parties in maximizing the joint surplus and then dividing it, according to their respective bargaining power. If a first-best contract involving vertical restraints could be imposed by a manufacturer on purely competitive dealers, then a first-best contract that maximizes the shared surplus between powerful parties is equally conceivable. However, vertical restraints have the potential to prove privately but not socially optimal, because a vertical restraint can supply parties on one side of the transaction with restrictions on competition that they could not impose on their own. Resale price maintenance and territorial restrictions could, for example, remove competitive pressures on retailers unable to reach or enforce such an agreement among themselves. It has been suggested that resale price maintenance may permit manufacturers to sustain price collusion on wholesale prices by reducing the efficacy of secret price cuts to dealers or by making it easier to detect the manufacturer's price cut when it is known to underlie any change in the retail price (Telser 1960; Posner 1977).[4]

Interrelation among Vertical Restraints

In both law and economics, each vertical restraint is normally regarded in isolation, whereas we expect to find (and frequently do) groups of them serving to balance the same manufacturer-dealer agreement. A sufficient basis for this expectation lies in models that point to the manufacturer's need to use multiple instruments to provide his distributors with the ideal incentive structures. However, the interdependence of vertical restraints is more general: whether distributors are atomistic or market power is enjoyed on both sides, a contract written to cover diverse and ill-predicted states of nature may require some vertical restraints in order to make other restraints acceptable. This balancing process reflects the familiar limitations of arm's-length contracts: elaborate *en ante* anticipations of states of nature are not cost-effective, and the preclusion of post-contract opportunism may require terms that would otherwise be inefficient.[5]

In this context, the familiar vertical restraints are usefully divided into those that can be conferred by the manufacturer and increase rents or restrict competition for the retailer, and those that can be conferred by the retailer and increase rents or restrict competition for the manufacturer. Whatever set of terms appears in a particular market bargain is assumed to reflect a mutual accord determined by the parties' preferences and relative bargaining power, and it presumably could not be changed so as to make both better off. Furthermore, which vertical restraints are included in the contract will depend on the going legal restrictions upon them. If the law is changed to exclude some restraint from the bargain, the remaining contractual terms no longer exactly reflect the parties' relative bargaining strength. In the long run, therefore, one expects other terms (including vertical restraints) to be added, dropped, or modified to push the bargain back into equilibrium. In addition, making some one vertical restraint illegal may permanently change the effective relative bargaining power of the two parties, so that the bargain (as recast) becomes relatively more favorable to one party than it was before the legal change.

We can now list these vertical restraints and show their interdependence in the manufacturer-retailer bargain.[6] The following vertical restraints, on their face, constrain the retailer and give some advantage to the manufacturer.

1. *Exclusive dealing* refers to a variety of practices by which the manufacturer may preclude a retailer from carrying other manufacturers' brands, commit him to obtain all his requirements from the manufacturer, or require him to carry the manufacturer's full product line. The particular terms normally can be resolved into some combination of a tying arrangement and an all-or-nothing offer. The manufacturer's motives therefore may be various, and we need not run through all the possibilities here. One typical motive for the manufacturer may be to cloak the retail outlet in the manufacturer's brand identity; this discourages on-the-spot comparison of his product to others and facilitates its differentiation. Another motive may be to carry out price discrimination by using exclusive dealing in its tying-arrangement capacity (Telser 1965, 492; Adams and Yellen 1976). The manufacturer may wish to avoid free-riding by the dealer who receives leads on potential customers from the manufacturers (Marvel 1982).

2. *Customer restrictions* usually preclude the retailer from seeking the business of certain large customers who are then pursued by the direct selling efforts of the manufacturer. One objective of the manufacturer is to maintain price discrimination among various markets and to preclude intrabrand

rivalry for certain strategic classes of customers. Another is to minimize customer-contact or other distribution costs when the manufacturer and dealers differ in their efficiency in serving differently situated final customers. Customer restrictions on wholesalers are used to implement whatever preferences the manufacturer has about the retailers who handle his product.

3. *Territorial restrictions* prevent a distributor from soliciting business outside an assigned territory. These function both to restrain dealers from seeking customers served more efficiently (from the manufacturer's viewpoint) by other of his dealers and to protect dealers from incursions into their territory.[7] Depending on the cost function of the distributive outlet, denial of the option of competing in another retailer's territory can lead the retailer to expand his efforts to contact customers at the intensive margin within his own territory—customers who are less cost-effective to contact because they are smaller or involve higher costs for servicing the account. This process is likely to increase the amount of price discrimination undertaken by the dealer, who is induced to charge different customers different prices net of the direct costs of serving them.[8]

4. *Volume requirements* are functionally similar to territorial restrictions, but act more directly to induce the dealer to cover his territory of primary responsibility more intensively (Travers and Wright 1962, 809). White (1971, chap. 9; 1981) pointed out that they amount to all-or-nothing quantity offers by the manufacturer that make sense on the assumption that the retailer faces a downward-sloping demand curve in his local market. The retailer then sets a margin (and distributes a quantity) that leaves him operating at a scale smaller than what would minimize his average unit operating costs. This is the equilibrium structure of the retail sector if entry is free (Gould and Preston 1965). The manufacturer's volume requirement can impel the retailer to operate at a scale large enough to minimize these costs. (Of course, the minimization of average costs of distribution is not necessarily optimal if distributors serve a spatially dispersed market.)

A corresponding list indicates the restraints that can be given by the manufacturer for the putative benefit of the retailer:

1. *Retail price maintenance* (RPM) directly protects the retailer's price-cost margin from competition. It has puzzled economists because the manufacturer who restricts retail competition among his distributors does not thereby minimize the retail price (given his factory price) and therefore seemingly cuts his own sales. Telser (1960) pointed out correctly that this concession could be for the manufacturer a rational if second-best way to get around the free-rider problem and induce the optimal number of pre-sale services. Earlier, however, Bowman (1952) urged that RPM could enter into the bargain between manufacturer and retailer as a reflection of retailers' bargaining power; competing retailers may be unable to collude effectively on

price, but they can agree to withhold sales-promotion efforts on behalf of a manufacturer's product when the manufacturer's own sales-promotion efforts aimed directly at the final buyer are not sufficient to make this tactic on the part of the retailers unprofitable.

2. *Exclusive territories* guarantee that the manufacturer will franchise no other dealers to supply a given territory or set of customers. A policy of granting exclusive territories does not by itself serve the interest of the manufacturer, but it can be used to purchase commitments desired by the manufacturer or as a payoff to bargaining power possessed by the dealer. In fact, exclusive territories and territorial restrictions are close to being equivalent, and territorial restrictions simply serve to implement exclusive territories. Exclusive territories (plus territorial restrictions) are functionally similar to RPM (equivalent, however, only under certain narrow circumstances). They share with RPM the capacity to restrict free-riding in pre-sale services and other activities carried on by the retailer. They may also reward retailers who enjoy some bargaining power, but cannot stifle competition among themselves directly.

3. *Limitation on the density of retailers* is a practice similar in its effects to exclusive territories, and probably fills the same function in the case of products whose buyers are anonymous, mobile, or otherwise cannot be clearly demarcated and assigned to retailer sellers.

The models of Mathewson and Winter (1983, 1984) make important points about the relative properties of RPM, exclusive territories, and density limitation. If dealers are differentiated from one another by spatial or service factors, the optimal contract for the manufacturer requires some provision to control the chain-of-monopolies problem, whatever externalities may be present. This problem for the manufacturer is worse (other things being equal) if dealers behave as parallel local monopolists (Losch conjectures) than if they behave independently (Nash conjectures). Exclusive territories impose Losch conjectures on the dealers, while RPM shifts their behavioral response to whatever conjectures they hold, from price to nonprice dimensions of competitive behavior. It is difficult to see how the manufacturer could rationally use either RPM or exclusive territories to deal with the chain-of-monopolies problem without also imposing minimum volume requirements. One wonders to what extent limits on dealers' densities effectively substitute for minimum volume requirements or permit their informal implementation.[9] In the same vein, the chain-of-monopolies problem by itself suggests that the manufacturer will generally favor RPM as a *maximum*-price constraint, and that exclusive territories should always be accompanied by minimum-volume requirements. If manufacturers impose resale price floors or exclusive territories by themselves in order to avert externalities among distributors, it is implied that these externalities are so strong that they more than offset the gains from squeezing dealers' gross margins to curb the chain-of-monopolies problem.

This list does not necessarily cover all terms of manufacturer-retailer agreements that affect competition, and it certainly does not cover all the types of terms included. The manufacturer may require the retailer to carry out a certain amount of advertising, provide a certain quantity of display space, maintain service facilities, and so forth. The retailer may seek advertising allowances, privileges of returning merchandise, training of salespersons, and so on. The bargain may be balanced with a variety of features, some restraining the manufacturer, some the retailer; most of these features are probably without significance for antitrust policy.

The preceding discussion sets the scene for a review of the empirical evidence on the incidence of vertical restraints. Much recent discussion implies that the task may be rather simple: many transactional reasons have been advanced by observers that may warrant vertical restraints, and the alternative market-power explanations demand rather stringent and specialized conditions. However, a simplistic view is inappropriate for at least two reasons. First, many economists who have proposed externality based reasons for vertical restraints assume that a restraint sufficient to internalize the externality is socially as well as privately desirable. However, the prevalence of signalling and information issues suggests caution: a quality signal implemented through a vertical restraint may, for example, be socially less efficient than a product-grading standard imposed by public policy.[10] If vertical restraints serve mostly to avert externalities in private contracts, we still should give close attention to whether these private externalities correspond exactly to social ones. Second, the interrelation of terms in manufacturer-dealer contracts raises at least the possibility that a normatively desirable restraint might be linked through the contract-balancing process to one that is undesirable. That is another reason for paying close attention to the full context of vertical restraints. Although this interrelation of contractual terms holds particular importance where dealers as well as manufacturers may possess some market power, the existence of substantial contracting costs and failures means that the terms imposed on dealers who are *ex ante* in elastic competitive supply need not attain a full optimum for the manufacturer.

Incidence of Vertical Restraints: Empirical Evidence

It would be highly desirable to obtain measurements of the incidence of vertical restraints as it varies from sector to sector and from one legal regime to another, in order to test the various explanations for the incidence of vertical restraints. Unfortunately, we lack even remotely suitable data. However, a good deal of informal evidence does exist on where vertical restraints have been employed in the United States economy. Some information stems from research on particular consumer-goods markets and from descriptive investigations of the various vertical restraints. Court decisions sometimes report enough information to indicate the structure of the manufacturer-distributor bargain that contained the challenged vertical restraint.[11] Resale price maintenance cases brought by the Federal Trade Commission have been reviewed and tabulated by Overstreet (1983). Economists and legal scholars have undertaken close investigations of some markets where vertical restraints were in use—notably, a group of investigations sponsored by the FTC. In the following paragraphs, I state a series of conclusions responsive to the preceding analysis and describe the evidence that underlies them.[12]

1. Some vertical restraints are clearly responsive to free-rider problems. In certain of the older antitrust cases, refusals to deal were employed apparently for the exclusive purpose of punishing parties who sought to free-ride on a shared intangible asset. In one instance, dress designers and textile producers jointly refused to deal with retailers who sold dresses that were copies of the designers' originals; in another case, a cooperative news-gathering organization prevented its members from reselling news material to nonmembers who had not contributed to the organization's operating costs.[13] The Coors brewery, whose beer requires special handling because it is unpasteurized, employed an extensive set of restrictions on distributors and a network of regional company representatives in order to prevent opportunistic shortcuts by distributors from the costly distribution processes mandated by the company. Territorial protection and some degree of resale price maintenance were used to reward distributors for adherence to these policies, and the length of the queue of applicants for distributorships suggested that the reward was generous.[14] Similar patterns appear in soft-drink and other franchise systems of distribution, where territorial protection reduces the temptation of franchises to debase the quality of the good they produce using inputs supplied by the franchisor (Caves and Murphy 1976; Katz 1978). At least some RPM has been for complex consumer durables (cameras, stereo equipment) for which pre-sales information could be an important consideration,[15] and efforts to enforce RPM were intensified in response to the rise of discount outlets offering low prices and little effort to advance a brand's goodwill value (Corey 1952). It is clear that manufacturers of products needing repair services assume that retailers will free-ride, and that this prospect motivates exclusive territories and territorial restrictions where quasi-contractual arrangements arise between distributor and final customer.[16] Customer restrictions are sometimes placed on wholesalers in order to effect some restraint on retailers that itself serves to mitigate a free-rider problem.[17] There are also examples of restraints that blunt an incentive for the manufacturer to underprovide some service; less training would be offered to mechan-

ics employed by franchised auto dealers if the resulting skills could be freely used on other manufacturers' vehicles (FTC 1978, 34–35).

2. Vertical restraints frequently serve to provide a quality signal that is implemented through the retailer's premises. The customer is assumed unable to judge a product's quality prior to purchase. The manufacturer provides a signal of high quality not so much through charging a high price per se as by assuring that the product is distributed only by retailers whose costly premises signal a quality image. Because this image is vulnerable to the product's sale through discount channels, the manufacturer must employ some combination of limited distribution and restriction on retail price competition. RPM or restricted distributorships have been used by many "quality" manufacturers (especially of goods frequently purchased as gifts, such as fine dinnerware, silverware, and fountain pens).[18] For goods that are made in different qualities and distributed through different sorts of retail establishments, the manufacturers imposing RPM and limited distribution are those who employ high-cost dealerships that emit a "quality" signal.[19] Sometimes RPM has been used by small-share or entrant producers to markets in which the dealer has considerable scope for influencing customers' perceptions of quality, with the negative effect on demand of the elevated price more than offset by the additional promotion that the deal can be induced to provide.[20] In short, vertical restraints and especially RPM have been strongly associated with signals emanating from the dealer.

3. Territorial restrictions seem commonly to serve in conjunction with exclusive territories as a vehicle for imposing volume requirements or otherwise attacking the "chain-of-monopolies" problem. The issue arises mainly with product lines whose distributors derive large proportions of their revenues from a few manufacturers' products.[21] Spacing limitations and volume requirements are revealed only indirectly in the vertical restraints cases because they are not generally under legal constraint. Still, they have evidently played a role in the distribution of hearing aids (Marvel 1984), automobiles (White 1971, 137–51), and soft drinks (Katz 1978). Examples can be found of RPM serving as a maximum-price constraint on territorially protected distributors for the same purpose,[22] but the combination of volume requirements and exclusive territories seems more common. In some sectors, however, the manufacturer's concern with the spacing of dealers reverses— where fixed costs per dealer are unimportant and the dealership itself serves as an advertisement for the product (as in franchised gasoline distribution). In such sectors, RPM has been used by manufacturers who presumably believe that demand for the product is increased by buyers' frequent observation of dealers' premises or the availability of the product close at hand when the whim to consume strikes—and increased enough to offset the higher distribution costs and product price.[23]

4. Territorial restrictions induce distributors to incur higher marginal

costs of customer contact within their territories. This model, which goes back to Preston (1965), is a special case of volume requirements as a control on chain-of-monopolies effects, and it operates where dealers incur significant contact costs that vary among customers, but do not get rolled into the resale prices quoted to them.[24] This pattern is documented in sales of soft drinks, trucks, and tools sold to auto mechanics and to others in mechanical trades.[25]

5. Customer restrictions serve in many cases to allow the manufacturer to maintain price discrimination among customer classes with different elasticities of demand. Territorial protection and/or RPM have served as adjuncts in these cases to compensate dealers for accepting customer restrictions. These practices have been present in the mechanics tools and truck markets, in passenger automobiles, drugs, and lightbulbs.[26] Other forms of price discrimination have also been effected through vertical restraints. These restraints allow the franchisor to extract the maximum rents from individual franchises through a tying arrangement that allows the manufacturer to meter the surplus accruing to each franchisee (Caves and Murphy 1976). Finally, some vertical restraints facilitate discrimination through the bundling of services together with the good sold.[27] Williamson (1979), analyzing the *Schwinn* case, argued that this bicycle manufacturer used a controlled distribution system to offer a package of a bicycle, guaranteed quality control, quality assembly at the time of sale, and guaranteed availability of service; this practice would segment buyer groups with high values of time or low aptitudes for making their own repairs.[28]

6. Customer restrictions also are used in conjunction with dual distribution by the manufacturer when customers are heterogeneous in the bundles of services that they require, and the manufacturer can provide some bundles more efficiently through direct distribution, others through intermediaries. Customer restrictions on arm's-length distributors are then required partly to avoid competition for rents captured by the manufacturer through direct sales, partly to avoid free-riding by distributors who promise a better bundle of services to the ultimate customer than they can deliver (Altschuler 1980, n. 6, pp. 42–43, 56–59).

7. There is no substantial evidence that manufacturers have used vertical restraints as an adjunct to collusion among themselves. No cases reveal convincing evidence of this form. Although it is possible to imagine circumstances in which vertical restraints would insulate horizontal price collusion among manufacturers from disturbances initiated in retail pricing, it is hard to imagine that manufacturers unable to forge a working collusive arrangement directly can achieve success by erecting parallel structures of vertical restraints.[29] Overstreet (1983, chap. 5) found that the seller-concentration ratios of manufacturing industries using RPM have actually been somewhat below the all-manufacturing median (59% of RPM industries with 4-firm

concentration below 40%), and that the manufacturers' absolute sizes similarly were on the small side. Because effective collusion usually requires fairly high seller concentration, his evidence tells strongly against the manufacturer-collusion hypothesis. In a few instances uncovered by competition policy in other countries (Canada, United Kingdom), oligopolies of manufacturers and distributors have joined forces to blockade entry,[30] but such instances are not evident in the United States. Exclusive-dealing arrangements hold the potential for erecting entry barriers to new manufacturers, but few of the U.S. antitrust cases on exclusive dealing seem to satisfy the necessary condition of natural restrictions on the entry of new, unattached distributors.[31]

8. Substantial evidence does support the hypothesis that some vertical restraints (notably RPM) have been sought by distributors who used their bargaining power to induce manufacturers to help restrict competition among themselves. The underlying hypothesis implies that vertical restraints may coincide with the bargaining power of retailers (as individuals or as collusive groups) and have nothing to do with problems of intangible assets. When RPM was widely legal in the United States, surveys found it especially prevalent among pharmacists' items (drugs and medicines, sundries, cosmetics and perfumes). It was also common among tobacco products and accessories, simple aim-and-shoot cameras and related photographic supplies, and inexpensive clocks and watches—also sold in part by drug stores. Most of these pharmacy items require little or no positive contribution by the retailer to the product's goodwill. Therefore, they broadly confirm Bowman's (1952) hypothesis that collusive behavior in this retail sector was directed against manufacturers who could not differentiate their products strongly through advertising.[32] It is also well established that groups of retailers such as the pharmacists were highly influential in lobbying for legislation that legalized RPM.[33] Restraints are common in some sectors for which retailers are highly concentrated in the relevant local market; eyeglass lenses supply an example (Bowman 1952). Among durable-goods manufacturers the incidence of RPM seems to be explained poorly by the market-failure model. RPM has apparently been less prevalent among major appliances than among small, simple appliances, which would seem to require less participation of the retailer in establishing and maintaining the manufacturer's goodwill (Corey 1952). It seems clear that "good dealers" capable of earning rents have in some instances collected them in the form of exclusive territories or other policies that confer some monopoly power on them (Travers and Wright 1962, 803, 805), which suggests that restraints may enter into some manufacturer-dealer agreements through rent-seeking rather than through dealers' market power.

9. The evidence clearly supports the proposition that vertical restraints, complementing or substituting for one another in the bilateral agreements

between manufacturers and distributors, are independent. Exclusive dealing imposes a particularly severe restraint and risk on the distributor, apparently compensated by requirements contracts (guaranteeing supplies) as well as pecuniary concessions, such as loans and preferential discounts.[34] Restrictions on customers to whom distributors can sell have commonly been compensated for by RPM or territorial restrictions on competition among the dealers.[35] Conversely, RPM and exclusive territories give the manufacturer an opportunity to make all-or-nothing quantity offers and force the protected retailer to discriminate within his territory.[36] The *Schwinn* decision, which made territorial protection illegal per se, provided a laboratory test of the hypothesis that restraints can substitute for one another; and, indeed, industries that had used territorial restrictions came up with a variety of substitutes in the following years (McLaren 1968; Timberg 1974). Similarly, a 1948 pronouncement by the Department of Justice that it believed territorial and customer restrictions to be illegal led to the substitution of "areas of primary responsibility" within the dealer had to fulfill a sales quota (Travers and Wright 1962, 796–97). A manufacturer may place territorial restrictions on his wholesalers while limiting competition among his retailers by clauses that confine their establishments to specified locations; the restraints are functionally equivalent and merely take account of the fact that the wholesaler goes out looking for customers while the retailer awaits the arrival of customers at his premises (Lewis 1976). Similarly, whether exclusive territories need to be buttressed with territorial restrictions depends on the mobility of customers; if they are immobile between distributors of the same brand, an exclusive territory may itself give the distributor an adequate local monopoly (Travers and Wright 1962, 809–11).

10. Vertical restraints substitute for vertical integration between manufacturer and dealer, in the sense that the parties' inability to devise satisfactory contract terms (including vertical restraints) at arm's length may be associated with increased use of vertical integration. This pattern accords with the predictions of the contractual approach (Williamson 1975) and indicates another frontier of adjustment in market institutions that will generally be affected by a change in the legality of any given vertical restriction. Franchising systems typically include a number of franchisor-owned outlets alongside those operating under contractual franchises, and one can get some distance explaining why the franchisor-controlled proportions vary as they do from sector to sector (Caves and Murphy 1976, 581–83), and many manufacturers seem ordinarily to employ a mixture of distribution directly and through agents (Altschuler 1980). Schwinn, precluded from imposing territorial restrictions on its franchised wholesale distributors, moved toward company-owned sales subsidiaries instead (Keck 1968). An in gasoline marketing, the use of company-owned stations has clearly supplied an alternative to franchises retail outlets, one used more heavily (in the United Kingdom, at least)

by petroleum refiners with samll shares of the market (Pass and Hawkins 1972, 589–91).

Selected Policy Implications

Evidence given here is much more fragmentary than one wishes, but it does suggest some conclusions about the incidence of vertical restraints that is relevant to public policy toward them. Clearly, the modern contractual explanations for vertical restraints do take us a substantial distance, but the market failures actually addressed by vertical restraints display a distribution somewhat different from what most builders of contractual models have had in mind. Most vertical restraints do serve to internalize externalities, attack the chain-of-monopolies problem, or otherwise minimize the costs of transaction and contractual enforcement between manufacturer and dealer. However, many of the vertical restraints seem designed to implement signalling equilibria or otherwise to maximize profits for manufacturers in conditions where the ultimate buyer possesses a severely limited set of information. To that extent, the more important policy question to ask about vertical restraints is not whether they are anticompetitive, but whether they commit avoidable excesses of resources to the transfer of information. Vertical restraints may in some cases have served to restrict competition—especially among distributors and especially through RPM. And in some cases they have contributed to entry barriers. However, these results have clearly not been their primary functions. Vertical restraints tend to appear in combinations in order to balance complex manufacturer-dealer contracts; although Pareto-optimal contracts will take this form, some evidence suggests that many such contracts are markedly second-best.

What do these conclusions contribute to the debate over the legal status of vertical restraints? The diversity of outcomes that they suggest certainly supports the *Sylvania* decision's placement of many vertical restraints under the rule of reason. In general, each restraint is capable of both averting a market failure and creating one through an exercise of market power. The analysis also helps to explain why the net welfare effect of vertical restraints may in many cases be difficult to infer. Forecasting the effect of legally excluding one vertical restraint from the manufacturer-retailer bargain requires a prediction of how the parties will recast that bargain after this disturbance to its mutual balance. The vertical restraints present in a given market situation may yield diverse effects on both competition and technical efficiency (cost minimization) at both the manufacturing and distributive stages. The standard judicial procedure of weighing effects on interbrand competition relative to intraband competition does not obviously capture the essence of the economic effects (White 1981).

The negative conclusions of the analysis can be overstressed, however, and some important positive propositions survive. Consider the question of whether an economic basis exists for different legal treatments of RPM and territorial restrictions. Bork (1966) and Posner (1977) argued that they are equivalent, so that the Supreme Court's newfound tolerance for territorial restrictions should by implication be extended to RPM as well. Indeed, if retailers were purely competitive, the effects of territorial restrictions and RPM would not differ, in the sense than any given resale price could alternatively be achieved by some restriction of the total number of retailers or their territorial spacing. However, if one drops the assumption that the retailers are purely competitive, this conclusion changes abruptly. Consider the following case.

1. As we mentioned above, volume requirements imposed by automobile manufacturers and others are an adjunct of territorial protection given to dealers and a method of keeping monopolistically competitive retailers from restricting their output below a level that minimizes average unit costs (the chain of monopolies). A *maximum* resale price could achieve the same effect, but the conventional *minimum* resale price could not avert this inefficiency.

2. The equivalence between territorial protection and RPM depends on price being the only dimension in which the retailer can vary his offer to the final buyer. However, the retailer may be able to offer trading stamps, free alterations, free delivery, credit, elaborate premises, and many other features that affect the quantity sold even if nominal price is not permitted to vary. Raising the resale price and imposing territorial restrictions will generally have different effects on these nonprice dimensions of the offer. One cannot be dogmatic about which result is preferred on welfare grounds. However, the choice may matter because some nonprice dimensions of competition involve significant commitments of resources. One example is the maintenance of excess capacity in the retail outlet's personnel and facilities to assure that randomly arriving customers are not put off by queues.

3. The effects of territorial protection and RPM on interbrand competition may differ. Assume that competing manufacturers of the product line recognize enough mutual interdependence to collude fairly effectively on price, but that their more numerous retail distributors do not collude with distributors of competing products (or collude less effectively than do the manufacturers). Retail price competition, if it occurs, probably prompts the brand's retailers to apply pressure for the manufacturer to cut the wholesale price and stay the erosion of their margins. Territorial protection, provided as a check on intrabrand competition, does nothing to dampen this form of interbrand rivalry at the retail level. RPM, however, blocks this form of retail rivalry and channels retail competition into dimensions less likely to transmit pressure back to the manufacturer.

4. We suggested that vertical restraints that serve to maximize the manufacturer's profits may be normatively questionable when information failures are involved. When RPM serves to emit a quality signal, the manufacturer can still replace it by limiting distribution to establishments that will maintain the desired "quality" image. However, either of them may be deemed a costly method of making credible the quality of the manufacturer's product.

The point of this comparison has not been to show that RPM is more objectionable socially than territorial protection—although the winds clearly blow in that direction—but rather to illustrate the subtle context in which the effects of alternative bargains between manufacturer and retailer are determined. A policy change that induces a shift from one to the other will have consequences for both intrabrand and interbrand competition—consequences that vary from product to product, depending on the cost structures of the retailers, the dimensions of nonprice rivalry available to them, and all structural conditions of the manufacturers' market that determine the extent and character of interbrand competition.

Notes

1. 433 U.S. 36 (1977).
2. Grieson and Singh (1985) showed why resale price maintenance might be employed where this condition holds.
3. Klein, Crawford, and Alchian (1978) wrote about this problem in the context of inducements for the parties to integrate vertically, but this approach also explains how arm's-length contracts may be structured so as to minimize the problem.
4. Bernheim and Whinston (1984) suggested a mechanism by which manufacturers exhibiting Cournot behavior among themselves could effect a collusive outcome through their process of contracting with a common set of marketing agents.
5. Williamson, 1983.
6. Precedents for this approach include Lewis (1976) and Porter (1976, 53–68). Schwartz and Eisenstadt (1982) provided a detailed survey of the analysis bearing on individual restraints.
7. White (1981) pointed out that rival dealers may spend excessive sums on various forms of nonprice competition, and the manufacturer can reduce total distributive margins by reducing their perceived rivalry.
8. This tradeoff in distributors' efforts between extensive and intensive margins requires that their marginal costs of customer contact be rising in the neighborhood of their normal levels of activity. See Travers and Wright (1962, 811); Preston (1965); Comanor (1968, 1430–32).
9. For an example, see Goldberg (1982, 482–86).
10. Scherer (1983) noted this point. He also investigated the logic underlying the proposition of Posner (1977, 18) and others that any output-increasing vertical restraint is economically efficient.
11. These decisions admittedly pose various hazards of interpretation. The facts revealed in the record may be incomplete or distorted by the way in which the legal issues were framed by the parties. Or the judicial inference from facts not stated in the opinion might not be the one an economist would draw. These uncertainties serve to qualify the conclusions that follow.
12. Notice that some of the evidence is rather old. I assume that the economic structure of distribution has not changed significantly in the last few decades.

13. Fashion Originators' Guild v. FTC, 312 U.S. 457 (1941); Associated Press et al. v. U.S., 326 U.S. 1 (1945); Groenke (1968).

14. Adolph Coors Co. v. FTC, 497 F.2d 1178 (2d Cir. 1974).

15. See, for example, Interphoto Corp. v. Minolta, 295 F.Supp. 711 (1969); Dictograph Products v. FTC, 217 F.2d 821 (2d Cir. 1954). My count of FTC cases for the 1965–82 period (from Overstreet 1983, chap. 5) suggests that free-riding problems might have been present in as many as twenty-five of sixty-three cases.

16. Travers and Wright (1962, 812); Altschuler (1980, 7–15). There seem to be several economic reasons for this, despite one's general expectation that no externalities would be involved. Repairs under warranty cannot always be compensated fully by the manufacturer. The dealer may trade on the final buyer's inability to tell whether poor performance of the product is due to faulty repairs or to faults of the product that are blamed on the manufacturer. Finally, the price of repairs may not ration demand to supply in the short run, in which case the dealer has an incentive not shared by the manufacturer to look after his regular customers first. These factors seem consistent with United States v. General Motors, 384 U.S. 127 (1966).

17. Customer restrictions also may directly protect the interest of distributors in an ongoing relation with customers in whom they make an initial investment that is not compensated directly. A lock manufacturer restricted customers who were expanding their master lock systems to the distributor who installed the original system. United States v. Eaton, Yale & Towne, Inc., CCH Trade Cases no. 73,889 (1972).

18. The case of Lenox china was discussed by Goldberg (1980). He also pointed out that RPM is responsive to the heavy fixed costs to retailers of providing services (such as bridal consultants) complementary to the sale of fine china. See Lee (1959) on pens and silverware, Corey (1952) on small appliances.

19. Whether the manufacturer sets a high margin in order to recruit dealers who will emit quality signals or to acquire the services of dealers who independently invest in sending quality signals is a question of whether the manufacturer employs specialized outlets or those that distribute many product lines. See Greening (1984) on Florsheim shoes, and Oster (1984) on Levi Strauss garments. Goldberg (1982, 456–60) showed how a quality signal can coincide with incentives for the generous provision of unpriced auxiliary services by dealers.

20. See Lewis (1976, 299) on TV receivers; Sandura Co. v. FTC, 339 F.2d 847 (2d Cir. 1964) on floor coverings; Hollander (1966, 85) on small appliances; McEachern and Romeo (1984) on stereo equipment; and Altschuler (1980, 39).

21. For manufacturers utilizing mass distributors, the problem is in effect solved by the close substitutes provided by other manufacturers' goods as inputs to the dealers' distribution activities.

22. See Albrecht v. Herald Co., 350 U.S. 145 (1968).

23. Corey (1952) suggested this pattern for small appliances as an explanation of why RPM should have prevailed for them and not for large appliances (where pre-sale information would seem more important). Hollander (1966, 92–93) associated the use of RPM with efforts of makers of nonprescription drugs to get their goods displayed in supermarkets and discount stores.

24. In such a case, territorial restrictions and exclusive territories avert the nega-

tive externality of duplicating contact costs when rival retailers both offer the manufacturer's brand to the same customer.

25. See Katz (1978) and Posner (1977) on soft drinks; Snap-On Tools Corp. v. FTC, 321 F.2d 285 (2d Cir. 1963), p. 829, on mechanics' tools; and White Motor Co. v. United States, 372 U.S. 253 (1963), pp. 256–57, on trucks. This mechanism may explain the full-line forcing of tires, batteries, and accessories with service stations; see Baker (1969).

26. See the cases cited in note 18; White (1971, 169) on automobiles; Bowman (1952) on lightbulbs; and United States v. Parke, Davis & Co., 362 U.S. 29 (1960) on drugs.

27. Adams and Yellen (1976). Tying arrangements that permit price discrimination, of course, may also allow transactional economies; see Markovits (1980). It should be noted, however, that a tying warranted by economic efficiency can be induced by competitive prices and does not require a contractual all-or-nothing offer.

28. An important part of this mechanism is the existence of fixed costs of maintaining the distribution network. Schwinn may have rejected discount stores as dealers in order to preclude the erosion of rents that might threaten the coverage of the repair facilities' fixed costs. Also see Goldberg (1980) on Lenox china.

29. However, Corey (1952) did conclude that this situation held in small electrical appliances, and some evidence supports it for gasoline distribution.

30. For example, the manufacturers agree with the distributors' association to supply no nonmember distributors or to impose RPM or territorial restrictions, and the distributors agree not to seek supplies from competing importers.

31. On farm equipment, see United States v. J.I. Case Co., 101 F. Supp. 856 (1951). Freishtat et al. (1974) applied the model to outboard motors, but not very convincingly.

32. Bowman places retail liquor dealers in the same situation. Also see Hollander (1966, 79–81).

33. Palamountain (1955, chap. 8). Pharmacists of course do provide auxiliary services with some items they sell, but not obviously the ones that were principally involved in conflicts over RPM.

34. Much of the evidence pertains to gasoline distribution. See Pass and Hawkins (1972) and Curran (1950).

35. Bowman (1952) on light bulbs; White Motor Co. v. United States, p. 257 on trucks; Snap-On Tools Corp. v. FTC, pp. 833, 835–36.

36. White (1971, 137–51) on automobiles; Hollander (1966, 84) on small appliances; Katz (1978) on soft drinks; and Travers and Wright (1962).

References

Adams, William James, and Janet L. Yellen. 1976. "Commodity Bundling and the Burden of Monopoly." *Quarterly Journal of Economics* 90:475–98.

Altschuler, Stuart. 1980. "*Sylvania*, Vertical Restraints, and Dual Distribution." *Antitrust Bulletin* 25:1–102.

Baker, Donald I. 1969. "Another Look at Franchise Tie-Ins after Texaco and Fortner." 14:767–83.

Bernheim, B. Douglas, and Michael D. Whinston. 1984. "Common Marketing Agency as a Device for Facilitating Collusion." Harvard Institute of Economic Research, Discussion Paper No. 1098.

Bittlingmayer, George. 1983. "A Model of Vertical Restriction and Equilibrium in Retailing." *Journal of Business* 56:477–96.

Bork, Robert H. 1966. "The Rule of Reason and the Per Se Concept: Price Fixing and Market Division." *Yale Law Journal* 75:373–475.

Bowman, Ward S., Jr. 1952. "Resale Price Maintenance—A Monopoly Problem." *Journal of Business* 25:141–55.

Caves, Richard E., and William F. Murphy III. 1976. "Franchising: Firms, Markets, and Intangible Assets." *Southern Economic Journal* 42:572–86.

Comanor, William S. 1968. "Vertical Territorial and Customer Restrictions: White Motor and Its Aftermath." *Harvard Law Review* 81:1419–38.

Corey, E.R. 1952. "Fair Trade Pricing: A Reappraisal." *Harvard Business Review* 30:47–62.

Curran, K.K. 1950. "Exclusive Dealing and Public Policy." *Journal of Marketing* 15:133–44.

Federal Trade Commission. Bureau of Competition and Regional Offices. 1978. *Report of the Vertical Restraints Task Force.* Washington: Federal Trade Commission. Mimeo.

Federal Trade Commission. 1984. *Impact Evaluations of Federal Trade Commission Vertical Restraints Cases.* Ed. R.N. Lafferty, R.H. Lange, and J.B. Kirkwood. Washington, Federal Trade Commission.

Freishtat, D., et al. 1974. "The Arrogance of Monopoly Power: Product Differentiation and Exclusive Dealing in the Outboard-Motor Industry." *Antitrust Law and Economics Review* 7, no. 4:55–78.

Goldberg, Victor P. 1980. "Enforcing Resale Price Maintenance: The FTC Investigation of Lenox." *American Business Law Journal* 18:225–58.

Goldberg, Victor P. 1982. "Resale Price Maintenance and the FTC: The Magnavox Investigation." *William & Mary Law Review* 23:440–500.

Gould, J.R., and L.E. Preston. 1965. "Resale Price Maintenance and Retail Outlets." *Economica* 32:302–12.

Greening, Timothy. 1984. "Analysis of the Impact of the Florscheim Shoe Case." In Federal Trade Commission (1984, 91–178).

Grieson, Ronald E., and Nirvikar Singh. 1985. "Resale Price Maintenance: A Simple Analysis." In *Antitrust and Regulation,* Ed. Ronald E. Grieson. Lexington, Mass: Lexington Books.

Groenke, T.A. 1968. "What's New in the Antitrust Aspects of Selecting and Terminating Distributors." *Antitrust Bulletin* 13:131–59.

Hollander, S.C. 1966. "United States of America." Chap. 3 in *Resale Price Maintenance,* Ed. B.S. Yamey. Chicago: Aldine Press.

Katz, Barbara C. 1978. "Territorial Exclusivity in the Soft-Drink Industry." *Journal of Industrial Economics* 27:85–96.

Keck, R.C. 1968. "Alternative Distribution Techniques—Franchising, Consignment, Agency, and Licensing." *Antitrust Bulletin* 13:177–91.

Klein, Benjamin, Robert G. Crawford, and Armen A. Alchian. 1978. "Vertical Integration, Appropriable Rents, and the Competitive Contracting Process." *Journal of Law and Economics* 21:297–326.

Lee, S.M. 1959. "Problems of Resale Price Maintenance." *Journal of Marketing* 23:274–91.

Lewis, M.B. 1976. "Restraints under *Schwinn* and *Sylvania*: An Argument for the Continued Use of a Partial Per Se Approach." *University of Michigan Law Review* 75:175–310.

McEachern, William A., and Anthony A. Romeo. (1984. "Vertical Restraints and Economic Efficiency: An Analysis of FTC Intervention in the Audio Components Industry." In Federal Trade Commission (1984, 200–259).

McLaren, R.W. 1968. "Marketing Limitations on Independent Distributors and Dealers." *Antitrust Bulletin* 13:161–75.

Markovits, Richard S. 1980. "Tie-Ins and Reciprocity: A Functional, Legal, and Policy Analysis." *Texas Law Review* 58:1363–1445.

Marvel, Howard P. 1982. "Exclusive Dealing." *Journal of Law and Economics* 25:1–25.

Marvel, Howard P. 1984. "Vertical Restraints in the Hearing Aids Industry." In Federal Trade Commission (1984, 271–377).

Mathewson, G.F., and R.A. Winter. 1983. "Vertical Integration by Contractual Restraints in Spatial Markets." *Journal of Business* 56:497–517.

Mathewson, G.F., and R.A. Winter. 1984. "An Economic Theory of Vertical Restraints." *Rand Journal of Economics* 15:27–38.

Oster, Sharon. 1984. "The FTC v. Levi Strauss: An Analysis of the Economic Issues." In Federal Trade Commission (1984, 47–90).

Overstreet, Thomas R., Jr. 1983. *Resale Price Maintenance: Economic Theories and Empirical Evidence.* Bureau of Economics Staff Report. Washington: Federal Trade Commission.

Palamountain, J.C., Jr. 1955. *The Politics of Distribution.* Cambridge: Harvard University Press.

Pass, C.L., and K.H. Hawkins. 1972. "Exclusive Dealing, Supplier Ownership of Outlets, and the Public Interest: The Petrol Case." *Antitrust Bulletin* 17:567–95.

Porter, Michael E. 1976. *Interbrand Choice, Strategy, and Bilateral Market Power.* Cambridge: Harvard University Press.

Posner, Richard S. 1977. "The Rule of Reason and the Economic Approach: Reflections on the *Sylvania* Decision." *University of Chicago Law Review* 45:1–20.

Preston, Lee E. 1965. "Restrictive Distribution Arrangements: Economic Analysis and Public Policy Standards." *Law and Contemporary Problems* 30:506–29.

Scherer, F.M. 1983. "The Econmics of Vertical Restraints." *Antitrust Law Journal* 52 no. 3:687–707.

Schwartz, Marius, and David Eisenstadt. 1982. "Vertical Restraints." U.S. Department of Justice, Antitrust Division, Economic Policy Office, *Discussion Paper* No. EPD–82–8.

Telser, Lester G. 1960. "Why Should Manufacturers Want Fair Trade?" *Journal of Law and Economics* 3:86–105.

Telser, Lester G. 1965. "Abusive Trade Practices: An Economic Analysis." *Law and Contemporary Problems* 30:488–505.

Timburg, S. 1974. "Territorial Restrictions on Franchisees: Post-*Schwinn* Developments." *Antitrust Bulletin* 19:205–16.

Travers, A.H., Jr. and T.D. Wright. 1962. "Restricted Channels of Distribution under the Sherman Act." *Harvard Law Review* 75:795–834.

White, Lawrence, J. 1971. *The Automobile Industry since 1945.* Cambridge: Harvard University Press.

White, Lawrence, J. 1981. "Vertical Restraints in Antitrust Law: A Coherent Model." Antitrust Bulletin 26:327–45.

Williamson, Oliver E. 1975. *Markets and Hierarchies: Analysis and Antitrust Implications.* New York: Free Press.

Williamson, Oliver E. 1979. "Assessing Vertical Market Restrictions: Antitrust Ramifications of the Transaction Cost Approach." *University of Pennsylvania Law Review* 127:953–93.

Williamson, Oliver E. 1983. "Credible Commitments: Using Hostages to Support Exchange." *American Economic Review* 73:519–40.

3
Special Interests, Bureaucrats, and Antitrust: An Explanation of the Antitrust Paradox

Bruce L. Benson
M.L. Greenhut

Robert Bork contends that there is an "antitrust paradox" (1978), while Peter Asch refers to the "antitrust dilemma" (1970). Others are critical of antitrust enforcement because of inconsistencies in application and a failure to apply economic theory towards the end of promoting efficiency. Asch proposes that:

> Economists are sometimes a critical, even cantankerous lot. We are especially prone to complain about public policies formulated in ignorance of the lessons of economic analysis or, worse yet, based in "bad" economics. Antitrust policy has thus been forced to compete with other areas for its share of criticism, but, all things considered, it has more than held its own (1970, vii).

Bork uses four observations to illustrate what he calls the antitrust paradox: (1) political choice in antitrust are being made largely by the courts rather than by the legislatures; (2) there is a concern for the status of each producer rather than for preserving competition; (3) emphasis centers on the welfare of specific groups rather than on the general welfare; and (4) equality of outcome and reward according to status is achieved rather than liberty and reward according to merit (1978, 10–11, 418–19). Bork proposes as the root of this paradox the idea that:

> A consumer-oriented law must employ basic economic theory to judge which market structures and practices are harmful and which beneficial. Modern antitrust has performed this task very poorly. Its version of economics is a mélange of valid insights and obviously incorrect—sometimes fantastic— assumptions about the motivations and effects of business behavior. There are many problems here, but perhaps the core of the difficulty is that the courts, and particularly the Supreme Court, have failed to understand and give proper weight to the crucial concept of business efficiency . . . this failure has skewed legal doctrine disastrously (1978, 7).

The purpose of this chapter is to explain that there really is no antitrust paradox. The paradox (really the dilemma that exists) arises because analysts start with the premise that the antitrust laws are "consumer-oriented" and that their basic goal is to promote economic efficiency. We shall propose instead that antitrust, as with virtually all government activity, is designed to benefit special-interest groups rather than to promote the "public interest." Under this focus, apparent inconsistencies and use of "bad economics" are readily explained. Economists educated in the tradition of positive analysis who view efficiency as a norm may not like the explanation. However, the political reality of antitrust must be recognized if any changes in the direction of antitrust toward efficiency, such as those proposed by Bork (1978), Posner (1970), and others, will ever be achieved. The fact is that efficiency has no strong politically active constituency. Thus the problem of antitrust has deep roots, based in fact on the general idea of economic regulation. Consider the following facts.

The once widely held Pigouvian view of government intervention as a mechanism to correct for market failures has recently begun to fall into disrepute, as economic *regulation* has increasingly appeared as a transfer mechanism whose design is to provide rents to politically powerful special-interest groups. Perhaps the most influential work in stressing the "special interest" rather than the "public interest" view of economic regulation is that of Stigler (1971). His seminal work along this line stimulated many follow-up theoretical extensions (for example, Posner 1971; Peltzman 1976; McCormick and Tollison 1981; and Becker 1983), besides fostering empirical verifications (for example, see Abrams and Settle 1978; Jarrell 1978; Kau and Rubin 1978; McCormick and Tollison 1981; and Smith 1982, among others).[1] One of the major conclusions of Stigler's demand-supply theory of economic regulation, where interest groups are viewed on the demand side and political representatives on the supply side, is that regulation is *not* designed to enhance economic efficiency. In fact, it is intended typically to restrict competition in ways that eventuate in deadweight losses and involve wealth transfers from one group (often consumers) to another (often business).

It is significant that the special-interest view of economic regulation recently found its way into the areas of antitrust laws (for example, Posner 1969; Faith et al. 1982; Weingast and Moran 1983; and Benson 1983b). Thus Posner has claimed that Federal Trade Commission investigations are seldom in the public interest and are undertaken ". . . at the behest of corporations, trade associations, and trade unions whose motivation is at best to shift the costs of their private litigation to the taxpayer and at worst to harass competitors" (1969, 87). Unfortunately, this approach has not yet been fully refined to account for antitrust problems per se. More specifically, there are several institutional differences between regulatory forms of market intervention and antitrust matters, with regulators typically being concerned with one or a few industries, whereas antitrust enforcement carries much broader scope. Perhaps a concentrated clientele is needed for interest group pressure to be effective (for example, for antitrust authorities to be "captured"). In addition, the courts play a much more visible role in antitrust than they do in regulation. Perhaps the courts effectively constrain antitrust enforcers and somehow limit their ability to generate rents. This chapter explores these issues in order to demonstrate that antitrust is indeed a component of the interest-group transfer process, just as is regulation. At the same instance, the chapter evaluates the intrinsic differences that characterize the two forms of government intervention and extends the regulatory interest-group perspective to include antitrust.

This chapter is divided into four sections. First, a generalized model of market intervention is proposed. This is needed because the interest-group theory of regulation has failed to account for the great influence and power of bureaucrats and/or commissioners in the regulatory (and in the antitrust) process (Hirshleifer 1976). Thus the first section offers predictions about interest-group behavior, particularly as it is influenced by the antitrust enforcers themselves. The second section then examines the passage and subsequent enforcement of various antitrust statutes in order to demonstrate the applicability of the interest-group model. The third section of this chapter considers antitrust institutions with emphasis on the role of the courts. The purpose of this is to show that the courts have not constrained, much less altered, the established interest-group transfer process. Our concluding section indicates that the paradoxical inconsistencies that economists find in antitrust are not really inconsistencies at all, given the special-interest view of antitrust proposed herein.

A Model of Market Intervention

There are three important parties to the market-intervention process: (1) interest groups, (2) legislators (or, more accurately, the potential legislators who compete for votes and contributions from interest groups), and (3) the commissioners and/or bureaucrats who actually regulate, interpret, and enforce the antitrust statutes. It should be stressed that these parties are not all mutually exclusive. In particular, bureaucrats and commissioners themselves constitute very important interest groups that wield considerable political power.

We shall define the object of special-interest demands for market intervention to be the transfer of wealth, as in Stigler (1971). However, for several reasons explained elsewhere (Benson 1984), it should be stressed that the wealth transfers are provided by governmental assignments or transfers of property rights. In fact, market intervention can be divided into two distinct elements: (1) the assignment of property rights, and (2) the enforcement of the resulting property-rights assignment.

The governmental assignment of rights is a rule-making or legislative function. However, interest groups demand more than just favorable property rights assignments, and governments perform more than just the legislative function. Once the rights assignment is made, it must be enforced. Interest groups demand that their rights be protected (or that opposition groups be prevented from using rights that are legally attenuated). The assignment and enforcement functions can, of course, be thought of as one commodity (one object of demand) because different levels of property rights enforcement are actually just varying degrees of property rights attenuation. Consequently, *the single object of interest-group demand is to obtain favorable property rights.*

In contrast to the Stigler-Peltzman model of regulation, there is good reason for distinguishing between the antitrust assignment and enforcement functions as legislators *do not* enforce rights assignments, even though they could, in theory, perform the overall regulatory function. Rather, as a practical matter, legislators delegate considerable independence and power to regulatory agencies. Ehrlich and Posner (1974) explain why this power is delegated. Specifically, they classify legislative bodies as firms whose costs of production are typically very high. Their costs actually rise sharply with increased output because legislative production must involve negotiations among members of a large group (legislators). Bargaining among large numbers of individuals creates high transaction costs that increase rapidly as the number of the bargainers is increased. Therefore, a legislature cannot respond efficiently to an increase in its workload by adding to its size. The fact of the matter is that as the amount of business grows (that is, as the demands of interest groups increase), a legislature can respond most efficiently by delegating more powers to commissions and bureaus.

Exchanges

Commissions and bureaus are supposedly extensions of Congress's assigned power to regulate commerce. They serve therefore as an arm of the legislature. Unfortunately, in a sense, we shall argue below that they have been given considerable independence along with the power to assign rights (in effect to legislate) as well as to enforce their rights assignments. There are, accordingly, two relevant transactions in the political process of market intervention. The first, which shall be referred to as the *political exchange,* is an exchange of political support from interest groups (votes, campaign contributions, and so on) for the allocative support of a legislature. That is to say, the legislature allocates property rights (or delegates authority to allocate rights) and provides budgetary support for the enforcement of rights. The second transaction, to be called the *budget exchange,* is between the legislature and the regulatory agencies or commissions.[2] The legislature trades (or allocates) budgets for the services provided by bureaucrats or commissioners—services including enforcement and, in many cases, the assignment of rights.

The Political Exchange. The Stigler-Peltzman theory of regulation is really a theory of the exchange of political support for favorable assignments of property rights. Their hypothesis that regulators are majority maximizers actually predicts the behavior of legislators in the political exchange. This situation results because law-givers face competition, whereas the interest groups that influence them have alternative sources of favorable property-rights assignments (that is, alternative political parties). When an incumbent does not assign rights to obtain support from the largest possible majority, there exists a political-rights system that results in a larger majority. Another candidate can offer that assignment and defeat the incumbent's reelection bid. Only an officeholder who behaves as a majority maximizer can maintain legislative tenure in the long run. Any nonmajority maximizing property-rights assignment (whether it occurs because a legislator prefers a different rights assignment, perhaps in deference to the public interest, or because the legislator misreads relative demand strengths of parties in interest) results in potential defeat in the next election. *Thus, the competitive political process moves the outcome (the assignment of rights) towards the equilibrium described by Peltzman's (1976) majority maximizing model.*

Peltzman's model need not be detailed here, but some of his conclusions are worth noting (1976).

1. The legislature will tend to favor the politically most powerful interest group(s).
2. More than one organization may be favored at the expense of others (that is, one rights assignment may benefit more than one group).
3. When there are differences among members of an interest group, the benefits or costs to the members involved in a property-rights assignment (that is, the welfare transfer resulting from a rights transfer) will differ among members.
4. The favored interest group(s) will not be favored to the extent that it (they) could otherwise be favored.

This last point warrants further discussion. Legislatures never act as the perfect broker for a single interest group. The reason this conclusion holds is that in order for an individual legislator to maximize his majority, the "marginal political return of a transfer must equal the marginal political cost" (Peltzman, 217). A legislative assembly wishes to assign rights so that the marginal benefits to the favored interest group(s) equal the marginal costs to the losers. In contrast, total benefits for the winning group(s) are maximized when marginal benefits equal zero. But legislators would not be majority maximizing if they allocated rights to maximize winners' benefits.

Legislators *wish* to meet the marginal conditions of the political exchange. Because of this, Stigler and his followers argue that the regulation process efficiently accomplishes what it is designed to do. For example, he proposes that "political systems are rationally devised and rationally employed, which is to say that they are appropriate instruments for the fulfillment of desires of members of society" (1971, 4). Posner reaches a similar conclusion, arguing that the process of regulation

> . . . can be expected to operate with reasonable efficiency to achieve its ends. The ends are the product of a struggle between interest groups, but . . . it would be contrary to the usual assumption of economics to argue that wasteful or inappropriate means would be chosen to achieve those ends (1974, 350).

In addition to the marginal-cost-equals-marginal-benefits goals of legislators, Posner notes that the legislature improves upon the political efficiency of the regulatory process by delegating powers to agencies and commissions. This strengthens Posner's belief that the economic theory of regulation implies that the regulatory process "can be expected to operate with reasonable efficiency." And yet, Posner observes that evidence exists that indicates that unnecessarily expensive methods of regulation are often used (1974, 354). Moreover, there is considerable empirical support for the contention that regulators are inefficient (1974, 337–39). He is also concerned because Stigler's theory fails to explain why "some forms of regulation generate costs in resource misallocation that seem large in relation to the benefits of the favored interest group" (1974, 353). It must be stressed that efficiency in this political arena does not imply that regulation will result in allocative efficiency or welfare maximization in the regulated market.

Actually, Stigler realizes, and Peltzman demonstrates, that a lawmaker prefers a politically efficient allocation of benefits in the sense of maximizing political support. Ehrlich and Posner explain that legislatures delegate powers to agencies to improve political efficiency. It does not follow, however, that bureaucrats and commissioners have incentives to operate efficiently. Examination of the budget exchange indicates that inefficiencies and unnecessarily expensive enforcement methods must arise.

The Budget Exchange. A transaction between a legislature and an agency (or appointed commission) involves the exchange of a specific output or combination of outputs for a specific budget. The output is a level of enforcement associated with legislatively determined property-rights assignments, or a combination of bureaucratically determined property-rights assignments and enforcement of the rights. Niskanen modeled this type of exchange, although he was concerned only with bureaucratic supply of goods and services (1968, 1975), not with the field of antitrust as such. Niskanen's work nonetheless serves as a foundation for a discussion of any budget exchange in the market intervention process, albeit several adjustments must be made in his presentation because:

1. Not all regulators and antitrust enforcers can be characterized as bureaucrats. One must account for differences in the incentives of commission and civil service bureaucrats.
2. There may be differences in constraints facing regulators and antitrust enforcers due to different institutional arrangements. These potential differences must be accounted for.
3. In Niskanen's model, legislative demand reflects the wishes of society rather than the preferences of the politically most powerful interest group or groups, as is contended below.[3]

Let us begin with incentives in regulatory and antitrust bureaus or agencies. Niskanen proposed a bureau manager's utility function of the form

$$U = a_1 Y^{b_1} p^{c_1} \tag{3.1}$$

where Y represents the present value of a civil servant's income and P is the set of nonmonetary perquisites associated with the bureaucrat's job (that is, prestige, power, leisure time, social and physical amenities, and so on [Niskanen 1975]). The parameters (a_1, b_1, and c_1) typically differ for each bureaucrat.

The output preferred by an agency is assumed by Niskanen to depend upon the bureau manager's incentive structure, as it relates to his utility function. He defines the incentive structure as

$$Y = a_2 Q^{b_2} (B - C)^{c_2}, \tag{3.2}$$

and

$$P = a_3 Q^{b_3} (B - C)^{c_3}, \tag{3.3}$$

where Q is the agency's output (for example, property-rights enforcement), B represents the maximum budget legislators will approve for production of Q, C is the minimum cost of producing this regulatory output, and $(B - C)$ denotes the agency's "discretionary budget," as in Mique and Belanger (1974).

Certain general observations can be made concerning the parameters of this incentive structure. Government regulators and antitrust enforcers probably have very low c_2 values because they cannot appropriate any of their agency's discretionary budget for personal income (unless promotions to higher-paying jobs are available). However, parameters b_2, b_3, and c_3 tend to be high for bureaucrats (that is, relative to the values for private managers). This conjecture applies because an agency manager's monetary and nonmonetary rewards increase as the output of the bureau expands. Salary and nonmonetary perquisites of the agency manager are positive, monotonic functions of agency size. A bureaucratic manager also is able to appropriate part of his agency's discretionary budget in the form of nonmonetary benefits because the legislature does not monitor the bureau to a degree sufficient enough to prevent such appropriation (as will later be stressed). A regulator can use a portion of the discretionary budget, for example, to improve his office environment (that is, large office, large desk, nice furniture, attractive secretaries, and so forth), enlarge his staff (and perhaps reduce his own workload), obtain a government limousine, and so on.

Now substitute equations (3.2) and (3.3) into (3.1) so that the utility function is expressed in terms of Q and $(B - C)$:[4]

$$U = aQ^b(B - C)^c. \tag{3.4}$$

Further adjustments are possible since the discretionary budget can be expressed as a function of Q. Assume for simplicity that both the legislature's demand for rights enforcement arising from market intervention (and reflecting the demand of the strongest interests), as well as the marginal cost of producing such rights enforcement, are linear. Then the discretionary budget is

$$(B - C) = (d - f)Q - (e + g)Q^2. \tag{3.5}$$

where d and f are the intercepts of the demand and cost functions respectively, and e and g are slope parameters of the two functions.[5] Therefore, equation (3.4) can be rewritten as

$$U = aQ^b[(d - f)Q - (e + g)Q^2]^c. \tag{3.6}$$

Maximizing with respect to Q leads to the bureaucrats' utility maximizing output where

$$Q^* = \left(\frac{b + c}{b + 2c}\right)\left(\frac{d - f}{e + g}\right). \tag{3.7}$$

The level of enforcement preferred by an agency manager (equation [3.7] is a positive function of the marginal effect of the level of enforcement on managerial rewards and a negative function of the marginal share of the agency's appropriated discretionary budget.[6]

A Natural Dichotomy of Choice

The legislature's preferred level of property rights enforcement, as we have seen, is determined by equating the politically marginal costs and marginal benefits (given the assumption that legislators are majority maximizers and therefore desire the politically efficient output of rights enforcement à la Peltzman [1976]). The maximization involved establishes

$$Q = \frac{1}{2} \left(\frac{d - f}{e + g} \right). \tag{3.8}$$

This is also the agency's preferred level of enforcement, provided that the bureau's output is completely unrelated to both managerial income and the perquisites of office (that is, when $b = 0$). If, however, $b > 0$, the bureaucrat would prefer to produce an output of property-rights enforcement greater than the politically efficient output. In other words, *bureaucrats do want to overenforce property-rights assignments, given the fact that their incomes or nonmonetary incentives are directly related to the level of enforcement* (that is, agency size). Of course, we still must determine whether the legislature will allow overenforcement, but clearly incentives to use the "unnecessarily expensive methods of conferring benefits" do exist, as Posner observed. But first, we must ask whether a bureaucrat also has the incentive to produce any given level of enforcement inefficiently.

If $c = 0$, then

$$Q'' = \left(\frac{d - f}{e + g} \right). \tag{3.9}$$

This output is twice the legislature's optimal output, *but* it is produced at minimum cost. A bureaucrat prefers this output *only* when no part of the discretionary budget can be appropriated. However, as long as a portion of the discretionary budget can be put to personal use ($c > 0$), the bureaucrat has incentives to enforce inefficiently.

A second question is, will the legislature allow regulators to produce inefficiently at levels of enforcement greater than the politically optimal levels? Given Niskanen's claim that the bargaining process between the legislature and a bureau (regulatory or antitrust agency) is a bilateral monopoly situation, the ultimate output, Q', should be

$$\frac{1}{2} \left(\frac{d - f}{e + g} \right) \leq Q' \leq Q^*. \tag{3.10}$$

This outcome depends upon the relative bargaining strengths and incentives of agency managers and of lawmakers. If legislators only had to monitor regulators and set their output, the outcome of the bargaining process would probably come very close to the legislators' optimum.

The Fundamental Causes of Over- and Excessive Enforcement

All this information indicates a need for us to examine the legislative demand for enforcement more carefully.[7] Up to now, we simply suggested that this demand function represents the legislature's perception of the dominant interest groups' demands. Lawmakers desire a property rights system and enforcement of that system. This objective results in the majority maximizing conditions described by Peltzman (1976). We further note that interest-group demand is a function of the alternative investments open to the group, the welfare the group expects to gain from a particular rights assignment (or the welfare loss it expects to prevent), and so on (see Benson 1984). If the group has alternative sources of regulation (for example, a choice between state or federal regulation), the legislative demand for a bureaucratic agency should be both lower and more elastic than otherwise.

Legislative Review. Will the legislature allow a regulator or antitrust agency to overenforce, and on top of that to enforce inefficiently? In this connection, consider the fact that a lawmaker performs more than one function. He must spend time choosing the appropriate rights assignment. This task can involve considerable time in direct contact with various interest groups (lobbyists, hearings, trips back to the home district, and so forth), since each legislator has to determine which interest group(s) is most powerful on each issue, as well as what that group wants done. In addition, the behavior of regulatory and antitrust bureaus must be controlled, and determination made as to whether they would efficiently meet the most powerful interests' demands. Legislators face (or must make) a tradeoff. When more time is spent monitoring regulators, less time is available for ascertaining interest groups' strengths and demands. Niskanen observed:

> Legislatures can use a variety of control devices . . . to reduce the misallocation and inefficiency of bureaucratic supply. These control devices are costly, however, and *they will be used only to the point where their marginal value equals their marginal cost* (1975, 623).

A legislator's majority maximization effort is, therefore, a *constrained* maximization problem.[8] If we assume lawmakers have two basic functions, (1) choosing appropriate rights assignments, and (2) controlling regulators, it follows that their time must be allocated between these functions while they attempt to maximize majority support.

Suppose for simplicity that the magnitude of a typical legislator's majority is a linear function (1) of the amount of time spent in assessing the demand conditions that determine the rights assignments, (2) the selection of property-rights assignments, and (3) the net welfare transfer that results from the enforcement of rights. Specifically, we have

$$M = uX + vN + wT, \qquad (3.11)$$

where M is the size of the majority, X represents the time spent choosing the rights assignments, N denotes the number of rights assigned to the favored interest group(s), and T is the value of the net welfare transfer. Just assigning rights has a positive effect on M. But because of overenforcement, the net welfare transfer tends to be negative.[9] The final net transfer is a function of the level of enforcement:

$$T = -zBN, \qquad (3.12)$$

where B is the actual budget for enforcement of each right assignment. Substituting (3.12) into (3.11) yields

$$M = uX + (v - wzB)N. \qquad (3.13)$$

A lawmaker's potential work time is limited. Actual budget allocations should approach the politically optimal allocation as additional time is directed to the controlling of bureaucrats. Time available for assessing relative interest-group demands (X) decreases as a legislator spends more time scrutinizing bureau performance. Niskanen (1975) suggests that a lawmaker's time constraint might be represented by

$$H = X + r(B - B^*)^{-1}, \qquad (3.14)$$

where H is the total work time and B^* represents the politically optimal budget for enforcing each rights assignment. This relationship implies that the actual cost of the subject government service (enforcement) converges to B^* as more of each legislator's time is devoted to control activities; moreover, the marginal time cost of reducing B increases as enforcement is produced more efficiently.

The time allocation of a majority maximizing legislator can be determined by maximizing equation (3.13) subject to (3.14). The resulting individual budgets that legislators are willing to approve are:

$$B = \left(\frac{ur}{wzN}\right) + B^*. \qquad (3.15)$$

This equation indicates that the budget that legislators are willing to give up—for enforcing each property right—is relatively large if the size of a legislator's majority is greatly affected by activities specific to his demand-assessing efforts (as represented by u). Budgets are also relatively large when the time cost of reducing B by closer scrutiny of the regulatory process is significant (as given by r). In turn, the budgets granted by the legislature relate negatively to the effect of a welfare transfer on the magnitude of a lawmakers majority (as denoted by w). They tend also to be small when the effect of the level of enforcement on the welfare transfer is large (since z is in the denominator of the fraction in equation [3.15]). In other words, the legislature is willing to allow regulators and antitrust enforcers to be inefficient and to overenforce, but not to the degree that the bureaucrats wish.

A legislator's choices are obviously not quite this simple.[10] But the implication, in any case, is that a lawmaker's vote-maximizing efforts are subject to constraints. Legislators simply cannot control agencies perfectly and, at the same time, determine the level of benefits and the appropriate interest groups to support.

One consequence of the increasing use of agencies to perform regulatory tasks is that the control efforts of a typical legislator are continually spread over more agencies or more functions within existing agencies (see Benson 1984). The underlying political efficiency of the system tends to be improved, as Ehrlich and Posner (1974) observe, but possibilities for individual agencies to produce inefficiently and to overenforce are increased.

Regulation or Antitrust Enforcement by Appointed Commissions. The presentation to this point has related exclusively to bureaucratic (or civil service) regulators and antitrust enforcers. Eckert (1973), Hilton (1972), and others feel that commission regulators face incentives that lead to a different output than that generated by civil service regulators. Antitrust can also be enforced by either type of organization (for example, the FTC or the Antitrust Division of the Department of Justice). The typical commissioner can readily be analyzed in the context of the above discussion.

Eckert (1973) argues that bureaucratic agencies seek to expand both their output or regulation and their budget, as predicted above. In contrast, he maintains that commission regulators prefer to minimize their efforts, hence the commissioner's output. The basis for Eckert's difference in workload objective is that a commissioner cannot easily increase his own salary as his output expands, whereas the bureaucratic manager's salary is directly related to output. Eckert's assertion implies that, for a commissioner, $b_2 = 0$ in equation (3.2). However, even if this observation is accurate, a commissioner's incentives, as they relate to the perquisites of the position, must be considered. Given that b_3 and/or $c_3 > 0$, commissioners also have incentives to expand their output and budget. We shall see that the combined effect is to make commissioner and bureaucratic actions very similar.

The Comparable Actions of Bureau Managers and Commissioners

Hilton (1972) describes commissioners as attempting to achieve "minimal squawk." Preference for minimal squawk is, of course, identical to a desire to maximize support. In other words, Hilton's commission regulator wishes to produce output at the legislator's most preferred level, as defined by Peltzman. Hilton's justification for his "minimal squawk" contention may be erroneous. He observed that a regulator builds human capital in his position and can sell this capital to the highest bidder (the regulated firms) after completing his term in office. In his view, the typical commissioner wishes to maximize his own opportunities for future employment and thus provides benefits to the dominant interest group. These benefits are enhanced when regulators improve the level of enforcement of property rights favorable to that group. Simply put, the possibility of future employment relates directly to the kind and level of enforcement. Thus, b_3 in equation (3.3) is positive (one of the perquisites of office is the possibility of future employment). *Even a commission regulator or antitrust enforcer has the incentive to overenforce* property-rights assignments.[11]

It may seem, at times, as if commission regulators are doing nothing. Posner (1974) notes, for example, that Stigler and Friedland (1962) and others have found that maximum price regulation has little or no effect on the pricing of public utility services. One obvious explanation for this is that regulators favor the dominant interest group (the industry) to such a degree that they overenforce the rights demanded by this interest—the essential right being freedom to price as it pleases.[12] The subject commissioners appear to be doing nothing when they are expected to have some impact on price (to favor interests with less political power). Actually, they are doing something—they are enforcing rights assignments demanded by the most powerful interest group.[13]

The fact is that commission regulators' b and c values may differ from those of bureaucrats, but the parameters are always positive.[14] The utility-maximizing output of a commissioner is therefore given by equation (3.7), where the basic model characterizes both bureaucratic and commission regulation with conclusions differing only in magnitude.

Further Implications of the Budget Exchange. Several important implications can be derived in addition to those already noted, with further examination of the budget exchange. An increase in the value of the parameter d, for example, represents an upward shift in demand (see note 5). Both the bureaucrat's (or commissioner's) and the legislature's desired output (equations [3.7] and [3.8]) and desired budget will obviously rise as a result. Thus an increase in enforcement output and budget can be expected. Since a bureaucrat's rewards in salary and perquisites, and a commissioner's in perquisites, are directly related to output level and budget size, it follows that regulators and antitrust enforcers often find it rewarding to shift their own demand functions. This conclusion has two important implications:

1. Regulators and antitrust enforcers may be willing to use some of their own resources and/or some of their discretionary budget to influence the demand for regulation and antitrust litigation. In other words, *regulators and antitrust enforcers constitute interest groups that demand regulation and antitrust actions.*

2. Bureaucrats and commissioners have incentives to inform lawmakers of the strengths and wishes of interest groups. Legislative delegation of regulatory powers increases political efficiency because it is a relatively low-cost means of producing regulation to meet interest-group demands (Ehrlich and Posner 1974). There appears to be a second reason for improved efficiency, however. The legislature's assessment of interest-group demands is enhanced because agencies report demand conditions to the legislature.[15] Bureaucrats and commissioners may actually be in a better position to read demand conditions than are legislators. This holds because agencies and commissions specialize in a narrow area of interest-group concerns (even antitrust enforcers have a considerably narrower range of concerns than legislators). Hence, they have a substantial amount of direct contact with interest groups, whereas the legislature must pay attention to a large number of diverse interests.[16]

Peas in the Pod. An interesting implication obtains when cost parameters f and g are varied. It turns out that over a specific range of output associated with elastic legislative demand, the bureau's or commission's budget rises as marginal costs fall. A typical regulator or antitrust enforcer wants to discover improved production (enforcement) techniques whenever such improvements can lead to an increase in the agency's budget; this desire is enhanced by the direct relationship that typically pertains to budget size and to the bureaucrat's or commissioner's own income and perquisites. When, however, legislative demand becomes inelastic, improvements in efficiency result in smaller budgets. Consequently, there is a willingness to improve efficiency only up to a specific point. The opposite implication holds, of course, if such efficient enforcement techniques exist that production is taking place in the elastic portion of demand. The bureaucrat or commissioner will choose less efficient enforcement techniques in order to justify an increase in the agency's or commission's budget. Thus, Posner's concern that unnecessarily expensive methods of enforcement are often used (1974, 354) conforms perfectly to Stigler's (1971) interest group theory, once the bureaucrats and commissioners are added to the model.

The Nonuse of Economic Theory. Another important conclusion of the budget exchange process is that agencies and commissions will benefit the interest groups that lawmakers favor (as Stigler [1971] and Peltzman [1976] obviously assumed), even though that support will tend to be stronger than the legislature wishes. Let us reemphasize that this conclusion implies that regulators or antitrust enforcers cannot be expected to use the most relevant economic theory available or to be overly concerned with empirical justification of their tools and rules. Their function is to improve the welfare of political interest groups rather than to promote economic efficiency.

Commissioners have generally been viewed as supporting the dominant interest group (Hilton 1972; Russell and Shelton 1974). However, the relevant incentives of bureaucrats may not have been examined adequately. Hilton, for example, demonstrates that his "squawk-minimizing" commissioner strives to support the most powerful interests, but "in contrast, a group of civil servants . . . might positively seek controversy since reconciliation of acrimony might provide them with reputations for statesmanlike behavior and with justification for seeking to extend their staff and budgets" (1972, 48). Hilton apparently believes that bureaucrats often attempt to implement the desires of a relatively weak party because controversy justifies an expanded budget. More is required than "justification," however. An agency is *constrained by demand conditions*. The agency will lose budgetary support by favoring a relatively weak interest group rather than increasing its budget. A bureaucratic regulator may overenforce rights which benefit the dominant interest group (and in doing so create some controversy), but he should not support less powerful interests.

It should be manifest that a property-rights assignment that is being enforced by an agency may not be desired by *any* nongovernment lobby group. Yet the legislature continues to grant it a budget. This can be understood by recognizing that antitrust enforcers and regulators themselves constitute interest groups. They can organize relatively easily, particularly when they are able to appropriate some discretionary budget to cover their costs. Commissioners and agency managers also have ready access to the legislature for expressing their wishes. They should be able to obtain the right to produce regulation or antitrust when no opposition interest group is effectively organized (perhaps because of the free-rider problem and small per capita gains from preventing antitrust and regulation). The politically dominant interest is actually being favored then, since this interest group is made up of regulators or antitrust enforcers and the property right in demand is the right to regulate or litigate antitrust.[17]

Conclusion to this Point

The preceding theoretical arguments are primarily drawn from various theories of regulation along with Niskanen's model of bureaucratic production. The question next to be examined is whether antitrust can really be characterized by the same general model, or are there institutional factors that distinguish antitrust from regulation? Two particular institutional distinctions shall be explored in the next two sections of this chapter.

First, regulators are typically charged with controlling one or a few industries. Antitrust, on the other hand, can be applied to virtually every industry. Perhaps it is the narrow focus of regulators that allows them to be "captured" by some interest group that is particularly concerned with that industry (for example, the industry itself). This would seem to be the implication of the simple capture theory of regulation proposed by many political scientists and some economists. (See Posner 1974 for a review of the capture literature.) However, when the general interest-group approach suggested above is employed, it becomes clear that a narrow focus is not required in order for interest-group demands to dominate either regulation or antitrust.

The second institutional factor to be considered below is the differential role of the courts. Regulators are, as is often noted, given the power to make rules (legislate) and to determine whether the rules are being broken (adjudicate). Superficial examination of the antitrust process may imply that antitrust agencies have neither legislative nor adjudicative power—they simply enforce laws made by Congress by bringing actions against suspected violators while the courts determine whether the law has actually been violated. However, examination of antitrust enforcement reveals that antitrust agencies have rule-making powers that compare directly to those of regulators and that the judgments of the antitrust enforcers and the rules they make are seldom overruled by the courts.

Interest Group Influences on Antitrust

There are really two separable aspects of interest-group influences on antitrust that can be examined. First, do the various antitrust statutes passed by Congress reflect the demands of identifiable interest groups? Second, does the antitrust policy carried out by the agencies selected to enforce the statutes reflect interest-group demands? Brief examinations of these questions follow.

The Statutes

The Sherman Act (1890). There was no overwhelming public demand for antitrust during the mid-1800s (Areeda 1974, 44). The impetus for the early legislation (for both antitrust and Interstate Commerce Commission regulation of railroads) began building in the 1870s and 1880s with the formation of many organizations ". . . with revealing names like the National Anti-Monopoly Cheap Freight Railway League . . ." (Neale 1970, 12). The primary source of pressure was from farm groups, which faced what they considered to be excessively high rail rates, as well as overly high prices on farm equipment and other manufactured goods "because of monopolies" and import tariffs. In addition, there was a strong belief among farmers that eastern financiers controlled the credit market and exacted unfairly high interest rates. "Dissatisfaction with manufacturers of farm machinery and other goods, railroads, and eastern financiers became a cry against monopoly . . . (Areeda 1974, 43), and since "the farmers were better endowed with political influence than economic strength, . . . organizations like the National Grange and the National Farmers' Alliance insistently demanded some control of the railways and of monopolies in general" (Neale 1970, 12). As Neale concluded, the chief goal of politicians in passing the Sherman Act was to meet this demand for action by such organizations.

Of course, the business interests that the farm groups were railing against were not without their political clout. Congress did not choose full-scale regulation or state ownership of these enterprises as a consequence of counterpressure from these businesses (Areeda 1974, 44). Thus, the Sherman Act reflects Congress's attempt to balance the conflicting demands of interest groups, just as Peltzman's (1976) model predicts. As Neale notes, "There is nothing in the form of the basic Sherman Act prohibition or its enforcement to ensure that it operates to produce optimum economic results" (1970, 473). Rather, the desire prevailed to meet the interest-group demands for legislation, and this led to the Sherman Act—not any "public interest" desire for economic efficiency. It is interesting to note that the courts have consistently refused to consider economic efficiency issues in judging whether an antitrust violation has taken place (Neale 1970, 473).

Federal Trade Commission and Clayton Acts (1914). According to Areeda (1974, 47–48), the Federal Trade Commission Act was passed as a consequence of several sources of political pressure. There was considerable pressure from business organizations for more clearly articulated standards to guide their activities than was provided by the Sherman Act. In fact, after observing the level of political pressure exerted by big business, some analysts concluded that the Federal Trade Commission Act reflected the triumph of this group. According to this view, big businesses wanted to rationalize (organize) the economy in a way that would ensure their political power and protect them from competition (Kolko 1963). Thus they turned to government, which created the FTC to advise businessmen, to approve their collusive organizations, and to establish order in markets.

The Kolko view is too simplistic. Clearly, the FTC act involved a compromise among conflicting interests, including big business, small business, and some of the same groups that were active in procuring passage of the Sherman Act. Many were dissatisfied with the Antitrust Division's enforcement of Sherman and sought a strong commission to enforce unfair practices.

Even the Ralph Nader study group in its report on antitrust recognized this when it wrote, "In 1914 both sides—those advocating a kind of business advisor and those seeking more energetic trustbusting—compromised to produce the Federal Trade Commission. From the beginning, therefore, its goals, powers, and constituency were quite ambivalent" (Green et al. 1972, 323).

Areeda reports that, "Similar differences of opinion were reflected in the Clayton Act, passed in the same year. . . . These differences were compromised in the ultimate enactment . . ." (1974, 48).

The Exemptions: Interest Group Pressures

Perhaps the most striking evidence of interest-group impacts on antitrust legislation are the statutory exemptions. As Walter Adams notes,

> The extent to which we have forsaken competition as a national policy is most dramatically illustrated by the simple listing of the statutory exemptions from antitrust laws . . . . Some of these exemptions are partial, others complete. Some apply to particular industries or organizations, others immunize specific activities and practices . . . . *All* were secured by political influence of special interest groups which succeeded in persuading Congress to accord them private commercial advantage—ostensibly to promote some legitimate public purpose (1965, 275).

Agricultural interests were major sources of pressure leading to the early antitrust statutes, so it is not surprising that such organizations were also able to obtain exemptions from most antitrust scrutiny. Section 6 of the Clayton Act partially exempts agricultural organizations in that farmers are allowed to form cooperative associations without the associations being held illegal. The Capper-Volstead Act (1922) extended Clayton Section 6 to exempt capital stock agricultural cooperatives that had not previously been exempted. This Act has been interpreted to allow farmers' organizations to "set association policy, fix prices at which their cooperative will sell their produce, and otherwise carry on like a business corporation without thereby violating the antitrust laws."[18] A similar exemption was given to fishermens' organizations in the Fisheries Cooperative Marketing Act (1934).

In 1908 the Supreme Court ruled in the case of *Loewe* v. *Lawlor* that a nationwide boycott organized by a union to persuade wholesalers and retailers not to buy a particular company's product was an interference with the interstate shipment of goods and was therefore in restraint of trade.[19] The Court awarded treble damages, with the union and individual union members being ordered to pay their share of the damages. Naturally, labor union officials were upset by this result and ". . . immediately commenced pressure for exemption of labor from the antitrust laws. This drive culminated in . . ." Section 6 of the Clayton Act's declaration that labor organizations were exempt from the antitrust statutes (Northrup and Bloom 1965, 313). The relevant passage in Section 6 is that ". . . nothing contained in the antitrust laws shall be construed to forbid the existence and operation of labor . . . organizations, instituted for the purposes of mutual help, and not having capital stock or conducted for profits, or to forbid or restrain individual members of such organizations from lawfully carrying out the legitimate objects thereof; nor shall such organizations, or the members thereof, be held or construed to be illegal combinations or conspiracies in restraint of trade under the antitrust laws." In addition, Clayton Act Section 20 prevents the use of federal injunctions against strikes, boycotts, picketing, and other similar activities ". . . in any case between an employer and employees, or between employees, or between persons employed and persons seeking employment, involving or growing out of, a dispute concerning terms or conditions of employment."

Yet, the Supreme Court maintained in *Duplex Printing Co.* v. *Deering* (1921) that labor unions still could be held accountable under the antitrust statutes for some of their actions.[20] In particular, a union that was trying to organize the Duplex plant had succeeded in getting members of other unions to refuse to handle the company's products. The Court ruled that Section 20 applied only in cases where union members were employed by the company so that the activity of this union was an illegal restraint of trade. Union pressure, therefore, continued to be applied, and, "in 1932 . . . the American Federation of Labor . . . achieved its greatest legislative triumph to date. After almost fifty years of sustained effort, the AFL succeeded in making the federal judiciary neutral in labor disputes" (Northrup and Bloom 1965, 315). The Norris–La Guardia Anti-Injunction Act had the effect of exempting most collective bargaining activities from the antitrust laws by depriving the federal courts of jurisdiction in almost all labor disputes.

There are numerous other exemptions that could be discussed. For instance, if the interest group theory of regulation that underlies this entire analysis is correct, then groups powerful enough to obtain benefits through regulation (typically, firms in the regulated industry, according to Stigler [1971]) should also be able to protect those benefits from potential challenges through antitrust litigation. It is therefore not surprising that regulated industries are largely exempt from antitrust laws (for example, see Areeda 1974, 105–14; Adams 1965, 277–84). Similarly, the Miller-Tydings Act (1937) and the later McGuire-Keough Act (1952) resulted from "a strong movement . . . especially among associations of small retailers in such trades as proprietary drugs and cosmetics . . . ." which had obtained passage of so-called fair trade laws in forty-five states prior to 1937 (Neale 1970, 283–86). This legislation made state laws that legalized minimum resale prices exempt from the antitrust laws. Such laws are widely seen as providing protection for small shopkeepers from the more efficient large retail chains. In fact, then, ". . . many political groups which would yield to none in zeal for trustbusting are to be found in the van of the so-called fair trade movement. . . ." (Neale 1970, 276). Thus, the exemptions, whether by legislation or by administrative preemption (for example, see Adams 1965, 284–97), can easily be shown to have arisen through interest-group pressure.

Small business lobbies were responsible for more than just the Miller-Tydings Act. The ". . . hard-headed lobby pressure . . ." which secured exemption of resale price maintenance also ". . . fashioned the intricacies of the Robinson-Patman (price discrimination) statute" (Neale 1970, 428). Without a doubt this statute was passed as a consequence of the growth of chain stores, primarily retail food markets, and of the resulting advantage these stores enjoyed because they could buy large quantities from wholesalers and producers at quantity discounts. Small retailers who could not buy in bulk and receive such discounts marshalled their political powers and demanded protection. The act was touted as part of the legislative package in the National Industrial Recovery Act period designed for the ". . . rescue of small business . . . ." (Neale 1970, 229). The very large number of cases brought under this act (as discussed below) are a major source of the criticism by economists that antitrust is largely concerned with protecting competitors rather than competition.

Antitrust Enforcement:
The Capture of Interest-Group Impacts

The fact that the antitrust statutes can be seen to have arisen in response to interest-group pressure is not sufficient proof that antitrust actually provides benefits to politically powerful interest groups. Since no single industry was to be regulated and the laws were largely (except perhaps for Robinson-Patman) written in fairly vague, nonspecific terms, one might anticipate that the benefits to be derived from enforcement would be difficult to capture. Indeed, some who have examined antitrust with at least the simple capture theory in mind have concluded that there is no strong evidence that one group is being favored (for example, see Katzmann's [1980] examination of the FTC). Baxter, for example, hypothesizes

> . . . that small business, usually making its political weight felt through the trade association, has effectively employed the antitrust laws to retard but not halt the continuous encroachment on its territorial enclaves by larger enterprises using superior production technologies and often achieving the attribute of propinquity through networks of branch outlets (1979, 10–11).

This would appear to be a natural hypothesis, given the major role noted above of small-business organizations in influencing the form and passage of several of the antitrust statutes. And yet, Baxter found no "unambiguous support" for the hypothesis (1979, 47). He did conclude that some modest support for the hypothesis could be found, but his results were, in his words, "disappointing." (It should be pointed out that he never actually performed any empirical tests, although he suggested several.)

Williamson, in his commentary on Baxter, points out a significant reason for the disappointing results. He notes that "Baxter processes the data . . . in a single-causal way. If, however, antitrust is commonly responsive to mul-tiple rather than single interests, single-causal analysis will predictably yield weak results" (1979, 77). The capture theory is, in fact, far too simple an explanation of the regulatory process. Even when a single industry is being regulated, there can be substantial conflicting interests within the industry; compromise is likely (Benson 1983b). When legislation is not specific to one industry, as in the case of antitrust, many conflicts may arise. Small-business interests may dominate in some cases, but not in others. Different small-business interests may even be in conflict in some instances.

Another problem with Baxter's analysis (and the simple capture theory in general) is that it does not allow for changes in policy over time. In fact, one clear implication of a theory of interest-group government is that policies change over time to reflect changes in relative interest-group strengths and demands (Benson 1984; Weingast and Moran 1983). And that is precisely what has happened in antitrust. Neale observes in this key that "there is evidence that the aims and scope of antitrust policy have changed a good deal since the passage of the Sherman Act, and may easily change some more in the future" (1970, 11). As interest-group demands change, antitrust policy changes.[21]

Consider FTC antitrust activity. Clarkson and Murio (1982) note that prior to 1969 the bulk of FTC antitrust enforcement was devoted to Robin-son-Patman enforcement towards the end of discouraging price competition when it threatened small firms. Over a considerable period, which culminated in two major 1969 reports, the agency was subjected to significant criticism for being ". . . too political, obsessed with trivia, and woefully inefficient" (1982, 137). Then, in 1969, the FTC suddenly appeared to respond to the criticism by closing about six hundred of its investigations, reorganizing the work of the commission, and undertaking major personnel shifts. Further-more, the agency deemphasized Robinson-Patman and began several large-scale industrywide cases. Between 1970 and 1979, the agency's budget grew from $21 million to about $70 million. However, negative reaction to the new FTC policies arose in the late 1970s. For three years the FTC did not receive congressional authorization, although a series of contingency resolu-tions allowed it to stay in operation. In 1980, the Federal Trade Commission Improvement Act, supposedly sanctioning the commission, was passed. The commission's emphasis seemed to change once again. As Clarkson and Murio noted, ". . . in its recent DuPont decision the committee retreated from an aggressive approach to dominant firms in an industry [which had charac-terized it] throughout the last decade" (1982, 145). These various changes are explained below as having arisen from shifts in interest-group demands.

The Generality of Interest-Group Theory

What appears to be significant inconsistency in antitrust enforcement, when judged from a single criteria (for example, efficiency, or a simple capture view), is perfectly consistent when one employs an interest-group theory of antitrust. ". . . There are always controversies in progress as the different groups seek to persuade the legislature or the courts that the letter of the law or its interpretation should be amended in this direction or that. Antitrust is a running compromise, in which . . . the voices of economist and businessman, social reformer and lobbyist are heard in varying strengths at different times" (Neale 1970, 431–32).

In fact, perhaps the most revealing way of thinking of antitrust is that it is largely couched in vague terms so that it can be flexibly applied in different ways as political demands change. Its primary purpose today appears to be to support potential political constituencies that may be able to influence the reelection of selected Congressmen, but that cannot be easily supported by (or do not have a political power base of sufficient size to command) overall regulation designed specifically for their benefit. Posner (1969), in his exam-ination of the FTC, points out that each Congressman must support the demands of powerful groups in his district. He further observes that ". . . the welfare of his constituents may depend disproportionately on a few key industries. The promotion of the industries becomes one of his most impor-tant duties as a representative of the district" (1969, 83). The FTC can pro-mote (protect) those industries that most influence the reelections of legis-lators—particularly those who have considerable power over the FTC.

Faith et al. directly tested the hypothesis suggested by Posner and found considerable support for what they referred to as Posner's "model of antitrust pork barrel" (1982, 329). They examined the case-bringing activity of the FTC and found a statistically significant bias in favor of firms operating in the districts of legislators who serve on committees having important bud-geting and oversight authority over the FTC. Remember that the FTC came under severe attack, particularly in the late 1960s, partly because a very large portion of its caseload was being devoted to Robinson-Patman violations. But the 1970s were supposedly a period of reform during which emphasis was said to have been shifted to a concern for preserving economic efficiency and competition. Faith et al, nevertheless concluded that their findings

. . . support a private-interest theory of FTC behavior over the entire period . . . [o]bservers who see the FTC as acting in . . . the public interest . . . have been misled . . . [W]e would not be so hasty in discarding budget-maximizing or congressional influence hypotheses . . . The tendencies . . . are hard to explain with other models (1982, 342).

In fact, the tendencies they described are easily explained by the interest-group model presented herein.

The Regulatory Dichotomy
Viewed in the Context of Antitrust

FTC commissioners and their bureaucracy have incentives to expand their enforcement output (and their budget) beyond that preferred by legislators. However, Congress monitors the FTC and controls its budget. Therefore, the FTC cannot act as a pure monopoly bureau, doing as it pleases. It pushes its output as far as possible given the constraint it faces in bargaining with Congress. But since Congressional oversight of government bureaus and agencies is dominated by specialized committees whose decisions are generally accepted by Congress as a whole (Benson 1981, 1983a; Weingast and Moran 1983), the FTC is most constrained by members of the relevant budgeting and oversight committees. Other members of Congress devote much less time and fewer resources to FTC oversight, as they are typically specialists in some other area of government production. Thus, the FTC is able to overenforce in those districts.

The findings of Faith et al. are perfectly consistent with the budget exchange portion of the model developed previously. Their findings also dovetail with the political exchange that found expression in the principle that the interest groups with strongest demands are the most favored, because legislative committee assignments are chosen so that each legislator can specialize in the area of government production that is of the greatest concern to (that generates the greatest benefits for) the powerful interest groups in the home district (Benson 1981; Weingast and Moran 1983). Thus, if firms in the districts of legislators on the FTC's oversight committees are being treated more favorably than firms in other districts, it is because they have expressed the strongest demand for such treatment.

Weingast and Moran (1983) tested a hypothesis similar to that of Faith et al. (1982), as well as several others, as they endeavored to apply the Stigler-Peltzman framework to the FTC. Their additional hypotheses were that the stability of FTC policy depends upon the stability of interest-group demands as reflected in oversight committees. In particular, they stated that "markedly different preferences on the committee lead to major shifts in agency policy" (Weingast and Moran 1983, 775). If agency production does not meet interest-group demands, congressional sanctions will result. Weingast and Moran concluded, as did Faith et al. (1982), that the FTC's output can best be ex-

plained by the interest-group theory. In addition, they found that "the statistical evidence implies that the FTC is remarkably sensitive to changes in its
oversight subcommittee and in its budget" (1983, 792).

Changes in FTC policy and its choice of the distribution of cases across
various laws result from changes in interest-group pressures on Congress:
Congressional sanctions were applied to the FTC in 1979–80, but Weingast
and Moran show that, "despite the political rhetoric about a runaway, un-
controllable bureaucracy bringing on the 1979–80 sanctions, the evidence
supports our interpretation that these sanctions reflected the new subcommittee's efforts [reflecting a change in relative interest-group strengths] to
reverse the policies of their predecessors [who had been dominated by different interests]" (1983, 793). Thus empirical support is given to the point made
above: as interest-group demands change, antitrust policy changes. In fact, if
the 1979–80 changes really did reflect Congressional efforts to rein in a
bureau run amok rather than to redirect the bureau's policies in the presence
of different relevant interest-group pressures, we should see reductions in the
bureau's powers and budget. However, the 1980 FTC Improvements Act left
virtually all FTC programs intact, and its budget continued to grow from $70
million in 1980 to $80 million in 1982. This reflects in part the fact that the
FTC itself acts as a political interest group that can exercise considerable
political clout, and ". . . in late 1979, the agency launched an effective lobbying and publicity counterattack" (Clarkson and Murio 1982, 156). Nonetheless, the observed changes in FTC policy arose because interest groups pressed
for a more active, aggressive FTC in the late 1960s and got one. Then the
backlash from groups threatened by such policies forced Congress to drop its
support for such activism in the late 1970s, and the FTC has responded.

Conclusion to this Point

It should be clear from the above that the lack of focus on one or a few industries that characterizes most regulation does not mean that antitrust is fundamentally different from regulation. Both are designed to promote the
demands of special-interest groups.

We are now in position to turn to the decision-making process within
the antitrust agencies. We do this in order to see how institutions have been
arranged to facilitate interest-group antitrust policy, and to demonstrate that
the involvement of the courts *does not alter or constrain* the process in any
significant way.

Antitrust Institutions and the Courts

There are two federal antitrust enforcement agencies in the United States,
The Department of Justice's Antitrust Division and the Federal Trade Com-

mission. They are quite different organizationally (see Neale 1970, 373–400 for detailed discussion), but for our purposes we shall emphasize a few of their basic similarities.

Similarities of the Agencies

First, how do the two agencies "detect" antitrust violations? Detection by each relies almost entirely on complaints that, for the most part, come from businessmen (but also, conceivably, from consumers, labor, and others) who feel they are being injured by other firms—generally competitors (Neale 1970, 374, 385). This is precisely what one should expect, given the previous discussion. If antitrust is designed for meeting the potentially widely differing demands of small, geographically dispersed interest groups whose political power is great within a congressional district, then antitrust enforcers tend to act when such demands are raised. In this way, as is often said, "the squeaky wheel gets the grease." A "react to the mail" procedure for choice of cases is what should be expected, rather than any systematic kind of "detective work" to discover lawbreakers. Of course, antitrust is so flexible that if substantial demand for a particular enforcement activity exists, an "antitrust campaign" can be undertaken and violators may be sought out (Neale 1970, 374–75).

It was suggested earlier that one reason why antitrust might differ from regulation in its ability to meet interest-group demands is that regulators are widely recognized to have been delegated rule-making (or legislative) powers—that is, powers to assign as well as enforce property rights—whereas antitrust enforcement involves charging suspected violators, with the courts determining whether a violation actually exists. This view is misleading. In fact, while the Department of Justice's Antitrust Division is organized as a prosecuting agency, the FTC is itself a tribunal dispensing judicial decisions, just as a regulatory agency does. And both agencies make rules. The Antitrust Division, for example, has ruled out mergers of banks in local markets when one of the banks is considered to be large in that market, by challenging every merger so characterized (Benson 1980, 1983b). Of course, all such rules must be backed by court decisions. However, the courts have supported the division to such a degree that such mergers (along with many other activities) are considered to be per se illegal. Indeed, the FTC has been called the "second most powerful legislative body in the United States. . . ." (Clarkson and Murio 1982, 135) because of the overwhelming number of rules (property rights assignments) it has made. In fact, "there has been a good deal of criticism of the commission in the past directed against its formulation of something like per se rules in the . . . field of antitrust . . ." (Neale 1970, 391).

Still, the courts play a major role in FTC antitrust decisions, as they do in those of the Antitrust Division. In each instance, major antitrust actions are reviewed. Once a particular action is legitimized by the Court, FTC findings may not be appealed to the courts; in point of fact, the same is true for the Antitrust Division. When it becomes clear that an Antitrust Division argument (ruling) is going to be accepted by the Supreme Court, the party charged can forego court review by pleading *nolo contendere* in a criminal case or by entering into negotiation for a consent decree in a civil case. A large portion of the Antitrust Division's caseload is so settled.[22] Thus, the apparent institutional differences between the two antitrust agencies are relatively insignificant in terms of the degree of court involvement. In each case, major new rulings are reviewed, while charges brought under established, court-accepted rules typically are not. (Of course, the same is likely to be true of all regulatory rulings.) Critically important is the question, how does the Court respond to challenges of rules established by the antitrust agencies? In virtually every instance the rules are accepted.[23] To demonstrate this claim we shall review the Court's treatment of a series of FTC decisions and related extensions of power.

Incipient Sherman and Clayton Act Violations: FTC Rule-making Legitimized by the Courts

Section 5 of the Federal Trade Commission Act made illegal "unfair methods of competition which have antitrust effects," where inclusion of the word "methods" was designed to support litigations extending beyond the practices of the common law, practices that for centuries had been treated as unfair competition. Thus, Senator Reed of Missouri, in response to an earlier (proposed) bill, stated:

> It is my opinion that if we employ the term "unfair competition" as it is employed in this bill, without adding anything to it, the courts will adopt as the meaning of Congress that meaning which has been affixed to the term by all of the law dictionaries and by a great many legal authorities.[24]

It is generally well accepted that the term "unfair competition" was designed to encompass the forms of competition considered illegal at common law, as well as the new forms of rivalry that had been emerging with the development of more advanced technology and commercial activity.[25] The FTC was, therefore, given the power to determine what should be considered to be unfair methods of competition, at least as far as the courts were concerned: "The Congress intentionally left development of the term 'unfair' to the Commission rather than attempting to define the many and variable unfair practices which prevail in commerce . . . ."[26]

Section 5 was held to encompass all Sherman Act violations in the *FTC* v. *Cement Institute* case.[27] This holding signified that commission jurisdiction reaches whatever action violates the Sherman Act; in other words, conduct illegal under the Sherman Act also violates Section 5 of the Federal Trade Commission Act. ". . . on the whole the Act's legislative history shows a strong congressional purpose not only to continue enforcement of the Sherman Act by the Department of Justice and the federal district courts but also to supplement that enforcement through the administrative process of the new Trade Commission."[28] And the same holds for Clayton Act violations (or for that matter Robinson-Patman and other antitrust statutes). In fact, the commission is authorized to enforce the Clayton Act directly (that is, to bring a suit under the Clayton Act distinct from the Federal Trade Commission Act, if preferred). This having been said, we are therefore in position to focus attention on the courts' acceptance of FTC extensions of its power *to include incipient violations of any antitrust statute*. This is a particularly relevant issue in the context of our effort to explain Bork's antitrust paradox, since Bork observed that ". . . the incipiency concept has proved to be an anticompetitive virus working . . . to protect the inefficient from competition" (1978, 17).

The Supreme Court held in the Fashion Originators Case that it was an object ". . . of the Federal Trade Commission Act to reach not merely in their fruition but also in their incipiency . . ."[29] This extension, reflecting oft--expressed desires to check "monopoly in the embryo,"[30] supports the claim that large size is per se bad. But clearly an oligopoly industry is not the monopoly firm of economic theory, and providing a set of commissioners (five in number) and their bureaucracy with the power to object to business practices—practices that per se may not offer any course of action to competitors or the public and that are objectionable only on the spurious, undefined grounds of potentially leading to a single firm market—is tantamount to unrestricted power. Along this line we might note that one of the most troublesome questions of Sherman Act enforcement has been that centering on behavior referred to as "conscious parallelism of action." The *incipiency* action makes virtually every oligopoly illegal; hence, all firms in the United States, including those in the service fields and retailing, can easily be considered as lawbreakers. Consider the following case.

In *Triangle Conduit and Cable Co.* v. *FTC.*[31] the manufacturers of electrical conduits were found to have utilized a basing-point scheme in order to stabilize price competition among themselves. The Seventh Circuit Court held this to be a conspiracy, a "present" violation of the Sherman Act. And we agree fully with this result and would condemn the violation, as in Greenhut (1956).[32] What is objectionable is the *obiter dictum* of the court (which, as we shall subsequently see, has become the present law) that the *unilateral adoption of basing-point systems by individual firms could also be prohibited* as long as those firms were aware that other firms were adopting similar practices and that pricing systems of this kind, *even if unilateral at the start,* represented the first step toward a conspiracy.

The Clayton Act carries extension similar to that of the Sherman Act. Thus the above case holds, notwithstanding the argument that the wording of the Sherman Act refers to present conspiracies, while the Clayton Act deals *futuristically* with conduct whose effect *may* be to lessen competition substantially *or* tend to create a monopoly. Manifestly, it would appear to follow that an "incipiency" application to the Clayton Act is clear cut, certainly in contrast to the Sherman Act. The subject issue was faced squarely in the *Brown Shoe* case. It was held there that the commission could arrest trade restraints ". . . in their incipiency without proof that they amount to an outright violation of Section 3 of the Clayton Act or other provisions of the antitrust laws."[33]

The case that followed, chiefly under the Sherman and Clayton Acts, provide evidence of a few guidelines. The incipiency rule clearly applies where a per se offense exists (for example, price fixing under the Sherman Act, or conspiring to receive illegal discounts under the Robinson-Patman extension of the Clayton Act). Simply put, an incipiency price-fixing conspiracy would be bad, as in the Grand Union case,[34] because *soliciting* discriminatory advantages are tantamount to granting them, and granting them would surely be illegal. But the extension may have gone so far as not even to require allegation of harm to competition, notwithstanding the wording of Section 5. Thus, in the *E.B. Muller and Co. v. FTC* case,[35] the court held that "the purpose of the Federal Trade Commission Act is to prevent potential injury by stopping unfair methods of competition in their incipiency."

Note further from the *Brown Shoe* case, where potentially little vertical foreclosure was involved (Brown Shoe's sales were about $110 million of $1.8 billion total), that the Section 5 incipiency test reached conduct that carried very little chance of even a reasonable possibility of eventually lessening competition substantially. It is apparently the extended court-approved law for the commission that neither actual nor present harm need be shown and that only some (any?) basis for predicted harm will suffice.

A related extension, which we shall not detail, is the condemnation of competitive actions that violate the *spirit* of the antitrust laws. Presumably an action based on the spirit of a law (for example, the Sherman Act) might be kept close to the original legislative intent. Any action under Section 5 that challenges, say, a merger would not contradict the spirit of the Clayton Act unless it also involved substantial lessening of competition. To this extent, the FTC would be restrained. But, as argued above, the real "spirit" of the antitrust laws is their vagueness and ability to change with changes in the political climate. In this regard, consider the conscious parallelism of action cases.

People trained in antitrust law can be expected to condemn as anticompetitive any collusive-like action, even though no conspiracy can be shown. Of course, the theory of incipient conspiracy would appear to apply to situations where firms exhibit interdependent, albeit not explicitly colluding, behavior. And yet, all of oligopoly involves taking account of rivals' actions (Greenhut 1970).

A principal case along these lines under Section 5 was the *FTC* v. *Beech-Nut Packing Co.* litigation,[36] as supported by the *FTC* v. *Cement Institute* case.[37] The elaborate resale price-maintenance system of the defendant was condemned in the district court, reversed on the appellate level, and finally struck down by the Supreme Court. This system had been imposed by the manufacturer on its jobbers and dealers. The Court held that the spirit of the Sherman Act damned parallel actions in restraint of trade, even in the absence of agreement.

To appreciate fully how the courts have extended commission powers, let us recall the *Brown Shoe* case. Note in this regard that exclusive dealing was proscribed by the Clayton Act (a substantive provision), whereas the Court condemned exclusive dealing in the *Brown Shoe* case only if the practice would have substantially lessened competition. But recall further that the Court nevertheless struck down the practice of *Brown Shoe* on *the premise of an incipient violation*. It went even further than that by adding as an alternative basis for its decision that *the practice violated the spirit of the Clayton Act*. It allowed this in terms that presumed that the commission is free to extend substantive Clayton Act provisions via Section 5 to the "spirit" of the Clayton. And it confirmed the presumption alluded to here in more recent decisions.[38]

The extended role of the commission was also approved in *FTC* v. *Gratz*[39] and *FTC* v. *Keppel and Bro., Inc.,*[40] as well as in many later cases. In Averitt's words: ". . . the Commission seems to be empowered to determine and enforce recognized standards of fair and competitive behavior, whether these have been declared by statute or have emerged as the generally accepted ethical norms of the community" (1980, 274). Beyond all this, the decision in *FTC* v. *Sperry and Hutchinson Co.*[41] allows the commission to pursue "public values" that are not contained in the letter or spirit of the antitrust laws. The Supreme Court considers the FTC to have the authority to *serve as the expert* in advising the court what the public considers to be ethical or not. To be sure, the commission will (probably) have to demonstrate some potential adverse effects on competition or on competitors, but then if and only if they "are not outweighed by other consumer benefits or by *bona fide* business justification" (Averitt 1980, 255). The scope of the commission's power is therefore virtually unlimited. In Averitt's view, ". . . The Commission is authorized to decide a case based on principles of conduct that have not yet won universal acceptance in the business community" (1980, 279).

Most significantly, Averitt's study of the legislative background to the enactment of the Federal Trade Commission Act convinced him that Congress *intended* broad commission scope and hence the courts are properly interpreting the intention of Congress (1980, 279–81). This is no surprise, since under our theory the U.S. Congress can be expected to design bureaucracies with the flexibility to meet the demands of interest groups. It is most interesting that Averitt's interpretation of the FTC's power, based on the *Sperry-Hutchinson* case,[42] is that the Supreme Court considers the commission to be "empowered to frame public competition policy on its own initiative" (1980, 283). That judicial review provides a safeguard against interest-group politics in antitrust is clearly not true. As Bork notes, "the modern Supreme Court, without compulsion by statute, and certainly without adequate explanation, has inhibited or destroyed a broad spectrum of useful [from an efficiency standpoint] business structures and practices . . . The Court has done these things, moreover, on demonstrably erroneous notions of the economics that guide the law" (1978, 5). *But all this is precisely what should be anticipated once an interest-group perspective of antitrust is adopted and the "public-interest" view abandoned.*

Conclusions: Clearing up the Antitrust Paradox

Bork observes that

> to study antitrust at length, to wonder at the manifold errors of economics and logic displayed, to see that the errors move the law always in one direction, is to begin to suspect that a process much deeper than mere mistaken reasoning is at work. It seems as though the intellectual terrain is regarded as important not in and for itself but as a field of action upon which the political order moves against the private order . . . I will not attempt here an examination of that process . . . (1978, 423).

We have examined that "deeper process," and the consequence is that antitrust does not seem paradoxical at all. Indeed, when a special-interest view of antitrust is adopted, the four observations that troubled Bork are easily understood. Certainly, the concern with the welfare of groups rather than the general welfare is no longer a paradox. Rewards according to political status, instead of merit, and reductions of liberty (attenuation of property rights) are also to be expected, as is a concern with producer well-being, not competition. The interest-group model also predicts that most political choices will be made by the antitrust enforcers and legitimized by the courts, rather than by Congress.

The very nature of the governmental process of rights transfer to benefit active interest groups creates incentives for more and more interest-group formation, and therefore greater demands for transfers (Benson 1984). It is to be expected that legislators seeking reelection will respond to increasing pressure by delegating more and more rule-making powers to commissions and bureaus. The FTC, for example, was given authority to enforce sixteen new statutes during the 1970s, and in the process, it developed more than forty new rules and sixty new programs to regulate business (Clarkson and Murio 1982, 141). Naturally, the agencies' power and budgets grow in the process—the FTC's budget was 3⅓ times larger in 1980 than it had been in 1970, for instance. A couple of implications of this process are worth noting. First, as agency power expands, the ability of Congress to monitor agencies effectively diminishes; thus, opportunities for inefficiency and overenforcement increase. Second, the commissioners and bureaucrats themselves become more powerful political interest groups as their resources and political clientele are expanded, and therefore, the interests of those in government become relatively more important as compared to the interests of those being governed (Benson 1984).

Is there much hope for reforming the antitrust process? Can we expect it ever to be used to actually support competition? Can the goal of economic efficiency be pursued rather than the present practice of providing rents to special interests through restrictions on market competition?

The Nader report on the FTC (Cox et al. 1969) concluded that the problems with the FTC were entirely attributable to the people employed there; it went on to suggest wholesale changes in staffing. But are antitrust enforcers (judges, legislators, and members of special-interest groups, for that matter) irresponsible, inefficient, or "bad" or "immoral" people? It is the political process itself that sets in motion forces that induce people to act as they do. The antitrust process cannot be reformed by replacing people. A fundamental institutional change that alters the incentives of commissioners, agency managers, and legislators would be necessary for radical adjustments to be observed. Behavior is more a function of the institutions and incentives (property rights) that arise with the development of such institutions than a function of the "efficiency" or "morality" of the individuals involved.[44]

Bork suggests that if the actors in the antitrust process (particularly the judges) just understood basic microeconomic theory, they would do a better job. He argues that "the reason for the inadequate performance of the legal institutions that shape antitrust is a complex topic. No single institution is wholly responsible, but perhaps it can be said that the factor common to the performance of all of them was, and is, the absence of a rudimentary understanding of market economics" (1978, 409). This view accepts economic efficiency as the goal of antitrust. When it is recognized that this is not the case, then economic education is not going to make much difference. Where "good" economics supports the demands that antitrust enforcers are trying to meet, they will use it; when it conflicts with such demands, they will adopt "bad" economics. As Clarkson and Murio note:

> . . . fundamental inconsistencies regarding economic analysis surface frequently in FTC programs . . . In general, the agency takes three approaches to economic analysis. Sometimes . . . the FTC concurs with the most accepted

view of economists. In other cases, the commission enthusiastically and apparently arbitrarily chooses one side in a raging debate among economists . . . In still other cases, FTC decisions run contrary to mainstream economic analysis . . . In this last group of cases, the agency not only deemphasizes economists' data but also often on ad hoc impressions of industry participants or observers (1982, 148).

Posner (1976) and Bork (1978), among others, suggest major legislative changes, including repeal of most of the antitrust statutes that have been heavily employed in the interest group process (for example, Robinson-Patman, Clayton, and Sherman Section 2). But the legislature is not going to make such changes unless a very strong political constituency arises to demand them. And even if such changes were made, the interest-group process would continue. After all, whatever antitrust laws are in effect, they are subject to interpretation by the antitrust enforcers and the courts. The nature of the interpretations and the level of enforcement are subject to the same political forces that operate under the current statutes. Retention of Sherman Section 1 is unlikely to change this, since, as Neale pointed out, there is nothing in the Sherman Act that can ensure that it will be used to promote economic efficiency, and ". . . the courts have consistently refused to take economic consequences as the criterion of antitrust right and wrong" (1970, 473).

The conclusions reached here are quite pessimistic. They imply that economists' continual complaints about the inefficiency-enhancing results of antitrust policy are going to fall on deaf ears. And that is probably true if the complaints are directed only at legislators, antitrust enforcers, judges, and other economists. On the other hand, if economists can convince a substantial number of the people who are losers in the antitrust process (that is, consumers) that they would be better off with policies that protect competition rather than competitors, perhaps a political constituency that demands efficiency can arise. The free-rider problems that are intrinsic to large-group actions where per capita gains are relatively small do not bode well for such a result (Stigler 1971). However, and unfortunately, the most visible so-called consumer advocates who denounce regulators and antitrust enforcers, inevitably advocate more reform, plus even more government control as the solution. This was indeed the Nader study group's (Cox et al. 1969) conclusion. Unfortunately, the fact of the matter is that in a representative democracy dominated by interest-group politics, more government is not likely to solve the problems that the governing process itself creates.

Notes

1. A parallel development to the literature on interest-group regulation is the rapidly growing literature on rent-seeking. See Tollison (1982) and Benson (1984)

for discussions of the relationship between the two developments and reviews of relevant literature.

2. It may be possible for interest groups to avoid the political allocative process (to bypass the legislature) because in many cases, agencies have been granted power to assign property rights (to legislate). Interest groups may pay regulators directly for desired rights (this situation creates the possibility of corrupting public officials [Benson and Baden 1985]). There is considerable direct contact between regulators and interest-group representatives. The result is that an agency may favor an interest group that the legislators does *not* want supported. This condition may explain, in part, the apparent political inefficiencies discussed below. The direct contact between interest groups and regulators is much less significant than it appears to be on the surface, however. Any large deviation between the interest groups that legislators wish to support and the organization favored by an agency should only be a short-run phenomenon. The legislature is the primary mechanism through which the demand of interest groups and the supply of agencies interact because legislatures control the agency budget, a claim we shall explain in greater detail below.

3. Several criticisms of the Niskanen theory of bureaucracy have been made. However, our presentation follows the relevant parts of Niskanen's most recent model, in which he resolves the most important criticisms (1975). Also, our discussion is designed to account for other problems in Niskanen's model (see Benson 1981, 1983a).

4. In equation (3.4)

$$a = a_1 a_1^{b_1} a_3^{c_1},$$

$$b = b_1 b_2 + c_1 b_3,$$

$$c = b_1 c_2 + c_2 c_3.$$

5. Let legislative demand for property rights enforcement arising from market intervention be

$$V = d - 2eQ,$$

where V is the dominant interest group's marginal value. The minimum marginal cost of producing any desired level of property rights enforcement, MC, is

$$MC = f + 2gQ.$$

An agency exchanges enforcement for a total budget. Total budget and total cost functions are integrals of a bureaucrat's demand and marginal cost functions:

$$B = dQ - eQ^2$$

$$C = fQ + gQ^2.$$

Thus, the discretionary budget is given by equation (3.5).

6. An agency manager's utility maximizing output can be substituted into the

budget function to yield the bureaucrat's desired budget in terms of demand and cost conditions and incentive function parameters:

$$B = d \left(\frac{b + c}{b + 2c} \right) \left(\frac{d - f}{e + g} \right) - e \left(\frac{b + c}{b + 2c} \right) \left(\frac{d - f}{e + g} \right)^2.$$

7. See Benson (1981, 1983a, 1984) for relevant additional discussion.

8. This constrained maximization argument is based on Niskanen's model (1975, 627–28). Several adjustments were, however, made in order to apply the argument to legislative response to interest-group demands for regulation. Furthermore, certain claims made by Niskanen are rejected—see Benson (1981, 1983a).

9. Those who benefit from regulation typically gain less than society as a whole gives up. This results from overenforcement and inefficiency, as well as from the welfare costs of rent-seeking (Benson 1984).

10. In particular, the legislative decision should be considered in the context of all budgeting and taxing decisions (that is, as a general equilibrium decision instead of a partial equilibrium), as in Benson (1981, 1983a). However, this does not significantly affect the conclusions reached here (Benson 1983a).

11. Mitnick and Weiss (1974) agree with Hilton's "minimal squawk" assertion (as does Jowkow [1974] and others), but they also make additional arguments to support their contention. They observe, for example, that the number of commissioners is generally fixed by statute. Any increases in workload will, therefore, have to be funneled through the same set of commissioners. Mitnick and Weiss conclude that commissioners will not increase their own workload. This conclusion is too extreme. If the expansion of output enhances the possibility of future employment (or perhaps the status of the position, and other things), then the utility-maximizing commissioner faces a tradeoff between increased work and the positive effects of expanded output. A commissioner's b and c may differ from a bureaucrat's b and c, but they should be nonzero.

12. Another explanation comes from the above discussion. It may be very costly to enforce the property-rights assignment in question. If the marginal cost of enforcement is very high, the level of enforcement may be so low as to be statistically insignificant.

13. One might ask why the industry bothers to enter the political market for property rights if the resulting regulation has no impact. This occurs because the regulatory process is uncertain. An interest group may enter the political arena to maintain the status quo because it cannot be sure of what opposition groups will do (Benson 1984).

14. The use of commission-type regulators is a potential legislative control device if commissioners have less incentive than bureaucrats to overproduce. One might ask, why is not all regulation and antitrust enforcement performed by commissions? It turns out that there may be some political disadvantages to using commission regulators in all cases—as we shall see below in note 15.

15. This observation explains, at least in part, why bureaucratic regulators and antitrust agencies exist when commissions appear to be politically more efficient. Commission incentives to assess demand conditions accurately and to report to the legislature appear to be weaker than the similar incentives of civil service regulators.

The legislature faces a tradeoff between supply efficiency and efficiency of demand assessment. In cases where lawmakers feel they do not have an accurate picture of demand conditions, they should choose to use bureaucratic enforcement.

16. One implication of this conclusion is that much of the direct contact between bureaucrats or commissioners and interest groups can probably be explained as part of the political exchange process rather than avoidance of the political exchange (see note 2). Interest groups inform regulators or antitrust enforcers of their wishes and political power, and they in turn advise the legislature. Legislators can determine when bureaucratic or commission assessment of demand is inaccurate or misleading, because a political disequilibrium results with the effect that the individual lawmakers' reelection chances are lessened. Of course, agencies have a definite bargaining advantage in the budgeting process if they are more efficient readers of demand; the consequence would be that legislators tend to accept the agencies' assessment of demand conditions. Nevertheless, they must support the dominant interests in order to maintain their advantage.

17. See Benson (1983b) for a detailed discussion of the interest-group role of bank supervisory agencies and of the Antitrust Division in the area of bank merger regulation and antitrust policy.

18. Maryland and Virginia Milk Producers v. United States, 362 U.S. 458, 466 (1960).

19. 208 U.S. 274 (1908).

20. 254 U.S. 433 (1921).

21. Of course, the same type of changes in interest-group concerns that are reflected in policy implementation can also be reflected in legislation. For example, ". . . the motives of the legislators in 1936 (when passing the Robinson-Patman Act) were quite different from those underlying the original Section 2 (the Clayton Act section concerned with price discrimination) in 1914" (Neale 1970, 226). Large retail chains were not of major importance in 1914, so small retailers were not overly concerned with being protected from them.

22. Between 1935 and 1955, for example, 72% of the Division's civil cases were terminated by consent decrees (Neale 1970, 381).

23. There are some exceptions, of course, but some regulatory rulings are also overturned by the courts. The Supreme Court is a bureaucracy that must sustain itself, and if it accepted *all* arguments put forth by the antitrust agencies, it would not be long before all cases were settled without litigation. Neither the Court not the antitrust agencies' lawyers want to see that happen.

24. 51 Cong. Rec. 12936 (1914).

25. Many cases have held that "unfair methods of competition" has a broader meaning than "unfair competition." Among those most prominently cited are FTC v. R.F. Keppel & Bro., Inc., 291 U.S. 304 (1934) and FTC v. Raladam Co., 283 U.S. 643 (1931).

26. Atlantic Refining Co. v. FTC, 381 & 357, 367 (1965).

27. 333 U.S. 683 (1948).

28. Ibid., 690.

29. Fashion Originators Guild v. FTC, 213 U.S. 457, 466 (1941).

30. Senator Newlands, 51 Cong. Rec. 12030 (1914).

31. 168 F. 2nd 175 (7th Cir. 1948).

32. See also Greenhut (1970), Chapter 7, on facets of the basing-point system, and also Chapter 14, where the system is shown to be a form of organized oligopoly, hence correspondent to a monopoly.
33. 384 U.S. 316, 322 (1966).
34. 300 F. 2d 92 (2d Cir. 1962).
35. 142 F. 2d 511, 517 (6th Cir. 1944).
36. 257 U.S. 441 (1922).
37. 33 U.S. 683 (1948).
38. Beatrice Foods Co., 67 FTC 473 (1965); Dean Food Co., 70 FTC 1146 (1966); U.S. v. American Building Maintenance Industries, 422 U.S. 271 (1975).
39. 253 U.S. 421 (1920).
40. 291 U.S. 309 (1934).
41. ???
42. 405 U.S. 233, 244 (1972).
43. In FTC v. Sperry and Hutchinson Co., 405 U.S. 233, 244 (1972) the Court held that like a court of equity, the commission could consider "public values" beyond simply those empowered in the letter or encompassed in the spirit of the antitrust laws.
44. The *Wall Street Journal* recently saw hope in the appointment of William Baxter as head of the Antitrust Division ("Baxter in the Pantheon of Antitrust," *Wall Street Journal,* January 6, 1984, p. 16). Naturally, short-term changes in policy can be achieved by replacing people, but as long as major institutional changes are not made, the changing of personnel and their policies will occur only as changes in interest-group demands produce policy alternatives. Obviously, the interest groups that dominate (benefit from) Reagan administration policy are different than the groups influencing the previous administration, so policy changes instituted through personnel changes were to be expected.

References

Abrams, Burton A., and Russell F. Settle. 1978. "The Economics Theory of Regulation and Public Financing of Presidential Elections." *Journal of Political Economy* 86 April:245–57.

Adams, Walter. "Exemptions from Antitrust: Their Extent and Rationale." 1965. In *Perspective on Antitrust Policy.* ed. Almarin Phillips. 273–311. Princeton, N.J.: Princeton University Press.

Areeda, Phillip. 1974. *Antitrust Analysis.* Boston: Little, Brown and Company.

Asch, Peter. 1970. *Economic Theory and the Antitrust Dilemma.* New York: John Wiley and Sons.

Averitt, Neil W., 1980. "The Meaning of 'Unfair Methods of Competition' in Section 5 of the Federal Trade Commission Act." *Boston College Law Review* 21, no. 2: 227–300.

Baxter, William F. 1979. "The Political Economy of Antitrust." In *The Political Economy of Antitrust: Principal Paper by William Baxter,* ed. Robert D. Tollison. 3–50. Lexington, Mass.: Lexington Books.

Becker, Gary S. 1983. "A Theory of Competition Among Pressure Groups for Political Influence." *Quarterly Journal of Economics* 98:371–400.

Benson, Bruce L. 1980. "An Examination of U.S. v. Philadelphia National Bank in the Context of Spatial Microeconomics." *Industrial Organization Review* 8: 27–65.

———. 1981. "Why are Congressional Committees Dominated by 'High Demand' Legislators?" *Southern Economic Journal* 48:68–77.

———. 1983a. "High Demand Legislative Committees and Bureaucratic Output." *Public Finance Quarterly* 11:259–81.

———. 1983b. "The Economic Theory of Regulation as an Explanation of Policies Toward Bank Mergers and Holding Company Acquisitions." *Antitrust Bulletin* 28:839–62.

———. 1984. "Rent Seeking from a Property Rights Perspective." *Southern Economic Journal* 51:388–400.

———, and John Baden. 1985. "The Political Economy of Government Corruption: The Logic of Underground Government." *Journal of Legal Studies.* Forthcoming.

Bork, Robert H. 1978. *The Antitrust Paradox: A Policy at War with Itself.* New York: Basic Books.

Clarkson, Kenneth W., and Timothy J. Murio. 1982. "Letting Competition Serve Consumers." In *Instead of Regulation: Alternatives to Federal Regulatory Agencies,* ed. Robert W. Poole, 135–68. Lexington, Mass.: Lexington Books.

Cox, Edward F., Robert C. Fellmeth, and John E. Schultz. 1969. *The Nader Report on the Federal Trade Commission.* New York: Barron Press.

Eckert, Ross. 1973. "On the Incentives of Regulators: The Case of Taxicabs." *Public Choice* 14:83–99.

Ehrlich, Isaac, and Richard Posner. 1974. "An Economic Analysis of Legal Rule-Making." *Journal of Legal Studies* 3:257–86.

Faith, Roger L., Donald R. Leavens, and Robert D. Tollison. 1982. "Antitrust Pork Barrel." *Journal of Law and Economics* 25:329–42.

Green, Mark J., Beverly C. Moore, and Bruce Wasserstein. 1972. *The Closed Enterprise System: Ralph Nader's Study Group Report on Antitrust Enforcement.* New York: Grossman Publishers.

Greenhut, M.L. 1956. *Plant Location in Theory and Practice.* Westport, Conn.: Greenwood Publishing.

———. 1970. *A Theory of the Firm in Economic Space.* Austin, Tx.: Lone Star Publishers.

Hilton, George. 1972. "The Basic Behavior of Regulatory Commissions." *American Economic Review* 62:47–54.

Hirshleifer, Jack. 1976. "Comment." *Journal of Law and Economics* 19:241–244.

Jarrell, G. 1978. "The Demand for State Regulation of the Electric Utility Industry." *Journal of Law and Economics* 21:269–95.

Joskow, P. 1974. "Inflation and Environmental Concern: Structure Change in the Process of Public Utility Price Regulation." *Journal of Law and Economics* 17: 291–327.

Katzman, Robert A. 1980. *Regulatory Bureaucracy: The Federal Trade Commission and Antitrust Policy.* Cambridge, Mass.: MIT Press.

Kau, James B., and Paul H. Rubin. 1978. "Voting on Minimum Wages: A Time-Series Analysis." *Journal of Political Economy* 82:337–42.

Kolko, Gabriel. 1963. *The Triumph of Conservatism: A Re-Interpretation of American History, 1900–1916.* New York: Free Press.

McCormick, Robert E., and Robert D. Tollison. 1981. *Politicians, Legislation, and the Economy: An Inquiry into the Interest Group Theory of Government,* Boston, Mass.: Martinus Nijhoff Publishing.

Mique, J., and G. Belanger. 1974. "Toward a General Theory of Managerial Discretion." *Public Choice* 17:27–42.

Mitnick, B., and C. Weiss. 1974. "The Siting Impasse and a Rational Choice Model of Regulatory Behavior: An Agency for Power Plant Siting." *Journal of Environmental Economics and Management* 1:150–71.

Neale, A.D. 1970. *The Antitrust Laws of the U.S.A.* Cambridge: Cambridge University Press.

Niskanen, William. 1968. "The Peculiar Economics of Bureaucracy." *American Economic Review* 58:293–305.

———. 1975. "Bureaucrats and Politicians," *Journal of Law and Economics* 18: 617–43.

Northrup, Herbert R., and Gordon F. Bloom. 1965. "Labor Unions and Antitrust Laws: Past, Present, and Proposals." In *Perspectives on Antitrust Policy,* ed. Almarin Philips, Princeton, N.J.: Princeton University Press. 312–54.

Peltzman, Sam. 1976. "Toward a More General Theory of Regulation." *Journal of Law and Economics* 19:211–40.

Posner, Richard. 1969. "The Federal Trade Commission." *University of Chicago Law Review* 37:47–89.

———. 1974. "Theories of Economic Regulation." *Bell Journal of Economic and Management Science* 5:335–58.

———. 1976. *Antitrust Law: An Economic Perspective.* Chicago: University of Chicago Press.

Russell, Milton, and Robert Shelton. 1974. "A Model of Regulatory Agency Behavior." *Public Choice* 20:47–62.

Smith, Janet K. 1982. "Production of Licensing Legislation: An Economic Analysis of Interstate Differences." *Journal of Legal Studies* 11:117–37.

Stigler, George. 1971. "The Theory of Economic Regulation." *Bell Journal of Economics and Management Science* 2:3–21.

———, and C. Friedland. 1965. "What Can Regulators Regulate? The Case of Electricity." *Journal of Law and Economics* 5:1–16.

Tollison, Robert D. 1982. "Rent Seeking: A Survey." *Kyklos* 35:575–602.

Weingast, Barry R., and Mark. J. Moran. 1983. "Bureaucratic Discretion or Congressional Control? Regulatory Policymaking by the Federal Trade Commission." *Journal of Political Economy* 91:765–800.

Williamson, Oliver. 1979. In *The Political Economy of Antitrust: Principal Paper by William Baxter,* ed. Robert D.Tollison. Lexington, Mass.: Lexington Books.

4

Voluntary Disclosure: Robustness of the Unraveling Result, and Comments on Its Importance

Joseph Farrell

U sed-car dealers have always had a poor reputation for revealing faults in their cars. In 1976, the Federal Trade Commission (FTC) proposed a strong rule requiring inspection by dealers of each of fifty-two systems or components, and revelation of the results, together with estimated repair cost, and other disclosures.

The National Automobile Dealers Association (NADA) claimed that such a rule was unreasonable, citing estimates of inspection cost of about $200, about ten times what the FTC estimated. NADA's protests were effective, and in May 1980 the FTC tentatively proposed a different rule, under which inspection would not be required, but defects known to the dealer would have to be disclosed to buyers. Having apparently defeated the compulsory-inspection rule, NADA and the National Independent Automobile Dealers Association (NIADA) turned on the new rule, claiming that difficulties in finding out what a dealer had known would make this rule equivalent to the previous proposal. However, in August 1981 the FTC adopted the second rule.

The rule did not immediately take effect, because in 1980 Congress had decreed that FTC rules should be subject to veto by both houses of Congress (acting together) within an uninterrupted ninety-day period. (This was called the Federal Trade Commission Improvement Act.) Because the Act required an *uninterrupted* ninety days, a Congressional recess extended the review period until May 1982, when both houses of Congress voted to veto the "known-defects" disclosure rule. (Incidentally, the rule was the first to come before Congress under the 1980 Act.) So, the rule seemed dead, especially after a move to attach a revised version of its provisions to an FTC funding bill was defeated in committee three months later.

However, the courts had been active meanwhile in the area of legislative vetoes. In January 1982 the U.S. Circuit Court of Appeals in Washington had ruled a "one-house veto" (either house of Congress could veto agency actions) unconstitutional in a case involving the Federal Energy Regulatory Commission (FERC). In October, the same court extended that finding to two-house vetoes, and in particular the veto provision of the 1980 Federal Trade Commission Improvement Act, in a case brought by the Consumers Union and Public Citizens against Congress. In July 1983 the Supreme Court upheld these rulings, on the grounds that vetoes violate the constitutional provision that everything must be presented to the president before becoming law (a somewhat illogical argument, since the agencies' rulings themselves are not normally presented to the president).

Thus the known-defect rule appeared to have been reinstated. However, the FTC then decided to take another look at the rule, and in July 1984 the five-member commission voted 3–2 to abolish it, citing difficulty of enforcement. So ended the tortuous history of one of the FTC's most controversial rules.

In this chapter, we ask: How much difference does this make to economic efficiency? A tentative conclusion—surprising to me—is that it makes rather little difference. The reader can judge whether or not this view is noticeably supported by the following analysis, which is the result of thinking about disclosure in general, rather than of trying to analyze this case in particular.

The principal existing model of voluntary disclosure is that (working independently) of Grossman (1981) and Milgrom (1981). It is summarized below in section 1. The "unraveling result" claims that voluntary disclosure will lead to the same results as compulsory disclosure and that therefore it makes no real difference whether disclosure is required or not.

Plainly, something is missing in that model, for the passion brought to bear in the 1980–1982 lobbying battle testifies that, whatever the results may be, disclosure *does* matter. A natural candidate for modification is the assumption made by Grossman and Milgrom that it is common knowledge that sellers are fully informed about their products. In section 2, I use a simplification of a model in Farrell and Sobel (1983) to examine the effects of having not all sellers informed. Although we reproduce the continuity result of Farrell and Sobel, we also see in this version that continuity may be misleading, in a sense I will discuss.

In section 3, I use the Farrell-Sobel model to examine whether disclosure requirements will actually increase the amount of information acquired and disclosed. The result is ambiguous.

In section 4, I try to evaluate the allocative gains from information. Although the models just discussed lack welfare benefits from information, there clearly are such benefits. However, by considering reasonable numerical examples, I will show that the benefits of simple allocative efficiency may be surprisingly small.

1. The Basic Model: A Basis for Departure

For completeness and to introduce notation, I will now describe the model discussed by Grossman and Milgrom.

Each of a large number of sellers has available for sale one item, which he does not value himself. Its value to each of many buyers, q, is initially known to the seller but not to buyers. The seller may make any true statement concerning q, and buyers will believe it; lies are assumed to be impossible or adequately deterred. Buyers are concerned with expected value and compete to buy, so that the price of an item certified to be of quality q will be q, while the price of an incompletely certified item will be the expectation of q. In forming expectations, buyers know the prior (overall) distribution function $F(\cdot)$ on $[0,1]$; buyers also take into account any equilibrium effects (see below).

For a full and careful treatment of the model, see Milgrom (1981). Here I simply give the unraveling result and a heuristic justification.

Suppose that a seller refuses to disclose q. What should buyers infer about q? Clearly, they should not infer that q is at the top of the range, for if they did so, then lower q's would follow that concealment strategy. But then buyers' beliefs have to be such that if q were in fact at the top of the range, then the seller would rather reveal q. Next, we apply the same argument to the range remaining after the top q's drop out . . . and so on.

A little more formally, suppose that the price for a wholly unlabeled item is p. Then, if $q > p$, a seller would rather label, so that all unlabeled items are of quality $q \leq p$. Since p must equal the average quality of unlabeled items, this implies that none has quality strictly less than p; but the only way that this can happen in equilibrium is for p to be zero. Thus we have:

PROPOSITION 1 (Grossman, Milgrom). With the assumptions discussed above, buyers are as pessimistic as possible—that is, if q is not revealed or is only partly revealed, buyers infer that q has the lowest value compatible with whatever has been revealed. As a result, in equilibrium buyers know the value of q for each item, and the allocation is as if revelation were compulsory.

In sections 2 and 3, we will briefly discuss the impact on Proposition 1 of allowing for imcompletely informed sellers. Another natural path to follow, which we will not do here, is to relax the very strong assumption that lies are in effect impossible.

2. Allowing for Uninformed Sellers: A Continuity Result and a Contrary Result

In this section, we briefly describe the model of Farrell and Sobel (1983) that allows for costs of sellers becoming informed; then we simplify it by making the fraction G of informed sellers exogenous. This enables us to show that the equilibrium price $p(G)$ of unlabeled items is continuous at $G = 1$, a result (due to Farrell and Sobel) that seems to suggest that the Grossman-Milgrom assumption ($G = 1$) is reasonable as an approximation. However, we then show that the derivative $p'(G)$ is (negatively) infinite at $G = 1$, and I argue that this suggests a certain nonrobustness.

Initially, sellers do not know q; they, like buyers, have prior beliefs $F(\cdot)$. However, a seller can, by paying a cost c, learn the quality of his item without this being observed by buyers. This information-cost c is distributed according to the distribution function $G(\cdot)$; c is distributed independently of q, and a particular seller's c is not observable to buyers.

Equilibrium will now be characterized by two related variables: a price p for unlabeled items, and a cutoff value c^*, such that a c^*-seller is indifferent to buying and not buying information. We consider only "unlabeled" and fully labeled items, because *partial* revelation of q would reveal that the seller was informed, and thus Grossman-Milgrom would apply to him. Informed sellers who conceal q are riding on the coattails of uninformed (therefore, on average quality) sellers.

We have two equations for p and c^*. First, the seller's *ex ante* decision problem yields as an equilibrium condition:

$$p = -c^* + \int_0^1 \max(p, q)dF(q) \tag{4.1}$$

Second, p must be the average quality of unlabeled items. This average includes the genuinely uninformed and the informed who found $q \le p$:

$$p = \frac{[1 - G(c^*)]\int_0^1 qdF(q) + G(c^*)\int_0^p qdF(q)}{[1 - G(c^*)] + G(c^*)F(p)} \tag{4.2}$$

Existence and properties of solutions to equations (4.1) and (4.2) are discussed in Farrell and Sobel. For the purposes of this section, we simplify by assuming that $G(\cdot)$ has a very special form:

$$G(c) = G \text{ if } 0 \le c \le 1$$
$$= 1 \text{ if } c = 1 \tag{4.3}$$

Thus a fraction G of sellers have zero information costs (and so will always be informed), while $(1 - G)$ have large enough information costs that they will never be informed. Then we have a single equation determining p:

$$p[1 - G + GF(p)] = [1 - G]\bar{q} + G\int_0^p qdF(q) \tag{4.4}$$

where $\bar{q}$ is the mean value, $\int_0^1 qdF(q)$.

Integrating by parts in (4.4) gives us:

$$H(p,G) \equiv p(1 - G) + G\int_0^p F(q)dq - (1 - G)\bar{q} = 0 \qquad (4.5)$$

The function H is differentiable in p and G, and has positive partials in both variables. This implies that p is uniquely defined given G, and that p is continuous and monotone decreasing in G. However, we have

$$\frac{\partial H}{\partial G} = (\bar{q} - p) + \int_0^p F(q)dq \qquad (4.6)$$

which becomes $\bar{q} > 0$ at $G = 1$, $p = 0$, while

$$\frac{\partial H}{\partial p} = (1 - G) + GF(p) \qquad (4.7)$$

which becomes zero at $G = 1$, $p = 0$.
Thus, $dp/dG = -\infty$ at $G = 1$. Summarizing, we have

PROPOSITION 2. Defining $p(G)$ by equation (4.4), the function $p(\cdot)$ is uniquely defined, continuous and monotone decreasing. However, at $G = 1$, $p'(G) = -\infty$.

The significance of the infinite derivative is the following. The continuity result shows a form of robustness of the unraveling result, in the sense that if G is *very* close to 1, then p will be almost zero. This is a one-term Taylor expression of $p(G)$ around $G = 1$:

$$p(G) \cong p(1) \text{ if } G \cong 1 \qquad (4.8)$$

For values of G, close but not *very* close, to 1, however, we ought to take another term in the Taylor series. This then gives us

$$p(G) \cong p(1) - \infty(G - 1) \text{ if } G \cong 1. \qquad (4.9)$$

Plainly, equation (4.9) gives a different sense from (4.8) concerning whether we should rely on the model with $G = 1$ to deal with cases in which G is "near" 1. (Of course, [3.9] does not claim that $p(G) = -\infty$ for $G < 1$, any more than [4.8] claims that $p(G) = 0$ for $G < 1$.)

To close this section, we solve a simple example explicitly. Let $F(\cdot)$ be the uniform distribution on $[0, 1]$ so that $F(x) \equiv x$. Then (4.4) becomes:

$$p[1 - G + Gp] = [1 - G]\frac{1}{2} + G\frac{1}{2}p^2 \qquad (4.10)$$

Multiplying by $2\,G$ and rearranging gives:

$$G^2p^2 + 2G(1 - G)p - G(1 - G) = 0$$

whose solution $p < 0$ is

$$p = G^{-1}\sqrt{(1 - G)} - (1 - G)]. \qquad (4.11)$$

Thus, for instance, if $G = 0.91$, then

$$p = \frac{0.3 - 0.09}{0.91} = \frac{0.21}{0.91} = 0.23$$

so that a 9% change in G, from 1 to 0.91, produces a change from $p = 0$ to $p = 0.23$. The lesson is that continuity results must be viewed with care. When we ask about robustness, we may be concerned with more than continuity.

3. Do Disclosure Requirements Increase Disclosure?

In this section, we apply the Farrell-Sobel (1983) model to ask whether more information emerges if the informed are more likely to be obliged to reveal their information. Given the amount of information acquired by sellers, this would be true; however, the prospect of compulsory revelation reduces the incentive to become informed, given the value of p. We will show that the net results of information flow are ambiguous.

In the Farrell-Sobel model, as described at the beginning of section 2, suppose that there is a probability $z \geq 0$ that a seller who becomes informed will be *obliged* to reveal his information. (We can think of z as measuring the degree of enforcement of disclosure rules, perhaps, although that interpretation might suggest that there would be more disclosure near p, and less near zero, than we will suppose.)

Then equations (4.1) and (4.2) are modified as follows: (4.1) becomes

$$p = -c^* + zq + (1 - z) \int_0^1 \max(p, q) dF(q) \tag{4.12}$$

and (4.2) becomes

$$p = \frac{[1 - G(c^*) + zG(c^*)]\bar{q} + (1 - z)G(c^*)\int_0^p q \, dF(q)}{1 - G(c^*) + zG(c^*) + (1 - z)G(c^*)F(p)} \tag{4.13}$$

It is easy to see that (4.12) represents a downward-sloping curve in (c^*, p) space, which shifts down and left with an increase in z. Equation (4.13) also represents a downward sloping curve, but this curve moves up when z increases. (A larger z makes buyers less cynical about unlabeled items, given c^*.) Thus we have two cases:

1. if (4.12) is steeper than (4.13), then $dp/dz > 0$ and $dc^*/dz < 0$. Both these effects tend to reduce the information transmitted: c^* falls, so less information is obtained by sellers; and p rises, so concealment is more attractive. These effects work against the direct revelation-producing effect of the increase in z, so overall the result is ambiguous.
2. if (4.13) is steeper than (4.12), the $dp/dz < 0$ and $dc^*/dz > 0$. Then both indirect effects, as well as the direct effect of z, lead to more information being revealed.

Can we say whether case (1) or (2) is to be expected? In an attempt to answer that question, we examine (4.12) and (4.13) when $F(\cdot)$ and $G(\cdot)$ are uniform on $[0, 1]$. Then (4.12) reduces to

$$(1 - z)p^2 - 2p + 1 - c^* = 0 \tag{4.14}$$

and (4.13) becomes

$$(1 - z)c^*p^2 + (1 - c^* + zc^*)(2p - 1) = 0 \tag{4.15}$$

The (absolute) slopes are given by

$$\text{slope of (4.14)} = \frac{-1}{2p(1 - z) - 2} = \frac{1}{2 - 2p(1 - z)} \tag{4.16}$$

$$\text{slope of (4.15)} = \frac{(1 - z)(p^2 - 2p + 1)}{2c^*(1 - z)p + 2(1 - c^* + zc^*)} \tag{4.17}$$

We can readily compare (4.16) and (4.17) only when z is close to 1: then (4.16) is greater, which tells us we are in the ambiguous case (1).

This ambiguity should not surprise us; we know that the "direct effect" of z increases revelation, but the prospect of compulsory revelation reduces the incentive to become informed, and the less cynicism of buyers about unlabeled items, the more tempting it is to conceal information.

4. Welfare Effects of Information

The alert reader may have noticed that in the models above there are no efficiency benefits of information. The reason is that the social value (as measured by market price) of an item of unknown quality is the expected social value of an item of known quality. Constructing models with a social value of information is a little more complicated: see Burdett and Mortensen (1980) or Farrell and Sobel (1983). However, the basic ideas described above will still hold. In this section, we will try to get a sense of the size of the allocative efficiency benefits of information.

Let us return to the used-car example. Used cars differ in their probability of breakdown, and people differ in their costs of experiencing a breakdown. Some of the reasons for the latter variation are that people's value of time differs, the probability of a breakdown's occurring far from a service station differs, and people vary in how well they cope with the consumer's nightmare of auto repair.

The direct allocative efficiency effects of more information lie in getting the most reliable cars to those who most value reliability. To gain some notion of these benefits, we carry out an illustrative calculation.

Percentage Savings from Information: Direct Effects

Suppose that cars differ in their probability p of having a breakdown,[1] and suppose p is uniformly distributed (among used cars) on [.1, .9]. Suppose, moreover, that the cost c to drivers of such a breakdown varies uniformly between \$100 and \$180, for the reasons suggested above. (One might expect those with the very highest costs of breakdown to choose new cars or to have their cars inspected; thus, the upper tails will be truncated.) Then efficiency requires that the car with breakdown probability p be assigned to the driver with cost

$$c = 180 - (p - .1)100$$
$$= 190 - 100p.$$

Such an arrangement will give total cost of breakdowns

$$C^* = \frac{1}{.8} \int_{.1}^{.9} p(190 - 100p)dp$$

$$.8C^* = 95[(.9)^2 - (.1)^2] - \frac{100}{3}[(.9)^3 - (.1)^3]$$

$$= 95 \times .8 - 33.3 \times .728$$

$$= 76 - 24.26$$

$$= 51.74$$

Now suppose instead that the revelation system is imperfect and that all cars with $p \geq .5$ are indistinguishable to buyers. Thus, those cars are matched randomly to the buyers in their lower half of the cost distribution. Now we have:

$$.8C = \int_{.1}^{.5} p(190 - 100p)dp + \int_{.5}^{.9} p \cdot 120dp$$

$$= 95[(.5)^2 - (.1)^2] - \frac{100}{3}[(.5)^3 - (.1)^3] + 60[(.9)^2 - (.5)^2]$$

$$= 95 \times .24 - 33.3 \times .124 + 60 \times .56$$

$$= 22.8 - 4.1 + 33.6$$

$$= 52.3.$$

This is only about 1.5% greater than the full information cost figure. If all cars are indistinguishable, we have random allocation, and

$$.8C'' = 140 \int_{.1}^{.9} p\,dp$$

$$= 70 \times [.9^2 - .1^2]$$

$$= 70 \times .8$$

$$= 56$$

Thus, the direct efficiency effects of information are rather modest:

$$\frac{c'' - c^*}{c^*} = \frac{4.26}{56} = .076 \text{ as a fraction of no-information costs.}$$

In other words, even if information does not emerge at all, this is the equivalent of a 7½% increase in breakdowns, a serious, but not a terrible problem.

We generalize this calculation by noting that

$$E(pc) = \text{cov}(p,c) + E(p)E(c) \tag{4.18}$$

and that, while random allocation makes $\text{cov}(p,c) = 0$, efficient allocation in this case makes $\text{cov}(p,c) = \sqrt{\text{var}(p)\,\text{var}(c)}$. Hence the proportional savings from efficient allocation are equal to

$$\left(\frac{\sigma p}{E(p)}\right)\left(\frac{\sigma c}{E(c)}\right) \tag{4.19}$$

the product of the "relative variations" $\sigma_p/E(p)$ and $\sigma_c/E(c)$. Note that (4.18) is general, but (4.19) applies only when efficient allocation gives a correlation coefficient of (-1) between p and c. In general, efficiency requires a perfect negative relationship between p and c, but it is only in special cases that this relationship is also linear, as required to obtain (4.19). Thus, in general, information is *less* valuable than (4.19) suggests.

We next derive a simple expression for (4.19) in the case where the variables are uniformly distributed. Suppose x is uniformly distributed on $[a, b]$, where $0 \le a \le b$. Then

$$E(x) = \frac{a + b}{2}$$

$$\text{Var}(x) = \frac{2}{b - a} \int_0^{\frac{b-a}{2}} y^2 dy = \frac{1}{12}(b - a)^2$$

So the relative variation of x is

$$\frac{\sigma_x}{E(x)} = \frac{1(b - a)}{\sqrt{3}\,a + b} = \frac{1}{\sqrt{3}}\left(1 - \frac{2a}{a + b}\right)$$

If $b = ma$, where $m = 1$, this becomes

$$\frac{1}{\sqrt{3}}\left(1 - \frac{2}{1 + m}\right).$$

Thus, as one would expect, large dispersions—that is, large values of m (for p and/or for c)—give greater cost savings, but in no case can information save as much as a third of the costs. The percentage savings for some reasonable values of *m* are given below.

	1.25	1.5	2	4	10
1.25	0.4	0.7	1.2	2.2	3
1.5	0.7	1.3	2.2	4	5.5
2	1.2	2.2	3.7	6.7	9.1
4	2.2	4	6.7	12.0	16
10	3	5.5	9.1	16	22

The notable thing about this is that only for quite large values of *m* do the savings become "substantial" (say, in excess of 10%). Remember also that this represents an extreme comparison: perfect information versus no information. As we saw above, if some of the information emerges, it already achieves quite a lot of the potential savings from full information. Thus, these direct allocative efficiency benefits from information are surprisingly small.

If the distributions have a central tendency, the gains from information will be smaller. For instance, suppose each distribution has λ of its weight uniformly distributed, with $(1 - \lambda)$ being an atom at the mean. Provided λ is the same for the two distributions (of p and of c), we still get a very simple formula for the proportional gain from information.

$$\lambda^2 \left(\frac{\sigma_p}{E(p)} \right) \left(\frac{\sigma_c}{E(c)} \right)$$

(With more general distributions, the efficient allocation is less simple to write down and manipulate.)

The intuition behind this surprising (to many people) result is the fact that, provided all cars have positive value, each will be allocated to somebody in the efficient allocation. Thus the social value of knowing about a repair whose cost is the same to every buyer is zero. One's intuition tends to start from the private incentive not to be the person landed with the bad car.

Indirect Effects

When goods of different qualities are not duly distinguished by the market, there will be feedback effects on incentives to maintain quality. In the used-car market, one will see this in two forms. First, car-owners intending to sell those cars used will not have enough incentive to maintain their cars. Second, auto-makers, who sell to new buyers (most of whom, at least traditionally, will sell the used car), will not have as much incentive as would be desirable to make the cars last longer than the tenure of first owners. These effects may well be important, but I do not know how to quantify them.

5. Conclusion

We tentatively view this episode as one in which market participants fought hard over rather doubtful distributional gains, and in which the direct efficiency stakes were smaller than one might think. Interest-group theories of regulation suggest that questions close to purely distributional will tend to produce a lot of conflict. However, it is far from clear in this case that all parties were behaving rationally.

Economic theory does a poor job of predicting the attitudes of market participants. It may be that theoretical predictions of the outcomes under different rules are mistaken. Alternatively, many market participants may have been wrong in their prediction. Sellers were almost uniformly against more disclosure enforcement. Consumer representatives were equally uniformly in favor, despite the fact that prices measure value under all sets of rules, so that not all consumers would benefit from more market information.

This raises an important methodological problem. In view of the ease of entry and exit, and very low level of sunk costs, few economists would hesitate to write down zero-profit equations for the used-car industry. Yet an industry with free entry and exit ensuring zero profits would naturally be expected not to have strong views on the rules of the game; whatever the rules, each firm would earn a normal profit. Evidently, something is wrong with this argument; perhaps it is that important comparative advantages translate into rents which will be affected by changes in the rules. This in itself is not a very interesting observation; but the caveat against a "natural" jump to a false conclusion may be important.

Note

1. This "probability of breakdown" may be an aggregate figure, weighting different breakdowns by seriousness, in the following sense. Suppose there are n different possible breakdowns, and a car has probability p_i of breakdown i. If buyer j has cost c_i^j of breakdown i, then the cost of assigning this car to him is

$$\sum_{i=1}^{n} p_i c_i^j \tag{A}$$

Suppose that, for all buyers j, k, and all i,

$$c_i^j / c_i^k = c_j / c_k. \tag{B}$$

for some c_j, c_k, independent of i. This says that, if j's cost for a certain repair is twice k's, then the same will be true for all other repairs. In this case (not likely to hold exactly, like most aggregation conditions, but a reasonable central case), we can write (A) as

$$\left[\sum_{i=1}^{n} \frac{p_i c_i^1}{C_1}\right] c_j$$

and write

$$\sum_{i=1}^{n} \frac{p_i c_i^1}{C_1} c_j$$

as p (for this particular car). Then the optimization problem reduces to minimizing Σpc, where the sum is over cars or buyers (equivalently).

References

Automotive News. 1979–1984. *passim.*

Burdett, K., and D. Mortensen. 1980. "Testing for Ability in a Competitive Labor Market." *Journal of Economic Theory.*

Farrell, J., and J. Sobel. 1983. "Voluntary Disclosure." Unpublished notes.

Grossman, S. 1981. "The Informational Role of Warranties and Private Disclosure about Product Quality." *Journal of Law and Economics* 24.

Milgrom, P. 1981. "Good News and Bad News: Representation Theorems and Applications." *Bell Journal of Economics* 12.

5
Competition and Collusion, Side by Side: The Corrugated Container Antitrust Litigation

Robert C. Goldberg
Craig S. Hakkio
Leon N. Moses

O n the face of it, the corrugated container industry would seem to qualify as a competitive industry. Economies of scale are quite limited, and there do not appear to be any other signficant barriers to entry. As a result, there are a large number of firms in the industry. During a crucial period in history, one in which it is alleged there was widespread collusion, the number increased significantly: 568, 709, and 863 in the years 1967, 1972, and 1977.[1] Since firms use virtually identical material inputs and standard machinery to produce containers, the containers of most firms are very close physical substitutes for one another. The 4- and 8-firm concentration ratios are low and were virtually unchanged during the period 1958 to 1977. The ratios were respectively 21 and 36 in 1963, and 19 and 33 in 1977. The fifty largest firms in the industry accounted for only 79% and 75% of industry output in the two years.[2] These last statistics indicate that the segment of the industry made up of very small firms has considerable capacity to survive.

Despite these characteristics of a competitive industry, in 1976 criminal and civil antitrust suits were brought which involved thirty-seven of the largest firms in the industry. These suits alleged a conspiracy to fix, raise, maintain, and stabilize the price of corrugated containers and the containerboard from which they are fabricated. In terms of the sheer numbers of defendants and plaintiffs and the number of attorneys involved, the case came to represent one of the largest antitrust actions in history. The settlements arising from the private civil actions were the largest of any class-action suit ever brought.

This chapter deals with the economic issues of the case. Our findings are somewhat supportive of an allegation of conspiracy. However, in our view, the collusion with which the defendants were legally charged was too broad and not supported by economic analysis. We do not believe that there ever was a conspiracy to fix *directly* the prices of the containers bought by most of the roughly two hundred thousand firms that purchase containers. The prices most purchasers paid was determined, *at least directly,* by competition between the hundreds of small producers and integrated firms who were the defendants in the case. We say "directly" because there seems little doubt that the defendants did conspire to fix the price of containerboard.

Our analysis leads us to question the basic claims involved in both the class-action suits and the opt-outs suits. The latter are the suits by large purchasers who felt that they had been especially injured by the conspiracy. These firms, almost all of them members of the Fortune 500, opted out of the class action in order to bring individual actions. We conclude that it was at most a small subclass of large customers, the multiplant-multiproduct firms we refer to as national firms, that were the victims of a system of discriminatory pricing founded in a conspiracy. These firms buy most of the output of the industry.

The chapter is divided into three parts. Part 1 provides some of the legal background of the case. Part 2 presents the results of an empirical investigation into a number of issues that are central to both the class and opt-out suits. We believe that our investigation of these issues provides new insight into a kind of industry structure that has not received much attention in the industrial organization literature, one in which price competition and price collusion exist side-by-side in the same product line and in the same geographic markets. We test the hypothesis that the prices paid by more than 90% of all users reflected the results of competition between large integrated firms and small, nonintegrated firms. The latter are called "sheet plants" in the industry. They purchase containerboard from the integrated firms and fabricate it into boxes. Many of the sheet plants concentrate on specialty boxes in small-volume runs.

The results of our investigation of prices raises questions as to whether the class that was presented for certification really did comprise a clearly identifiable group of consumers that had demonstrably been damaged by the alleged conspiracy. The findings reported in part 2 of the chapter support the claim of a conspiracy to allocate and practice market segmentation and price fixing with regard to a certain class of large consumers, the multiproduct-multiplant firms that serve national markets. *So far as corrugated containers are concerned, the only conspiracy that we have been able to detect is one in which large national firms conspired to gouge other large national firms.*

Part 3 of the chapter accepts the claim of plaintiff's attorneys that the defendants, the large, integrated firms, monopolized the supply and fixed the price of the board from which containers are made. We attempt to explain why a group of firms that were in a position to control the corrugated container industry, because of their control of the basic input, permitted and even encouraged the growth of a truly competitive sector within the industry that was made up of many small firms. The argument is made that such a strategy was profit maximizing for the smaller integrated firms. This position is supported by an analysis of costs and of economies of scale, and by reasoning based on differences in the demand curves of national, as against other, purchasers.

1. Legal Background

Our chapter has its origin in *In Re Corrugated Containers* Antitrust Litigation, MDL 310. Litigation began with an investigation into the industry by a grand jury convened by the U.S. Department of Justice in Houston, Texas, in 1975. Subsequently, private civil actions were filed throughout the country. Later, these actions were transferred to the federal district court in Houston by a judicial multidistrict panel. They were ultimately consolidated and certified as a national class action, which later was distinguished to include a subclass of sheet plants. Thereafter, criminal indictments were returned against a group of corporations in the corrugated container industry and key employees of those corporations who were alleged to have engaged in a conspiracy to fix, raise, maintain and stabilize the price of corrugated containers and containerboard. The private class action plaintiffs alleged the same conspiracy in violation of the Sherman and Clayton Acts, 15 U.S.C. § 1, 2, 15. To explain the group of firms that was named in the conspiracy, the members of the class of plaintiffs in the class action suit, and the consumers who opted out of the class after it had been certified in order to pursue individual remedies, we comment briefly on the industry, its product, and the consumers of the product.

Corrugated containers are used as shipping containers by many firms in a wide variety of industries because they are strong, lightweight, and relatively inexpensive. They are made from a category of paperboard referred to as containerboard. There are three steps in the manufacture of corrugated containers. In the first step, woodpulp is converted into containerboard, the inner, fluted sheets of which are the corrugating medium that is glued between two liners of flat facings. In the second step, the containerboard is made into corrugated sheets. Finally the sheets are fabricated into containers. Containers are fabricated in many different sizes and shapes, but the medium from which they are made is substantially the same, regardless of which integrated firm has manufactured it. The containers are fabricated from sheet that is essentially homogeneous, a bit of glue, some printing material to denote ownership and contents, using standard machinery that is broadly available, so, the boxes of different firms tend to be close physical substitutes for one another.

The defendants in the litigation were a group of integrated firms. It was alleged that these firms controlled the supply of containerboard because of their dominant positions in upstream operations, timber production, and pulpmill output. Defendants produced corrugated containers, but they also sold board to small, nonintegrated firms (or sheet plants) who also produced and sold containers.

The purchasers of containers, and therefore plaintiffs in the class action, included processors of food and beverages, and manufacturers of paper and printed materials, glass and ceramic products, metals and machinery, chemicals, paints, drugs, soaps, cosmetics, appliances, electrical equipment, clothing, textiles, leather goods, rubber and plastic products, furniture and wood products, and transportation equipment. As indicated above, the defendants also sold containerboard to plants that produced and sold corrugated containers. These sheet plants were also plaintiffs, but they were segregated into a separate subclass.

As explained earlier, litigation began with the convening of a grand jury in Houston. This was followed by the filing of a number of private civil actions that were transferred to and consolidated in the federal district court in Houston. After the transfer, the grand jury returned two criminal indictments against fourteen corporations, all of which became defendants in the civil actions, and twenty-six individuals. The indictments consisted of felony indictments against nine corporations and nine individuals, and misdemeanor indictments against five corporations and seventeen individuals. The indictments alleged the same conspiracy noted above, with the exception that they alleged a conspiracy "East of the Rockies" only. The criminal indictments resulted in pleas of *nolo contendre* by many of the corporations and individuals. The remaining corporations and individuals who did go to trial in the criminal case were found not guilty by a jury.

The private class action, which involved thirty-seven corporate defendants, was one of the largest antitrust class actions in history. It was prosecuted by a coalition of thirty-nine law firms located in many parts of the nation. Fifty-five separate class actions and seven individual actions were consolidated and constituted by the multidistrict litigation. The class action was brought by fifty-eight companies on behalf of a class of over twohundredthousand purchasers of corrugated containers and sheets. Although most of the named plaintiffs were small companies, the one-hundred class members who filed the largest claims were among the Fortune 500 companies. As already stated, virtually every significant business in the nation was represented in the category of purchasers making up the class. The thirty-seven corporate defendants had numerous plants spread throughout the nation, but it should be noted that no defendant had more than 7% of the market for corrugated containers and sheets.

The conspiracy was alleged to have lasted for eighteen years, from 1960 through 1978. The sales of corrugated containers and sheets by all of the defendants during this time period exceeded $60 billion. The complexities of the case from a legal standpoint were mammoth. Several appeals were taken to the United States Supreme Court, and the Fifth Circuit Court of Appeals set up a separate panel to hear appeals regarding the corrugated container litigation. Ultimately, all but one of the corporate defendants settled with the class action plaintiffs. The only defendant that did go to trial in the class action was found guilty by a jury. Settlements with all of the class plaintiffs, including interest, totalled over $550 million, a record.

Prior to settlement with all the defendants in the class case and before trial in the class action, certain plaintiffs elected to opt out or exclude themselves from the class action. This procedure, set forth in the Federal Rules of Civil Procedure (Rule 23), allowed these plaintiffs independently to pursue actions against the same defendants. Opting out of a class action can be advantageous. In this case the "opt outs" were significant purchasers of corrugated containers. The opportunity to prosecute their own antitrust action against the same defendants held out the possibility of proving specific anticompetitive conduct against themselves and corresponding damages which varied from that of the overall class. The opt-out actions resulted in the majority of the defendants settling with all of the opt-out plaintiffs. Those defendants who did not settle were found by the jury to have conspired. However, the jury also determined that there had been no impact on the opt-out plaintiffs who therefore received no damages.

In order to win their case, the plaintiffs, both class and opt-outs, had to do more than prove a violation of the antitrust laws. They also had to prove impact on and damages to the class plaintiffs. A major obstacle that faced the plaintiffs during the prosecution of their case was the massive invocation of the Fifth Amendment privilege against self-incrimination by many of the employees of the corporate defendants. This seriously hampered the plaintiffs' efforts to discover the facts of the conspiracy. Nevertheless, through the process of regular discovery, and on the basis of testimony obtained after certain employees were ordered to testify, lawyers for the plaintiffs felt they had achieved enough understanding of the nature of the conspiracy to allege that it went beyond an effort to fix particular prices at certain levels. They claimed there was a conspiracy to refrain from competition at all on the basis of price; that there was a common anticompetitive understanding and attitude in addition to the practice of engaging in specific exchange of price information among employees of the defendants. It was alleged that this shared prevailing understanding and attitude in the industry compensated for the fact that the industry tended to be localized because shipments from plants to customers rarely exceeded three-hundred miles. The analysis that we present in part 2 of this chapter leads us to the conclusion that these allegations were much too broad and, at least for the container industry as distinct from containerboard, substantially incorrect.

For their part, the defendants argued that there was no conspiracy and that, even if there had been, there were no damages. They asserted that the product was low in value and that the cost of transporting it was high in relation to that value. As a result, the defendants claimed, geographic markets for containers were highly localized. They asserted that the prices charged in these hundreds of localized markets reflected local cost and competitive conditions. The localized nature of markets was used by the defendants to support their claim that there could be no national conspiracy. They also claimed that the highly specialized and customized nature of the containers required by different customers ruled out the possibility of a national conspiracy to fix prices, since it would have required agreements as to tens of thousands of prices (that is, an industry with a highly diverse product line could not be subject to a nationwide conspiracy to fix prices on all of its products). It should be mentioned that our analysis fails to support the claim of significant regional variations in costs of production and prices. This completes our presentation of the legal background of the case.

2. Prices, Costs, and the Conspiracy in Containers

As stated earlier, the authors of this chapter accept the proposition that the defendants acted collusively in setting the price of the basic material from which containers are fabricated. The evidence is incontrovertible that, acting directly and through the Fibre Box Association, the defendants exchanged information on the cost of making containerboard, on the output of each of the major firms (even by division), announced changes in prices practically simultaneously, and so forth. The defendants were able to act as a group of collusive oligopolists in sheets because they were dominant in its production and the production of other products that were upstream from it. Thus, while the 8-firm concentration ratio was 33% in the corrugated container industry, it was much higher in activities directly upstream from containers: 51% and 73% respectively in unbleached (26311) and bleached (26312) paperboard in 1977.[4] The control that the defendants had over the supply of the paperboard came from their dominance in activities that were still further removed from the production of containers: forestry and pulpmill operations. The 8-firm concentration ratio for the pulpmill industry (2611) was 76% in 1977.[5]

While we accept the validity of the arguments put forward by the plaintiffs' attorneys in the class action suit that the defendants fixed the price of containerboard, the plaintiffs' allegations of a conspiracy to fix the prices of containers are not in our view supported by economic analysis. The conspiracy their allegations envisaged was much too broad. Moreover, our analysis fails to support most of the settlements that have taken place. The research on which we report below raises questions as to whether the broad class of all users of corrugating material and containers should have been certified and should have remained certified as a very broad class of purchasers and a small subclass of sheet plants. Our research also raises questions about the basic claim involved in the opt-out suits, that large users were especially damaged by the conspiracy. We do not find that being a large user, as distinct from being a member of the class of national users, led automatically to a firm's becoming the victim of a collusive arrangement which foreclosed competition and resulted in price discrimination. We begin our investigation of these matters by taking up the question of whether the class of all users of containers was too broad and whether it should have been certified.

As indicated earlier, the number of defendant corporations in the case was 37, but the total number of companies in the industry exceeded 700 in 1972, just three years before the grand jury was convened. While the 37 were conspiring to fix prices, if that is what they were doing, what were the 670 or so other, small firms doing? We believe that they were doing what all small firms do in a highly competitive environment. They were producing as efficiently as possible and struggling to get as much business as they could. Were they able to compete effectively with the large, integrated firms? Our answer is that they were able to compete for the business of most customers. However, as we explain in part 3, for a variety of reasons, one of which may have been the result of collusion, they may not have been in as good a position to satisfy the requirements of the subset of large users we call the national firms. At this point we wish to begin to test a central hypothesis of the paper: namely, that there was competition between small and large firms for the business of most customers, but that this competition was accompanied by a system of collusive price fixing. We frame our investigation in a way that initially leaves open the question of whether the collusive arrangement was directed against large purchasers in general or the small subclass of large purchasers we call the national firms.

The price lists that the integrated firms distributed to their customers carried explanations of prices based on costs of converting containerboard into containers. The lists indicated that an important element of those costs was machinery set-up cost. The same machinery is used to produce many different sizes of containers, but the machines have to be adjusted. Where set-up costs are significant and there is competition, we should find that customers who order in large quantities pay lower prices. The explanation is obvious. The more large orders a supplier fills, the lower its unit costs for any given rate of overall plant output, and the higher will tend to be its rate of profit. As a result, suppliers will vie for the business of large customers, who will tend to pay lower prices. Taken together, the impact of set-up costs on the prices paid by different size customers, and the hypothesis of the side-by-side existence of competition and collusion directed against large purchasers imply a U-shaped price function.

Let us be clear about the point we are making. A monopolist with a cost function that entails significant set-up costs and who also faces certain demand functions can end up charging large buyers lower prices than small ones. Hence the finding of a negative relationship between prices and order sizes does not prove the existence of competition or the absence of collusion. However, a finding of a U-shaped relationship, one in which prices fall over some range of order sizes and then increase, could be interpreted as supportive of the hypothesis.

The data we employed in our analysis of prices, as well as a later analysis of costs, are for a very large firm in the corrugated container industry. This firm operates a large number of plants that are spread out across the lower forty-eight states. Our data sets are for January 1973 and January 1976. We have employed information on all of the customers and accounts served by our firm in those two months. The inclusion of 1976 in the analysis provides an opportunity to see what effect the convening of the grand jury early in 1975 had on competition and collusion.

The data we used came directly from invoices that indicate the total amount of money billed to a customer each month. Some of the customers, those we call national, had multiple accounts; That means that the customer had operations at more than one site. Our company assigned a separate account number to each of the sites to which containers were delivered, and its records showed which of its plants served each site. Thus, for multiple-account customers we had data on each account as well as the total for the entire corporation.

We worked with two data sets. One we call CORP. It contains corporate totals for all customers, but does not contain data on the separate accounts of the multiple-account customers. The second body of data, MULTI, contains the separate accounts of each multi-account customer but not the corporate totals of these customers. There is a significant overlap in the two bodies of data because single-account customers, who constitute a majority of all customers, appear in both bodies of data.

Customers buy many different sizes of containers. However, our company kept its financial records in terms of the thousands of square feet of corrugated sheet (MSF) involved in the order; this is the convention in the industry. The Fibre Box Association publishes output and other data in terms of board feet, a practice that offers some support for the position taken earlier that sheet is an essentially homogeneous product and that the containers of most firms in the industry are substantially the same, at least physically.

We divided the dollars billed to each customer by the thousands of square feet involved in producing the boxes purchased by each customer and each account of each multiple-account customer. These average revenues per MSF are our measure of prices paid by different customers and accounts. MSF is our surrogate for the quantity of containers bought by each customer and account. Price lists are available for some sizes of boxes, but the information is not comprehensive. We believe that the average prices we have derived from invoice information constitute a reliable body of data to use in a study of competitive behavior. Clearly, the company would not have kept its own records in terms of dollar billings for thousands of square feet of sheet if such figures were not meaningful.

As indicated earlier, our interest was in testing for the existence of competition and seeing whether the data would support the allegation of a pervasive conspiracy in the pricing of containers. We wished to investigate whether economic analysis supported certification of the class. Finally, we wanted to investigate the basic claim involved in the various opt-out suits: namely, that large customers were especially victimized by the alleged conspiracy. For these reasons and the existence of set-up costs we chose to estimate a quadratic price relationship. This relationship involved the log of the amount of containerboard, *lnMSF,* used to produce the containers shipped to customers and the square of this amount, $(lnMSF)^2$ The equations that were estimated incuded a dummy variable. This variable requires some explanation.

Testimony taken during the criminal and civil suits suggested that the prices certain large customers paid for containers were set at the home offices of the integrated firms. In telephone conversations with each other, representatives of the integrated firms used the term *equity customers* in referring to these large purchasers. The plaintiffs' attorneys alleged that the defendants agreed not to compete in price for each other's equity customers. It was also alleged that when price changes were announced, these customers received identical price lists from the integrated firms that were serving them. When these customers requested bids from integrated firms that were not currently serving them, the plaintiffs' attorneys asserted that the prospective suppliers checked the prices charged by current suppliers and then submitted essentially identical bids. Unclear from the testimony are the precise characteristics that allegedly placed a customer in the equity category. Certain parts of the testimony suggest that all large customers were the victims of collusion. Elsewhere in the testimony is the suggestion that it was only the multiple-account, national customers whose prices were set in the home offices of the integrated firms. Since our variable, *lnMSF,* was designed to catch the effect of pure size, we felt that we could test the above ideas by entering a dummy variable, *NATL,* that was unity for a customer that was a national or multiple-account customer. Thus, the equation that was estimated was:

$$lnP = \beta_1 + \beta_2(lnMSF) + \beta_3(lnMSF)^2 + \beta_4 NATL \qquad (5.1)$$

Table 5–1 presents the results of estimating this equation for the two bodies of data described above. The constant and the coefficients on *lnMSF*

Table 5–1
Price Functions

	CORP		MULTI	
$\ell nP = \beta_1 + \beta_2 \ell nMSF + \beta_3 (\ell nMSF)^2 + \beta_4 NATL$				
	1973	1976	1973	1976
Constant	4.193	4.479	4.270	4.522
	(82.0)	(81.5)	(84.4)	(83.3)
$\ell nMSF$	−.329	−.294	−.356	−.306
	(−14.9)	(−13.2)	(−15.5)	(−13.5)
$(\ell nMSF)^2$	.021	.017	.025	.018
	(9.2)	(7.7)	(9.8)	(7.8)
$NATL$	.124	.085	.038	.013
	(6.6)	(4.3)	(2.1)	(.8)
R^2	.25	.24	.24	.23
MIN	2291	5863	1320	4996
N	1946	1914	2439	2542

Notes: Estimation was done by OLS. t-statistics are underneath each coefficient. N denotes sample size. The number of observations for 1973 and 1976 are complete counts.

and $(\ell nMSF)^2$ are highly significant in each of the years for both bodies of data. Clearly, what we have are U-shaped price functions. A great deal should not be made of the similarity between the CORP and MULTI price functions in each of the years. As explained earlier, most customers were single-account customers, so the invoice entries for them are the same in the two data sets. In addition, the overall or CORP prices for the multiple-account customers are weighted averages of their individual entries.

The minima of our price functions, *MIN*, are shown in the tables. More than 90% of the customers had orders that placed them on the falling portion of the price functions in 1973. More than 96% of them had order sizes that placed them on the falling part of the 1976 price functions. In our view, defendants could have used price findings of the kind we have presented to argue effectively against certification of the class. It would have been eminently reasonable to hold that competition between small and large firms determined the prices paid by customers whose sales corresponds to the falling portion of the CORP price function; that is, it was competition and the spreading of set-up costs with increasing order size that explains why prices fell over a large part of the range of prices. On the other hand, the significance of $(\ell nMSF)^2$ and of *NATL* in the CORP data-set appear to support the position of the opt-outs that large and national customers were victimized by collusion and price fixing.

As had already been noted, the range of customer and account sizes over which prices fall is far greater in 1976 than in 1973. The values of *MIN* are approximately three times greater in 1976 than in 1973. The coefficient on *NATL* is much smaller in 1976 and lacks significance in the MULTI estimation. The above changes are somewhat supportive of a position in which it is held that the calling of the grand jury led to an increase in competition and to an abatement of collusion on the part of the integrated firms.

We argue that if systematic and extensive price discrimination in the sale of containers can be proved, then it is also proved that there was collusion. However, to prove that there was price discrimination requires more than implicitly taking into account of the costs of producing containers for different customers. We had data on the costs of converting containerboard into containers, customer by customer, account by account, and plant by plant. Therefore, we undertook an investigation of actual conversion costs and their impact on prices. However, before presenting the results of that investigation we have one final set of remarks to make that relate to our study of prices and the issue of the extent of collusion.

Because the estimation of functions with higher-power terms can lead to misleading results we decided to check on the results reported in table 5–1 by estimating a higher-order equation, one that contained the cube of the log of *MSF*. The following result was obtained using the CORP data set for 1973:

$$\ell nPrice = 4.465 \quad - .554\,(\ell nMSF) + .074\,(\ell nMSF)^2$$
$$(54.9) \qquad (-9.7) \qquad\qquad (5.9)$$

$$- .004\,(\ell nMSF)^3 + .117\,NATL$$
$$(-4.3) \qquad (6.3)$$

$$R^2 = .26 \hspace{6cm} (5.2)$$

This result agrees with that found in table 5–1 in that the signs on $\ell nMSF$, $(\ell nMSF)$,[2] and *NATL* are unchanged. The significance of these coefficients is also essentially unchanged. However, the equation leads to a somewhat different view of the extent of collusion.

The coefficient on the cubic term is small, though significant. Its negative sign leads to the following result: over the range of actual customer sizes, price falls continuously with order size, but, for national customers, price is everywhere above the prices paid by other customers. In other words, the cubic differs from the quadratic equation in its suggestion that large customers who were single-account customers appear to have received discounts. Rather than having been discriminated against, they appear to have been part of the competitive segment of the industry. This is the same result we come to when we introduce costs into the analysis, *whether we use the quadratic or the cubic form in the cost-price analyses.* We turn now to the cost analysis and the impact of costs on prices.

The conversion cost data available to us included a number of directly measurable costs, such as set-up costs and the cost of materials, such as glue and ink for printing, electric power, and direct labor. It also included a number of items that involve cost allocation, including indirect labor, maintenance cost, and corporate costs. The allocations were based on directly measurable conversion costs. We divided the cost of converting the thousands of square feet of containerboard (*MSF*) associated with the month's purchase of each customer or account to get unit cost. It is important to state that our cost data are incomplete because they do not include the cost of containerboard. According to testimony in the case, it accounts for 50% to 60% of variable cost. The practice our company followed was to add the value of the containerboard to the conversion cost in arriving at the price that was quoted to each customer.

Our investigation of costs employed both the CORP and MULTI data sets to estimate cross section conversion cost functions. The form we initially selected for the estimations was the same as the one used in the estimation of prices in table 5–1.

But why should the amount bought by a customer in a month influence the cost of serving the customer? As explained earlier, there is a set-up cost associated with fabricating containers. Therefore, we might expect that the larger the order size and length of run associated with satisfying the requirements of a customer, the lower the average cost of the run. There are several reasons why the average cost per MSF might increase after a certain point. First, if underlying cost functions of plants exhibit the traditional U-shape, then as the rate of output associated with a given length of run approaches the capacity of the plant used to satisfy the order, costs might be expected to rise. In part 3 we show that plant functions have such shape. Second, a large month's purchase by a customer might represent orders for a number of different sizes of containers rather than for a long run of one type. Third, in their depositions, a number of defendant and plaintiff witnesses made the point that there were important differentials in the quality of the service provided by different container manufactures. The purchasing agents of some opt-out firms indicated that while the prices they were quoted by different suppliers were the same, the conditions surrounding the sales were not. Agents stressed the need for reliability in promised delivery data because their firms kept small inventories of containers. In other words, these agents attempted to shift the inventory function to their suppliers. If large and powerful customers demanded and received a higher than average quality of service, the cost of serving them would have been higher. The dummy variable *NATL* was entered in order to gain insight into this issue.

The following conversion cost equation was estimated:

$$\ell nC = \beta_1 + \beta_2(\ell nMSF) + \beta_3(\ell nMSF)^2 + \beta_4 NATL \qquad (5.3)$$

The results that were obtained appear in table 5–2. The left side of the table, labeled CORP, is for the body of data that contains only the total purchases of the multiple-account customers. The right side of the table contains the results obtained when the estimation was carried out using the separate accounts of multiple-account customers, as well as the data for the single-account customers.

The first thing to note about the results shown in the table is that costs exhibit the same U-shape as the table 5–1 price functions, whichever body of data is used, and that is the case for both years. There are cost economies associated with serving customers and accounts whose monthly purchases are large, but costs do finally turn up.

We are able to say at this point that our cost functions are very much like our price functions. They do not have the same minima, but that is not surprising, since our cost functions are derived from data that are incomplete. As has been noted, the data omit the cost of containerboard, a major input in the production of containers.

Our cost findings support the position that for the great mass of customers in the corrugated container industry, prices were determined by competition between the small sheet plants and the integrated firms. We have

Table 5–2
Conversion Cost Functions

$$\ell nC = \beta_1 + \beta_2 \ \ell nMSF + \beta_3 \ (\ell nMSF)^2 + \beta_4 \ (NATL)$$

	CORP		MULTI	
	1973	1976	1973	1976
Constant	3.517	3.480	3.570	3.612
	(51.8)	(48.1)	(56.3)	(50.5)
$\ell nMSF$	−.510	−.461	−.532	−.516
	(−17.4)	(−15.7)	(−18.5)	(−17.3)
$(\ell nMSF)^2$	.037	.030	.041	.036
	(12.2)	(10.3)	(12.9)	(11.8)
$NATL$	.130	.119	.009	.001
	(5.3)	(4.6)	(.4)	(.1)
R^2	.25	.25	.25	.25
MIN	961	2189	672	1322
N	1946	1914	2439	2542

shown that costs fall over a considerable range of order sizes and monthly customer purchases. In a competitive environment we expect the prices different customers pay to reflect any cost economies or diseconomics associated with serving them. The reference to diseconomies brings us to the dummy variable.

The cost function estimated using the CORP data-set reveals that there is a clear and statistically significant effect on costs of the *NATL* dummy variable for national customers. We cannot say why costs shift up for multiple-account customers. We do not know whether they tend to order a large number of different sizes of boxes, order more frequently within a month, or demand special- or higher-quality service than other customers; but the cost function estimated with CORP data reveals a clear shift up in the costs of serving multiple-account customers.

The only important difference between the two sides of table 5–2 is that *NATL* is not significant in the function that was estimated for the body of data that did not include corporate totals for the multiple-account customers. We have no explanation for the difference, but, as we will shortly show, it does not change or affect our conclusions regarding collusion and price discrimination. We turn now to our investigation of the effect on prices of the costs functions depicted in table 5–2.

To see whether conversion cost differences can explain the price differences reported in table 5–1, we entered $\hat{C}$, predicted costs, into a predicted price equation. *NATL* is entered as an explanatory variable in order to test for the kind of price discrimination that could be accomplished through a conspiracy to allocate national customers and to fail to compete for their business, as had been alleged by the plaintiffs' attorneys in the opt-out suits. Our goal was to determine whether these customers paid more in relation to costs than did other customers. We also entered *ℓnMSF* in the new equation. We did so because the conversion cost functions do not take into account all elements of production and distribution cost. We wished to see whether size alone, as distinct from *NATL,* had any impact on price. By including both *NATL* and *ℓnMSF* in the new equation we hoped to determine whether large, single-account customers were part of the competitive segment of the market or were treated as equity customers. The equation that was estimated was:

$$\ell n P = \beta_1 + \beta_2(\ell n\hat{C}) + \beta_3(\ell nMSF) + \beta_4 NATL \qquad (5.4)$$

The results of the estimation appear in table 5–3. Again there are two parts to the table, one for each of the data sets employed.

The first thing to observe is that the coefficient for predicted cost is the largest of all of the coefficients and is highly significant. This is reassuring because it suggests that our cost data and our methods of estimating conversion cost functions are reasonable. It should also be noted that the coeffi-

Table 5–3
Cost-Based Predicted Price Functions

$$\ell n\hat{P} = \beta_1 + \beta_2\hat{C} + \beta_3\,\ell nMSF + \beta_4\,NATL$$

	CORP		MULTI	
	1973	1976	1973	1976
Constant	2.178	2.509	2.107	2.712
	(12.4)	(12.0)	(11.8)	(14.6)
$\ell n\hat{C}$	.573	.566	.606	.501
	(9.2)	(7.7)	(9.8)	(7.8)
$\ell nMSF$	−.037	−.033	−.033	−.48
	(−3.2)	(−2.5)	(−2.8)	(−3.9)
NATL	.049	.018	.033	.013
	(2.3)	(.8)	(1.8)	(.8)
R^2	.25	.24	.24	.23
N	1946	1914	2439	2542

cients are less than unity, but that is expected because linerboard, which tends to account for about 50% of variable cost, is not included in conversion costs.

We observe from the table that the coefficient on *NATL* is positive and significant in 1973, according to both data sets. It will be recalled that the cost analysis we carried out using CORP data revealed that it was more expensive to serve national customers. We now see that the prices paid by national customers exceed what can be explained by cost differentials, regardless of which data set is used. We conclude that national customers were the victims of a system of discriminatory pricing based on collusion.

It should be noted that the value of the coefficient on *NATL* in 1976 is much smaller than in 1973 and is not significant. Earlier it was pointed out that the grand jury was convened early in 1975. The change in the size and significance of the coefficient supports the claim that the discriminatory prices national customers were charged was the result of a conspiracy and that the calling of witnesses by the grand jury terminated the conspiracy. Our findings clearly support the allegation that multiple-account customers, the so-called equity customers, whose prices were set in the home offices of the integrated firms, were the victims of a system of discriminatory pricing based on collusion.

Finally, concerning the table 5–3, it should be observed that the coefficient on *ℓnMSF* is negative and significant in each of the estimations. From this we conclude that large, single-account customers did not tend to be the victims of collusion and discriminatory pricing. They appear to have been part of the competitive segment of the market and to have received discounts, perhaps because, as was explained earlier, there are cost economies in long runs. However, it should be noted that there were large, single-account customers among the opt-outs with whom defendants settled.

In equation (5.2) above we reported on an investigation of prices that involved the cubic term, $(\ell n MSF)^3$. The interpretation of collusion and price discrimination yielded by this equation differred in one regard from that based on the quadratic estimation, equation (5.1). In particular, equation (5.2) carried the implication that large, single-account customers tended to be part of the competitive rather than the collusive segment of the market, even in 1973. The price-based cost analysis on which we reported in table 5–3 led to the same conclusion. As a final check on this conclusion, we carried out a price-based cost analysis for 1973 in which CORP data was used and the conversion cost function involved the cube of the log of *MSF*. The results agreed completely with those reported in table 5–3. National customers were the only ones who were clearly in the collusive segment of the market. The prices paid by all other customers, better than 90% of all customers, appear to have been determined by competition in 1973, at least directly.

We conclude this part of the paper with a report on our efforts to investigate one of the arguments that the defendants advanced in opposition to certification of the class. They held that containers were rarely shipped more than three-hundred miles because transport cost was high relative to their value. As a result, markets tended to be localized. Price, it was asserted, varied greatly from market to market because of differences in cost and competitive conditions within them. Therefore, defendants claimed, it was not possible to identify a class of consumers who had been damaged by the alleged conspiracy.

Our investigation of the above line of reasoning involved the estimation of separate price functions, conversion cost functions, and cost-based predicted price equations for most of the more than twenty-five plants that our firm operated in different parts of the country. The form as well as the types of functions that were estimated were the same as those on which we have already reported in tables 5–1, 5–2, and 5–3 above. We found very few instances of significant variations in parameter estimates. For example, our separate plant price function, the equivalent of table 5–1, each involve estimation of four parameters. The constant term for only one plant was found to differ by more than two standard obviations from the mean of all the constant terms. There were no significant variations in any of the other parameter estimates. The same result was found for the conversion cost functions. The constant term for one plant was found to differ significantly from the mean of that for all the plants, and there were no significant variations in any of the other parameter estimates. Much the same result was found for the separate plant cost-based predicted price functions.

3. Scale Economics, Demand Conditions and Industrial Structure

A central thesis of this chapter is that, during a crucial stage in the history of the corrugated container industry, competition and collusion in pricing existed side-by-side in the same geographic markets. We believe that the data and analyses of the preceding parts of the chapter provide strong empirical support for this thesis. The goal of this final part of the chapter is to provide additional understanding of why this competitive-collusive form of industrial structure came to characterize the industry. The arguments we present rest on an economic condition that seems incontrovertible to use, namely that the integrated firms controlled the supply of and acted collusively in the pricing of board. They were able to do so because of their dominance in such upstream operations as pulp and timber production. Given this control of the major input used in the production of corrugated containers, we attempt to provide answers to three questions in this part of the chapter. First, why did the integrated firms allow, and perhaps some of them even encourage, the entry of small sheet plants into the container industry? These small plants competed with the large firms for some of the business, including that of the large, single-account customers. Second, why did the integrated firms continue to produce containers—which is to say, why didn't they restrict themselves to the production of the intermediate product, price it monopolistically, and leave the container business to the small firms? Third, why were the integrated firms able to enforce the system of market segmentation, that is, the equity customer arrangement described in the previous part of the chapter. If national customers were the victims of collusion and price discrimination, why didn't they purchase their containers in the competitive segment of the market? They could have arranged to have their container requirements provided by a group of small sheet plants rather than one or two of the integrated firms. Why didn't they do so?

Our answer to the first question, why hundreds of sheet plants were allowed—perhaps even encouraged—to enter the container business, rests on differences in economies of scale for different stages in the operations of integrated firms. It is our position that economies of scale at the level of the plant were very much greater in pulpmill operations and in paperboard production than they were in the downstream operation, the production of containers. We will shortly show that the optimum scale of plant is quite small in container production and that large container firms are not large because they operate large plants. Rather, they are large because they operate many small plants. On the other hand, there appear to be very significant economies of scale in pulpmill operations. There are relatively few firms in the industry. The top firms in the industry are not large because they operate many plants but because they operate a few large plants. Paperboard production tends to fall between pulpmill and container operations; large firms operate large plants, but they also operate more plants than do small firms.

It is our position that the smaller integrated firms either could not or chose not to engage in extensive multiple-plant operations in the container end of the business. They chose to sell a large percent of the output of their pulpmill–paperboard mills to sheet plants, which were essential to the successful operations of the smaller, integrated firms. They may have even encouraged entry of sheet plants into container production. However, to keep peace with each other and with the larger, integrated firms, the smaller and larger firms colluded and fixed the price of the input that was sold to the sheet plants. Much of what has just been said is speculative, but we can provide some concrete evidence in support of our position. We begin with economies of scale at the level of the plant in the production of containers.

As indicated earlier, in our MULTI data-set we have the conversion cost of serving every single-account corporate customer and every account of each multiple-account customer *at each plant.* We also know the associated MSF figures. For each plant we were therefore able to derive two figures, total conversion cost expenditure and total (*MSF*) output for January 1973 and January 1976. Our firm operates enough plants for us to be able to estimate a plant cost function. Our basic decision was to employ pooled data to estimate a form of cost function that resembles that of microeconomic theory, namely, the cubic form. However, we added a variable, *MED,* for the median size of account of each plant. This variable was included because we believed that, other things remaining constant, the larger the average size of account served by a plant, the lower would be its operating cost. The logic behind the choice was straightforward. That is, there are costs of handling customers, and the larger the average size of order for any given plant output, the fewer would tend to be the number of customers and the lower the cost of operating the plant. The results are shown in equation (5.5). The variable Q is now used to represent *MSF,* the thousands of square feet of linerboard used by a plant in producing all of the containers ordered by all customers and accounts of that plant. The stars (*) represent multiplication.

$$TC = 345.6^* \ YRDUM \ - \ 21143.5 \ + \ 16.10Q \ - \ .355^*10^{-3}\ ^*Q^2$$
$$ (.04) (.62) (3.92) (2.47)$$

$$+ \ .407^*10^{-8}\ ^*Q^3 \ - \ 269.6^*MED (5.5)$$
$$ (2.65) \phantom{^*10^{-8}\ ^*Q^3 \ - \ } (3.79)$$

$$R^2 = .90$$

The fit is excellent. All coefficients are significant at the 5% level, save that for the year dummy. This suggests that factor price and technological changes were not significant in the period. If we treat the above result as an estimate of a long-run cost function, then the optimum or least cost rate of output is 34,783 MSF per month or 417,391 per year. The output of the industry was 216.371 billions of square feet in 1976.[6] Clearly, the output of an optimal size plant is trivial compared to the output of the container industry. Additional evidence concerning our argument about differences in scale economies at different stages in the operations of integrated firms comes from Census data.

From table 5–4 we observe that the top twenty firms in pulpmill and paperboard operations do not operate a large number of plants, and that there is not a great deal of difference between the number of plants operated by the top eight firms and the number operated by the next twelve. Much the same situation holds in paperboard operations. In these two industries, the large firms operate large plants. The situation is quite different in containers, where the largest firms operate many plants. The average for the top four firms is twenty-nine, which is six times as many as the number operated by firms that rank in the nine to twenty category. On the other hand, the output per plant for the largest class of firms is only 1.5 times as great as the output

Table 5–4
Scale and Extent of Multiplant Operations

	Value of Shipments Per Firm (millions)	Numbers of Plants Per Firm	Value of Shipments Per Plant (millions)
Pulpmills 2611			
Top 4 firms	1008	2.7	93
Next 4 firms	577	2.0	72
Next 12 firms	483	1.7	57
Next 30 firms	23	.2	4
Remainder	X	X	X
Paperboard mills, 2637			
Top 4 firms	458	7.0	66
Next 4 firms	246	5.2	47
Next 12 firms	135	3.1	44
Next 30 firms	64	2.8	23
Remainder	11	1.1	10
Corrugated Boxes, 2653			
Top 4 firms	353	29	12
Next 4 firms	259	28	9
Next 12 firms	153	17	9
Next 30 firms	40	5	8
Remainder	2	1	

Source: Census of Manufactures, table 8, volume I, 1977.

per plant for the nine to twenty group. These differences suggest that the optimum scale of output of pulpmill and paperboard plants, but especially the former, is much greater than that of container firms. Some integrated firms adjusted to this disparity by building and operating numerous container plants. Other, smaller, integrated firms lacked the means or desire to engage in extensive multiplant operations. They chose to sell much of their paperboard output to sheet plants. This was the way the smaller integrated firms competed with the giants, but the entire group accepted the need for collusion in the pricing of board.

If we are correct in our claim that scale economies are quite limited in the production of containers, why did the integrated firms bother to produce them at all? (Which was our second question.) Why didn't the large firms simply turn over all production of containers to the sheet plants and price the board monopolistically? The answer to this question has already been given. We saw in part 2 that the large, national firms pay higher prices for their containers and buy more of them than do the small and medium size firms. This is evidence that the container demand functions of the national firms tend to lie outside those of the small and medium size firms. This demand situation is a basis for price discrimination. We are not arguing that the demand functions of the national customers were necessarily less elastic than that of other customers. Rather, our position is that there are expenses involved in acting collusively and that there was money to be made in a collusive arrangement that was directed against the few, large national customers. It was profitable for the integrated container firms to bring about a segmentation of the market in which they satisfied the demands of the national firms and priced to those firms in a discriminatory way. *Through collusion and price discrimination they were able to extract more revenue (and profit) from the national firms than they could have obtained indirectly through the conspiracy to fix the price of corrugated material, because the sheet plants could not practice price discrimination.*

We now turn to our last question. Why were the integrated firms successful in their practice of market segmentation and price discrimination? Why didn't the national firms contract with a number, possibly even a large number, of sheet plants to satisfy their container needs? If the costs and difficulties of doing that were too great, why didn't a type of brokerage or middle-person arrangement emerge for satisfying the large requirements of the national customers? We have no firm answer to this question, only a speculation.

As indicated earlier, the practice of many container purchasers is to hold small inventories. Rapid and reliable delivery is then very important. There are repeated references to the need for such service in deposition testimony. Because the integrated firms controlled the output of containerboard, they would have been in a position to cut off or delay shipments to sheet plants that attempted to compete for the business of equity customers. These plants would then have had difficulty meeting delivery dates. The impression would have been created that the small firms were an unreliable source.

Notes

1. 1982 Census of Manufacturers, April 1984, Preliminary Report Industry Series, Table 1, Historical Statistics for the Industry: 2653, Corrugated and Solid Fibre Boxes.

2. 1977 Census of Manufacturers, Volume I, Table 7: Share of Value of Shipments of Each Class of Product.

3. Two things that detract from the usefulness of concentration ratios are large differences in the products of firms that are assigned to an industry, and a high percent of industry output produced by firms that are assigned to a different industry. The concentration ratios for 2653 do not suffer from either of these defects. The primary product specialization ratio of the firms assigned to the industry was 9910 in 1977. The firms assigned to the industry also accounted for 99% of the output of corrugated containers in 1977. Both of the above percentages were virtually the same in 1963.

4. 1977 Census of Manufacturers, Table 8: Share of Selected Items of 4 Largest Companies and Complementary Groupings Ranked on Value of Shipments.

5. 1977 Census of Manufacturers.

6. Fibre Box Industry, 1983 *Annual Report,* Fibre Box Association, p.5.

6

Resale Price Maintenance: A Simple Analysis

Ronald E. Grieson
Nirvikar Singh

Resale price maintenance's minimum retail (resale) price provision arouses the suspicion of economists and policy makers. One's straightforward intuition is that higher resale prices, with the manufacturer's price constant, will cause less of the good to be sold, most probably reducing manufacturer's profits. Furthermore, resale price maintenance (RPM) is often suspected of reducing retailer competition, or aiding retailers or manufacturers in price collusion.

Posner (1976) argues that as long as it is not part of collusion, price fixing, or monopolization, there is nothing wrong with RPM per se. It is certainly true that one can argue that it would be the collusion, and the other things, that ought to be outlawed per se, but that RPM cannot per se produce it. There is, however, something unconvincing about an argument that does not show why a noncollusive manufacturer might want to have RPM. If there is no reason to justify something, and it may be antisocial, why not minimize enforcement or collusion costs and prohibit it? If it can never be socially optimal, its prohibition will have benefits (reduced enforcement costs and collusion costs) and almost no costs.

To justify RPM, therefore, the retailer service provision and free-rider problems have been advanced.[1] However, Telser (1982), among others, indicates that dealer service fees and manufacturer-provided services may be used in place of RPM. We present arguments against this position, and construct a simple model that is characterized by the provision of externalities (or quasi-public goods) in addition to higher private goods service levels on the part of some retailers. Holahan (1979) presents a somewhat similar argument (where information is the externality) for the optimality of RPM for some manufacturers. To some extent, our model is complementary to Holahan's, in that all firms in his model are identical, so that each firm affects all others identically. We allow for this, but focus on unidirectional externalities. Our

Financial support from the University of California, Santa Cruz, Faculty Research Grant Committee to N. Singh is gratefully acknowledged.

model is more general, in allowing for types of externalities other than information and private good service levels, as well as differentiated products. It is also significantly simpler, clearer and empirically useful.

The model is one of independent (of the manufacturer) dealers and is consistent with free entry, zero profits, competition or monopolistic competition among one or all types of dealers. Examples of the point-of-sale services involved are advertising, information, display, guarantees and other amenities. The provision of a private service may also create an externality. For example, if only some retailers carry spare parts, the search time of the consumers who buy originally from retailers who do not carry them goes down with the number of part-carrying firms. The product-specific externality or public goods nature of these services nullifies the separate provision for fee argument. Furthermore, the service-externalities may be inseparable from the type of product or to those who merely visit the retail establishment without buying anything. Contrast the services available at an exclusive department store to those available at a mail-order or an 800-phone-number discounter. To require all retailers to provide department-store type services would effectively bar any other type of retail outlet and may be infeasible or legally risky. Furthermore, it may not be optimal from the manufacturer's point of view to have all retailers provide these costly services. An alternative policy, selling to department stores at a lower price, could be viewed as discriminatory or predatory, and therefore legally prohibited or risky. Subsidies to the externality-producing sector may have similar legal difficulties or be otherwise similarly infeasible: these stores might wholesale to the nonexternality-producing outlets. Last, the transaction costs of enforcing an externality- or service-production requirement on retail outlets may be much higher than simple enforcement of a minimum price rule, due to measurability or observability problems with the former.

Given the constraints on the feasibility of alternatives, therefore, we derive a condition for RPM to be beneficial to the manufacturer. We consider a market where there are two types of retailers, those who provide the services and those who do not. One or more of the types of services discussed in the previous paragraph may be provided. Their number and type will obviously affect the strength of the externality. The service-externality-producing retail outlets may simply have higher average or marginal costs and may be monopolistic competitors as well. The other sector may be lower cost and/or perfectly competitive. We allow, therefore, for product differentiation at the retail level in specifying the consumer demand functions. We also allow for the externality in both types of retailers' demand functions. The sufficient condition for RPM to increase the quantity sold depends on the demand elasticities, the elasticity of demand with respect to service-externality provision, and the relative sizes of the service-externality and "purely competitive" (nonservice externality) sectors at the retail level.

Model

The crucial specification of the model is that of the demand functions. We assume that the products of the service-externality and nonexternality sectors of the retail market are viewed differently by consumers. Thus the service-externality is not simply information, but includes factors such as display and after-sales services. The level of provision of these service-externalities depends positively on the size of the service-type retailing sector. Hence we allow this effect to enter demand functions in a general way, through the inclusion of an extra variable, the number of firms in the service sector. Therefore we have the following aggregate consumer demand functions:

$$Q_c = D_c(p_c, p_s, n), \tag{6.1a}$$

$$Q_s = D_s(p_c, p_s, n), \tag{6.1b}$$

where subscript c denotes the "purely competitive" or nonservice-externality sector; subscript s denotes the monopolistically competitive[2] or service sector; p denotes price, Q, quantity; and n, the number of firms in the service sector. We have the following signs on partial derivatives:

$$\frac{\partial D_i}{\partial p_i} < 0, \quad \frac{\partial D_i}{\partial P_j} > 0, \quad \frac{\partial D_i}{\partial n} \geq 0, \qquad i, j = c, s, i \neq j. \tag{6.2}$$

The second pair of inequalities embodies the fact that the two sectors sell substitute goods. The third pair of inequalities reflects the assumption that consumers may be better off with more stores that provide service-externalities. As an example of the above demand specification, we may consider something similar to Holahan's formulation, with $Q_c = D_c(p_c + vt(n), p_s)^3$, where v is the cost per unit of time, t is the time spent searching or acquiring information, and $t' < 0$.

Next, we discuss assumptions concerning both types of retail outlets. We need not be very explicit on assumptions concerning competitive conditions or costs, since this is not at all necessary for the exposition or analysis. An essential feature, clearly, is that the average costs of s-type firms are higher, since they provide additional services whether they are monopolistically or purely competitive. Costs include, of course, the price charged for the good by the manufacturer to the retailer. In equilibrium with free entry, p_s and p_c will equal respective average costs, with $p_s = p_c$. For simplicity we assume that all retail firms are price takers. Hence, s-type firms are not monopolistically competitive in the traditional sense. This assumption is not essential, but implies that the amount sold by each s-type firm in equilibrium is independent of n. Let q be this amount, that is to say, $Q_s = nq$. Hence, q is the output at which the average costs of the *s*-type firm attain a minimum. The number of *s*-type firms, *n,* is determined by free entry and the zero profit condition, as usual.

The above assumptions are all that we need. In the next section we analyze the effects of increasing p_c, that is, the effect of resale price maintenance on total sales and perhaps profits of the manufacturer. Assuming that firms maximize either sales or profits is consistent with the analysis.

Results

The following result is the keystone of the analysis.

Lemma: $\dfrac{dQ}{dp_c} > 0$ if and only if $\dfrac{1 + r\epsilon_{cn}}{1 - \epsilon_{sn}} > -r\dfrac{\epsilon_{cp}}{\epsilon_{sp}},$

$$\epsilon_{cn} \equiv \frac{n}{Q_c} \cdot \frac{\partial D_c}{\partial n}, \ \epsilon_{sn} \equiv \frac{n}{Q_s} \cdot \frac{\partial D_s}{\partial n}, \ \epsilon_{cp} \equiv \frac{p_c}{Q_c} \cdot \frac{\partial D_c}{\partial p_c},$$

$$\epsilon_{sp} = \frac{p_c}{Q_s} \cdot \frac{\partial D_s}{\partial p_c}, \ r = \frac{Q_c}{Q_s} \text{ and } Q \equiv Q_c + Q_s.$$

Proof: Differentiating (6.1a) and (6.1b) with respect to p_c, we have

$$\frac{dQ_c}{dp_c} = \frac{\partial D_c}{\partial p_c} + \frac{\partial D_c}{\partial n} \cdot \frac{dn}{dp_c},$$

$$\frac{dQ_s}{dp_c} = \frac{\partial D_s}{\partial p_c} + \frac{\partial D_s}{\partial n} \cdot \frac{dn}{dp_c}.$$

But

$$\frac{dn}{dp_c} = \frac{1}{q} \cdot \frac{dQ_s}{dp_c} = \frac{n}{Q_s} \cdot \frac{dQ_s}{dp_c}$$

Furthermore,

$$\frac{dq}{dp_c} = \frac{dQ_c}{dp_c} + \frac{dQ_s}{dp_c}.$$

The result follows by a simple sequence of algebraic manipulations.

The significance of $dQ/dp_c > 0$ is that a manufacturer can increase sales through RPM if this condition is met, without altering the price at which it sells to retailers. Since the demand curve for the manufacturer's product has shifted to the right, the manufacturer's profit must go up with p_c, whatever it chooses to do in terms of a profit-maximizing (price-quantity) policy. The final effect of raising p_c on consumers' welfare is ambiguous, reflecting the familiar ambiguity of a profit-maximizing imperfect competitor's response to a demand shift. However, consumers' welfare may increase whether the manufacturer's price rises, remains constant or decreases. The last situation clearly represents the strongest case for RPM.

Note that this analysis can be applied to perfectly competitive homogenous product manufacturers if they collectively impose RPM. One of many manufacturers raising P_c for its dealers alone would not increase sales significantly. If manufacturers themselves sell differentiated products, the same analysis applies for each manufacturer's product market.

To summarize, we have

PROPOSITION 1. A sufficient condition for RPM to increase the quantity sold (profits) of one manufacturer is

$$\frac{1 + r\epsilon_{cn}}{1 - \epsilon_{sn}} > -r\frac{\epsilon_{cp}}{\epsilon_{sp}}. \tag{6.3}$$

Clearly, the higher is ϵ_{cn}, the more likely is this condition to be met. This elasticity measures both the sensitivity of the level of service-externalities to the number of providing stores and the sensitivity of consumer demand for the competitive retailers' product to the level of services. ϵ_{sn} has a similar interpretation. To take Holahan's case,

$$\epsilon_{cn} = \epsilon_{cp} \cdot \frac{nvt'}{p_c} = \epsilon_{cp} \cdot \epsilon_{tn} \cdot \frac{vt}{p_c}$$

is the product of the price elasticity, the elasticity of search time with respect to the number of firms, and the ratio of the two components, vt and p_c, of the "full price." A necessary condition for inequality (6.3) is $\epsilon_{sn} < 1$, which seems a reasonable condition. In fact, it may even be the case that $\epsilon_{sn} = 0$: a customer at an s-type retail outlet is already benefitting from the externality. RPM can still increase total quantity sold and welfare in this case. The right hand side of (6.3) is greater than one, from restrictions on the demand functions imposed by the utility functions from which they are derived (own-price effects exceed cross-price effects). Hence, $\epsilon_{sn} > 0$ or $\epsilon_{cn} > 0$ is necessary for (6.3). The impact of the relative size of the nonservice and service sectors is less transparent. Assuming $\epsilon_{sn} < 1$, (6.3.) may be rearranged to give:

$$r[\epsilon_{cn}\epsilon_{sp} + \epsilon_{cp}(1 - \epsilon_{sn})] > \epsilon_{sp} > 0. \tag{6.4}$$

A necessary condition for (6.4) to hold is that the term in square brackets be positive. If this is the case, then increasing r clearly makes (6.4) more likely to hold. Hence we state:

PROPOSITION 2. If the demand elasticities satisfy the necessary conditions for (6.3), RPM is more likely to benefit the manufacturer if the relative size of the nonservice sector is larger.

Conclusion

In this chapter we have presented a simple model that shows how resale price maintenance may benefit a manufacturer and possibly consumers through increasing the level of provision of services that create an externality in the retail market. A sufficient condition for this to be the case for the manufacturer is derived in terms of demand elasticities of general demand functions.

Whether consumers are benefitted depends on the manufacturer's precise incentives, but since in the absence of resale price maintenance the externality is underpriced and hence underprovided, it seems that total welfare, measured by manufacturer profits plus consumer surplus, will go up with resale price maintenance, if total sales do increase in that case. The condition we have provided is potentially verifiable, and empirical investigation might help to settle the public policy issue.

Notes

1. Marvel and McCafferty (1984) have recently provided an alternative explanation of RPM in terms of quality certification.

2. See Grieson (1976) for a discussion of information, location, and so forth, that creates monopolistic competition. The provision of these services at no charge by the retailer results in a more preferable allocation.

3. This kind of formulation, borrowed from Becker, relies on very specific assumptions. See Becker (1965).

References

Becker, G.S. 1965. "A Theory of the Allocation of Time." *The Economic Journal* 75:493–517.

Grieson, R.E. 1976. "Welfare Implications of Various Pricing Schemes in Monopolistic Competition Due to Location." In *Public and Urban Economics,* ed. R.E. Grieson. Lexington, Mass.: Lexington Books.

Holahan, W.L. 1979. "A Theoretical Analysis of Resale Price Maintenance." *Journal of Economic Theory* 21:411–20.

Marvel, H.P., and S. McCafferty. 1984. "Resale Price Maintenance and Quality Certification." *The Rand Journal of Economics* 15, no. 3:346–59.

Posner, R.A. 1976. *Antitrust Law: An Economic Perspective.* Chicago: University of Chicago Press.

Telser, L.G. 1982. "Why Should Manufacturers Want Fair Trade." *Journal of Law and Economics.*

7

Voter Participation and Voter Choice: An Empirical Examination of Massachusetts' Proposition 2½

Ronald Krumm
George Tolley
Austin Kelly

Much attention has been given in recent decades to the theory of public decision making and public choice. One strand of inquiry has been the explanation of voter choices and the related question of participation in the voting process. From the beginning, benefits and costs to individuals have been central to economists' attempts to explain voting behavior (see, for example, Arrow 1951 and Tullock 1970). In the absence of voting participation costs, theories have attempted to explain an individual's voting choice in terms of the expected net benefits accruing to him from the outcome of the voting. In early theories, given differences among individuals, the voting outcome was visualized as resulting in a service level at which the net benefit to the median voter was zero.

Adding the costs of voter participation to the above analysis results in several complications. The median voter and others with preferred service levels near that of the median voter would not find it worthwhile to vote. On the other hand, incentives to vote might be small for even those individuals with preferences on the tails of the distribution because their vote would make only a miniscule difference to the outcome and would not be sufficient to outweigh the costs of voting. Thus, as a result of the introduction of the costs of voting, the description of voter participation patterns becomes quite

Partial financial support from the Committee on Public Policy Studies at the University of Chicago is gratefully acknowledged. We thank the participants in the Conference on Regulation and Antitrust, University of California, Santa Cruz, and participants in the Workshop on Economics and Public Policy at the University of Chicago for helpful comments and suggestions. We also thank Julie Wilson for access to and permission to use the survey data collected by herself and Helen Ladd as reported in Ladd and Wilson (1982). The usual disclaimer applies.

complicated, even to the point of being indeterministic. Nevertheless, it is often the case that voter turnout is high, even in countries where participation of eligible voters is not required. One factor that might account for this is that there is an instilled predilection for voting that gives an added personal gain to voting in addition to the gains or losses that accrue to the individual as a result of the vote outcome. Nonetheless, intensity of feeling (the magnitude of loss to voters from an outcome different from their most preferred outcome) can still influence voter participation. Intensity of feeling is particularly likely to induce people of similar views to vote if they band together and continuously vote as a block in order to maximize their influence.

The roles of intensity of feeling and information costs were examined by Tullock and Buchanan (1962). They suggested that taxes tend to be more diffuse and general than the benefits of public-spending programs. As a result, many individuals would not be aware of the slight costs that they bear from a particular program. In this case, the beneficiaries of the program would dominate the voting process. Using the same concept, Downs (1957) argued that political parties might propose policies that would benefit particular minority groups, with the costs of the policies spread out among all groups; then none of the minority groups would bear the full costs of the program that directly benefitted them. And if they were unaware of the costs of the programs aimed at benefitting other minority groups, the whole set of policies might be adopted. One result might be that the level of total government expenditures would be in excess of what it would be if all persons had full information.

Another strand of thought stems from Tiebout's (1956) famous analysis of how people "vote" ("with their feet") by choosing to live in jurisdictions that give them a desired mix of services and taxes. Extensions of the work by Tiebout and empirical testing of the implications of the framework have focused on property values (for example, Oates 1969, 1973; Hamilton 1976; Orr 1968, 1970, 1972; Wales and Wiens 1974; and Grieson 1974). While these studies have not led to conclusive results, they have illustrated the myriad of factors that could affect the outcome.

In addition to such considerations, Haurin (1978) has used rent gradient analysis to illustrate the proposition that since land values at the edge of a city cannot be increased above their opportunity costs in alternative uses, the incidence of differential property tax rates between cities might be expected to go into wage differentials. Also, with respect to the property value change impacts initially taken up by Oates (1969), Edel and Sclar (1974) and Hamilton (1976) have argued that impacts on property values of such property tax differences would be evidence that a complete working out of the Tiebout equilibrium would not occur. Epple, Zelenitz, and Visscher (1978) have considered this aspect more fully and suggested that such a distinction could only be made by seeing if property tax differentials resulted in deadweight losses and thus reduced nonmedian voters' demands for housing. They point out that this result is not even useful when community boundaries are flexible or when supply is perfectly elastic. Such considerations fit in well with Haurin's analysis.

The analyses listed above have not explicitly addressed the question of how different people might be expected to vote on local government tax and expenditure propositions. One interesting question that is raised, however, is the different incentives that renters and owners of property in a local jurisdiction might have with regard to support of local tax or expenditure issues in the presence of property tax capitalization. Moreover, given the findings in Haurin (1978), a much broader set of issues might also be involved.

Another interesting line of research has dealt with analysis of voting patterns on property tax rate limitation initiatives. As indicated in Picus (1974), while almost forty states have enacted tax or expenditure limitations since the passage of Proposition 13 in California in 1978, in only three states have voters enacted initiatives to reduce property taxes (California, Idaho, and Massachusetts). Analyses of surveys of voter opinions in California (Citron 1979; and Sears and Citron 1982), Michigan (Cournot, Gramlich, and Rubinfeld 1979), and Massachusetts (Ladd and Wilson 1982) have generally been interpreted as showing that support of the tax limitation measures was based primarily on the desire to reduce tax burdens, but not to reduce the size of government. One implication of this result, is that support for these tax measures shifts the burden of taxation to some other groups (presumably to those voting against the tax limitation proposals).

The purpose of this study is to investigate more fully voter participation and voter choices (decisions or patterns) as they pertain to property tax rate limitation measures. In particular, we examine these decisions for Massachusetts' Proposition 2½, which was passed in November of 1980 by about a sixty to forty margin.

Part 1 of this chapter summarizes the characteristics of Proposition 2½ and reviews empirical studies of voter behavior in this and related situations. Part 2 considers alternative empirical approaches to analysis of voter participation and voter choice in this setting. One concern of our analysis is to examine more fully the implications of spatial diversity in conditions for specification of voting choice models. The variables used in our empirical analysis of voting behavior are described in part 3, and part 4 presents estimates of their impacts.

Description of Property Tax Limitations

The major provisions of Massachusetts' Proposition 2½ are outlined in Davis (1982). As illustrated there, a number of issues were considered in this proposition besides limitation of community tax rates. However, most attention has been focused on the implications of the limits on local government property taxation. This component of the proposition limits the amount that communities may tax property to 2.5% of the total fair cash value of all property, or to the taxes levied in 1979, whichever is less. For communities exceeding this limit, the proposition requires a roll-back of the tax levy by 15% per year until the 2.5% limit is attained. Further, there is a 2.5% limit on the yearly rate of increase in the tax levy in following years.

Proposition 2½ was passed in November 1980 during the general election. Immediately after the passage, a survey was conducted in Massachusetts in an attempt to determine why support for the proposition was so high. Analysis of the results from this survey are presented in Ladd and Wilson (1982). The approach taken in the Ladd and Wilson study was to model voter choice with regard to Proposition 2½ on those individuals who voted on it. The voter choice was specified as a function of attitudinal and opinion variables measured in the survey. The findings were interpreted as indicating that preferences for lower taxes and spending led to votes for the proposition, while preferences for lower levels of service did not contribute significantly to this vote. On the other hand, Ladd and Wilson conclude that the fear of service loss was the most important cause of votes against the proposition.

The Ladd and Wilson study is only one of many analyzing property tax limitation voting behavior. Attiyeh and Engle (1979), for example, examined voting results for Proposition 13 in California in fifty-eight counties. Their concern was to determine the extent to which voting patterns were consistent with alternative expectations of the impact of the proposition. The alternatives they considered were whether voters behaved as if they expected (1) the level of local expenditures to remain the same, (2) slight reductions in property taxes and thus slight reductions in local expenditures, or (3) large property tax reductions and thus large expenditure cuts. They interpreted their findings as consistent with the last set of expectations. In another analysis of the California experience, Citron (1979) examined the vote in terms of demographic characteristics of the voters (age, income, tenure status, education, and race) as well as in terms of voter ideology (conservative, liberal) and party affiliation. He found that homeownership and higher levels of income led to an increase in the probability of voting for the proposition, and that higher levels of education led to an enhanced probability of voting against the proposition. The study also found that voter ideology and party affiliation significantly affected vote choice.

The empirical findings in the studies discussed above indicate that property tax limitation voting behavior is significantly related to demographic as well as attitudinal characteristics of voters. Implicit in these results is that the perceived net benefit from passage of a property tax limitation measure is a function of these characteristics. However, these studies lack an explicit formulation of how variation in voter characteristics corresponds to variation in the perceived net benefit measures. Such a formulation is required before serious econometric analysis of voting behavior can take place. The next part of this chapter provides a beginning in that direction.

2. Model Development

One approach to analysis of voting decisions is to relate voter decisions to voter preferences. Empirical studies of such relationships should not be interpreted in terms of structural causality between preferences and voting decisions: expression of preferences using a voting ballot is not unlike expression of preferences on a survey questionnaire.

Nevertheless, it may be useful to examine the relationships involved. One reason is that the observed choice of vote represents the preference for a measure which involves potential changes in many conditions. The vote choice thus reflects the sum of the net benefits to the voter for each particular issue. Information on each of the component net benefits may then be used in the measurement of overall net benefits. In this section we consider more fully the structure of the relationship between individuals' preferences as stated in the Ladd and Wilson study and their voting decisions. First, we consider the voting participation decision, and then we turn to the question of vote choice.

Preference Measures and Voting Participation

Let $B(i) = A(i) - 3$, where $A(i)$ is the response for the ith service preference variable. A value of $A(i)$ equal to 1 corresponds to a preference to decrease the level of service provision substantially, a value of $A(i)$ equal to 3 corresponds to a preference for continuation of the current level, and a value of $A(i)$ equal to 5 corresponds to a preference for a large increase in the service level. The sign $B(i)$ gives the direction from the current level of service provision that is desired by the individual. Further, let $Z(i)$ be the absolute value of $B(i)$. $Z(i)$ thus measures the magnitude of the difference between the desired and current service levels.

Consider a proposition whose passage would slightly increase the ith service level and whose defeat would slightly decrease that service level. Only individuals with $Z(i)$ (or $B[i]$) equal to zero would be indifferent with respect to the outcome of the vote or vote outcome. If individuals voted as if their vote "counted," those with higher values of $Z(i)$ would have greater incentives for participating in the voting process because they have more to gain or lose from the vote outcome than would individuals with lower values of $Z(i)$. With random variation among individuals in their costs of voting, the above discussion suggests that the probability that an individual would participate in the voting process is usefully specified as

$$P(v) = f[Z(i)] \tag{7.1a}$$

In this case $f()$ translates alternative values of $Z(i)$ into their net benefit value.

For a proposition involving changes in more than one service level, off-setting as well as augmenting values of the $B(i)$, several terms need to be considered in the specification of $P(v)$. Consider, for example, the specification given by

$$P(v) = f[B(1), \ldots, B(n)] \tag{7.1}$$

where n is the number of service categories involved and $f()$ translates the series of $B(i)$ terms into the absolute value of the net benefits for the individual as a result of the vote outcome.

Implicit in equation (7.1) is that the benefits of passage of the proposition (either negatively or positively) are related to a function of the absolute difference of preferences from their current levels. In many cases, however, the voting choice is between a vote to change conditions and a vote to maintain them as they are. In this situation an individual with a $B(i)$ equal to zero would not be indifferent to the passage of the proposition. Further, when more extreme changes would result from passage of a proposition, individuals preferring only slight changes from current conditions (in the direction of the proposed change) may find that they would be better off with the current conditions than with the extreme ones.

The inappropriateness of the $B(i)$ for measurement of the benefit associated with the outcome of the vote is especially relevant when considering Proposition 2½. In some communities, passage would not affect property tax revenue capabilities at all, as tax rates were substantially below the ceiling. In other communities, only the future growth of tax revenues would be affected. In still other communities, passage of the proposition would reduce both current and future tax revenue capabilities by varying amounts. As a result of this variation in impact, a particular value of $B(i)$ would not represent the same net benefit measure in different communities. Below, we outline a procedure to take this into account in specification of the voting participation expression.

Community Variation in Implied Expenditure Impacts

Let $A'(i)$ be the level of service that would result from passage of the proposition. If the proposition is defeated, however, the level of service would remain unchanged and equal to a value of 3. For a person with $A(i)$ less than 3 to begin with, if $A'(i)$ is between $A(i)$ and 3, the individual unambiguously gains through passage of the proposition. We estimate this amount to be an amount proportional to $\{[A(i) - 3]^{**}2 - [A'(i) - 3]^{**}2\}$. The first quantity inside the brackets in the above expression is the amount the individual would gain if the service level were brought totally into line with the desired value. Subtracted from this amount is the loss that occurs because this desired quantity is not fully achieved. In the case in which $A'(i)$ is less than $A(i)$, but still less than three, the corresponding net benefit calculation is $\{[A(i) - 3)^{**}2 - [A(i) - A'(i)]^{**}2\}$. This may be either positive or negative in sign. While gains are associated with movement toward the desired amount, losses result from movement past that amount.

If $A'(i)$ is greater than three, the individual with $A(i)$ less than three unambiguously loses if the proposition is passed. The loss incurred is given by $\{[A(i) - A'(i)]^{**}2 - [A(i) - 3]^{**}2\}$. For persons with $A(i)$ equal to 3, the loss from passage of the proposition is merely $[A(i) - A'(i)]^{**}2$. For persons with $A(i)$ greater than three, the calculation of benefits proceeds symmetrically to that considered above for a person with $A(i)$ less than three.

Let the net benefit measures described above be denoted $B(i)^*$. The voting participation decision is then specified by

$$P(v) = f[B(1)^*,...,B(n)^*]. \qquad (7.2)$$

The same comments made with respect to functional form for equation (7.1) apply in this case.

It is important to note that the values of the $B(i)^*$ will differ among communities depending on their current property tax status, so that equation (7.1) would represent a misspecification of the voting model. One problem with the specification in equation (7.2), however, is that the values of the $A'(i)$ are not directly observed, and even if they were observed for one year, the whole future time pattern of these values would sometimes be needed to capture the effects adequately. The approach taken in our analysis is to replace $A'(i)$ with variables from the Ladd and Wilson survey that measure individuals' expectations of service levels that would result from passage of the proposition.

Preference Measures and Vote Choice

Having discussed the structure of voter participation decisions above, we now turn to the related question of vote choice. The probabilities of voting for and against passage of the proposition conditional upon the decision to participate in the voting process are denoted $P(y/v)$ and $P(n/v)$, respectively. Studies of voter choice such as that of Ladd and Wilson (1982) have dealt entirely with these probability functions. These functions fit into the more general setting which concerns us here because they can be expressed in terms of the joint probabilities of voting and vote choice $[P(y,v)$ and $P(n,v)]$

and the probability of voting participation $P(v)$. It is important to note, however, that the probabilities of voting for or against the proposition [$P(y)$ and $P(N)$] are not necessarily the same as the conditional distributions considered above.

A likely candidate for specification of the conditional vote choice probabilities is given by

$$P(y/v) = h[B(1)^*, \ldots, B(n)^*] \tag{7.3}$$

Unlike $f()$ in equation (7.2), $h()$ in equation (7.3) does not transform the series of $B(i)^*$ terms into the absolute value of their overall benefit counterpart. Rather, vote choice depends on the sign as well as on the magnitude of the net benefit impact. In any case, it is the $B(i)^*$ terms and not the $B(i)$ terms which enter on the right hand side of equation (7.3).

The Joint Participation and Vote Choice Model

It is clear that the same variables that explain the vote decision in equation (7.3) also affect the voting participation decision in equation (7.2). As a result, use of a sample of individuals who chose to vote in a study of the vote choice, may result in a misinterpretation of the nature of the impacts. One goal of the analysis carried out in our study is to examine the separate impacts of preference variables on the voting participation decision and on the vote choice decision.

3. The Variables

Preferences and Expectations

The Ladd and Wilson study examined the influence of forty-five attitude and expectation variables on the vote choice for the sample of voters in their survey. The consideration of so many variables is not possible in our study. We have therefore limited our analysis to only some of the variables that they employed and found significant. A summary of the variables we employ is presented in table 7–1. Below we summarize their construction.

Service Level Provision. The variables that we consider to represent preferences and expectations regarding local service level provision are: *EDUC, SAFETY, HUMAN,* and *WELFARE.* The preference measures, $A'(i)$, and expectation measures, denoted $E(i)$, each range from 1 (decrease a lot) to 5 (increase a lot).

Table 7–1
Preference/Expectation Variable Descriptions

Variable	Description
EDUC	Preferences relative to expectations regarding the level of education
SAFETY	Preference relative to expectation regarding the level of safety
HUMAN	Preference relative to expectation regarding public provision of human services
WELFARE	Preference relative to expectation regarding public welfare provision
OVERPAID	Attitude regarding extent to which government employees are overpaid
EFF	Expectation regarding efficiency in local government
EFFMOST	Single most important impact of Proposition 2½ would be more efficient government
CONTROL	Expectation of more local control over school spending
LOCALP *LOCALE*	Preference and expectation regarding local spending and taxes
STATEP *STATEE*	Preference and expectation regarding state spending and taxes
SCHOOLP *SCHOOLE*	Preference and expectation regarding school spending and taxes

Inefficiency and Waste. The attitude variable used to represent presence of inefficiency and waste in local government is called *OVERPAID*, which runs from a low value of 1 to a high value of 4. The expectation variables *EFF*, *EFFMOST*, and *CONTROL* are all dummy variables. It is expected that *OVERPAID*, *EFF*, and *EFFMOST* will interact in some manner similar to the service level variables. For example, the greatest benefit to a voter from an increase in government efficiency would be expected to come from those individuals who have high values of *OVERPAID*. The approach taken here is to consider two interaction terms in addition to these variables in order to capture any of these effects.

Spending and Taxes. The preference variables used to measure spending and tax preferences are called *LOCALP*, *STATEP*, and *SCHOOLP*. The corresponding expectation variables are termed *LOCALE*, *SCHOOLE*, and *STATEE*. All of these are measured by dummy variables with a value of 1 representing a desire for lower spending and taxes, expected decreases in school funds and property taxes, and the expectation that state taxes will increase. For local and school tax issues we consider the following scheme: If $A(i)$ and $E(i)$ are each unity, then $B(i)$ is equal to unity. If both of these measures are zero, we set $B(i)$ equal to zero, since the individual would be indifferent to the passage effects in this regard. If the value of $A(i)$ is zero while that of $E(i)$ is unity, the value of $B(i)$ is set equal to -1. If $A(i)$ is unity while $E(i)$ is zero, $B(i)$ is also set equal to zero since there would be no change from the desired position regardless of passage. On the state tax issue, if $A(i)$ is zero and $E(i)$ is zero, then $B(i)$ is set equal to zero, presuming that no change is desired or expected. If $A(i)$ is 1 while $E(i)$ is 1, then we set $B(i)$ equal to -2. If $A(i)$ is 1 while $E(i)$ is zero, then we set $B(i)$ equal to zero. If $A(i)$ is equal to zero but $E(i)$ is equal to 1, we set $B(i)$ equal to -1.

Demographic Variable Modeling

As discussed in part 1, an alternative approach to the analysis of voting behavior in terms of effects of individuals' preferences is to consider voting decisions as a function of their underlying demographic characteristics. Many of the same specification issues discussed in part 2 arise in this case. In particular, the influences of demographic characteristics on voting participation decisions are closely related to the influence on the vote choice. Hence it is useful to examine the structure of demographic variable impacts on voting decisions for the same set of individuals examined with respect to their preference and expectation responses.

The demographic variables employed in this analysis include *AGE, EDUC, INCOME, RACE,* and *SEX*, where *AGE, EDUC,* and *INCOME* are continuous variables. Community size effects are captured using the level and squared value of *PEOPLE*. The type of school system in which children of the household were enrolled is captured by inclusion of dummy variables for private and public school enrollment. Effects of family size are captured through the number of children in the household, *KIDS*. Finally, we include variables representing government employment status and tenure choice.

In the absence of any differences between communities in the expected impact of passage of Proposition 2½, households might have already located themselves among alternative locations in order to receive the desired level and mix of services. In this case, benefits from passage of Proposition 2½ might not be considered as a function of, for example, income differences among individuals living in different communities. A more adequate specification of voting behavior using demographic variables might then proceed along the lines suggested by the work of Tiebout. Instead of pursuing specification issues along these lines, however, we decided to focus attention on voting differences as a function of community differences in the existing property tax rate. We now turn to analysis of the empirical results.

4. Empirical Results

Preference and Expectation Results

Logistic estimates of equation (7.2) indicated that the $B(i)^*$ variables did not perform well in explaining voter participation decision. This might be expected, however, because the vote on Proposition 2½ occurred at the time of general election. Hence, preferences specific to the proposition were not likely to have been the motivating factor behind the voter participation decision. In light of these findings, the focus of the analysis presented here is on the joint voter participation and vote choice estimates. These findings stem from estimation of a multinominal logistic specification of these decisions.

Table 7–2 shows the chi-squared statistics for each of the preference/expectation variables. These statistics indicate the significance of the variable in explaining the voting behavior decisions. A value equal to 5.99 corresponds to significance at the 95% confidence level. Below, we examine the impacts of these variables on the probability changes when the individual would otherwise have a probability of voting of .8, a probability of voting against the proposition of .36, and a probability of voting for the proposition equal to .45. In this case, the ratio of individuals voting for the proposition to those voting against the proposition is 1.25. Table 7–3 summarizes the results.

Variable Impacts

An increase in *BEDUC* by 1 results in an increase in $P(v)$ of .010, a decrease in $P(n,v)$ of .038, and an increase in $P(y,v)$ of .048. These impacts imply that the value of $P(y,v)/P(n,v)$ would increase to a value of 1.55. An increase in *BSAFETY* by 1 leads to an increase in $P(v)$ of .016, a decrease in $P(n,v)$ by .052, and an increase in $P(y,v)$ of .068. This results in an increase

Table 7–2
Chi-squared Statistics for Preference/Expectation Model

Variable	Chi-Squared for Vote Choice and Voting Participation
BEDUC	9.85
BSAFETY	17.85
BHUMAN	3.63
BWELFARE	3.52
OVERPAID	24.64
EFF	9.13
EFFMOST	4.43
OVER*EFF	0.73
OVER*EFFMOST	6.31
CONTROL	22.51
BLOCAL	8.92
BSCHOOL	2.13
BSTATE	10.07
log likelihood	− 648.70
Number of observations	804

Table 7–3
Summary of Preference/Expectation Effects

Variable	Change in Probability		
	P(v)	P(n,v)	P(y,v)
BEDUC higher by one	− .010	− .038	.048
BSAFETY higher by one	− .016	− .052	.068
BHUMAN higher by one	− .007	− .020	.028
BWELFARE higher by one	− .005	− .005	.010
EFF and EFFMOST higher by one with OVERPAID equal to three	− .151	− .270	.421
CONTROL higher by one	− .066	− .179	.245
BLOCAL higher by one	.128	− .061	− .067
BSCHOOL higher by one	.003	− .075	.072
BSTATE higher by one	.084	− .009	− .076

in $P(y,v)/P(n,v)$ to 1.68. An increase in *BHUMAN* by 1 leads to an increase in $P(v)$ of only .007, a decrease in $P(n,v)$ of .020, and an increase in $P(y,v)$ equal to .028. Again, the odds of voting for rather than against the proposition increase. Impacts in the same direction as those for the above variables are induced by an increase in *BWELFARE*. The effects are much smaller in magnitude, however. In all of the above cases, the expected impacts on voting behavior are verified by the coefficient estimates.

An increase in *OVERPAID* by 1, when *EFF* and *EFFMOST* are equal to zero, yields a decrease in $P(v)$ of .034, a decrease in $P(n,v)$, and an increase in $P(y,v)$ of .112. The result is an increase in $P(y,v)/P(n,v)$ to 2.62. For *OVERPAID* equal to 3, an increase in both *EFF* and *EFFMOST* from zero to a value of 1 results in an increase in $P(v)$ of .151, a decrease in $P(n,v)$ by 0.270, and an increase in $P(y,v)$ equal to .421. The result is an increase in $P(y,v)/P(n,v)$ to a value of 9.68.

An increase in *CONTROL* by 1 results in an increase in $P(v)$ of .066, a decrease in $P(n,v)$ of .179, and an increase in $P(y,v)$ of .245. This change affects $P(y,v)/P(n,v)$ by a large amount also, increasing it to 5.52.

Higher values of *BLOCAL, BSCHOOL,* and *BSTATE* all lead to decreases in $P(v)$, most dramatically for the cases of *BLOCAL* and *BSTATE*. In all cases, the effect is to decrease $P(n,v)$ but also to decrease $P(y,v)$ in the case of *BLOCAL* and *BSTATE*. Only in the case of *BSCHOOL* does the value of $P(y,v)/P(n,v)$ increase (to a value of 1.83).

The empirical findings described above indicate the often substantial impact of differences in the $B(i)^*$ variables on voting behavior. However, these findings are not to be interpreted as a test of the conceptual modeling approach developed in part 2.

Demographic Variable Results

Table 7–4 presents the chi-squared statistics for the demographic variables as they enter each of the three specifications considered in our analysis. In cases involving voter participation choice, the sample includes 1,042 observations. In the case of vote choice only (conditional upon voter participation), the sample includes 860 observations. The square roots of the chi-squared variables in the first and second columns of table 7–4 correspond to *t*-statistics in the normal regression setting. In the third column, where three choices are involved, a chi-squared value of 5.99 corresponds to significance at the 95% confidence level.

For voter participation choice considered alone, the only very precisely estimated effects are for *PEOPLE, SEX, PUBLIC, KIDS,* and *RENTER.* In the vote choice analysis, effects of *INCOME, RACE,* and *GOVEMP* are also quite precisely estimated. In the joint voter participation and vote choice analysis (the third column in table 7–4), variables significant in explaining either choice remain important in the joint analysis. Also, the effect of education becomes significant. Below, we highlight the signs and magnitude of the implied effects for the case of the joint decision model.

Table 7–4
Chi-squared Statistics for Demographic Variables

Variable	Voter Participation	Vote Choice	Vote Choice and Voter Participation
AGE	0.09	0.04	0.22
AGE2	0.54	0.05	0.48
EDUC	0.83	0.61	1.29
EDUC2	0.04	1.83	1.38
PEOPLE	2.68	13.02	15.94
PEOPLE2	1.97	13.78	15.70
INCOME	2.33	9.08	11.42
INCOME2	0.54	7.00	7.31
RACE	0.41	5.28	4.72
SEX	7.39	4.99	11.64
PRIVATE	1.34	0.07	1.36
PUBLIC	4.86	2.13	7.94
KIDS	7.18	0.38	6.99
OWNER	11.00	5.49	16.49
GOVEMP	3.86	33.51	38.84
UNDER	0.12	0.51	0.79
OVER	0.34	2.73	3.14
log likelihood	− 382.8	− 527.9	− 910.6
number of observations	1042	860	1042

Variable Effects

Table 7–5 shows the implied impacts on probability category changes due to discrete changes in the explanatory variables. The effect of higher age is to increase the odds of voting and to increase the odds of voting against the proposition. The magnitude of the effect is small, however. The effect of higher levels of education is to increase the odds of voting. On the other hand, $P(n/v)/P(y/v)$ at first declines with increases in education and then increases at higher education levels. When the probabilities are taken at their sample means, to begin with, the highest ratio of $P(n/v)/P(y/v)$ occurs at a value of $EDUC$ equal to 7.2. Based on the same sample of average probabilities for a person with twelve years of education, the impact of increasing education to sixteen years is to increase $P(v)$ by .129, decrease $P(y/v)$ by .050, and increase $P(n/v)$ by .178. In this example, the increase in voter participation leads to a decline in $P(y/v)/Pn/v)$ from a value of 1.25 to a value of .742.

The effect of variation in *PEOPLE* on voting behavior depends quite significantly on the value of *PEOPLE*. At low values of *PEOPLE,* the probability of not voting is relatively high, but for those voting, the tendency is to vote for the proposition. A similar situation applies to persons in areas with high values of *PEOPLE*. The odds of voting and the odds of voting against the proposition increase to a level of *PEOPLE* equal to approximately 400,000.

The odds of not voting and $P(n,v)/P(y,v)$ are both negatively influenced by higher income. Consider the case in which an individual with income equal to $20,000 per year had average voting behavior propensities. The effect of an increase in income to $30,000 per year is to increase $P(v)$ by .023, decrease $P(n,v)$ by .030, and increase $P(y,v)$ by .053. The effect of this is to increase $P(y,v)/P(n,v)$ to a value of 1.52.

Table 7–5
Summary of Effects of Demographic Variables

Variable	Change in Probability		
	$P(v)$	$P(n,v)$	$P(y,v)$
$EDUC$ higher by four years	− .129	.178	− .050
Nonwhite racial status	.047	.131	− .178
Female	− .068	.101	− .033
PRIVATE equal to one	− .038	.006	.032
PUBLIC equal to one	− .052	.070	− .018
KIDS higher by one	.066	− .047	− .019
Renter	.140	.010	− .151
Government employee	− .075	.268	− .193
0.005 more under 2½ limit	− .008	− .016	.024
0.005 more over 2½ limit	− .004	− .010	.014

Nonwhite racial status leads to a decrease in $P(v)$ of .047, an increase in $P(n,v)$ of .131, and a decrease in $P(y,v)$ equal to 0.178. These results indicate that there was a tendency for white individuals to participate in the voting process more than otherwise identical nonwhite individuals. Further, nonwhites tended to vote against passage of the proposition compared to otherwise identical whites.

The findings indicate that females tended to participate in the voting process more than their male counterparts. They also tended to vote against the proposition, compared to males. For example, female, rather than male status, is predicted to increase $P(v)$ by .068, increase $P(n,v)$ by 0.101, and decrease $P(y,v)$ by .033.

Households with school age children tended to participate in the voting process more than other households. Those households with children in private schools tended to vote for the proposition, while those with children in public schools tended to vote against it. Homeownership leads to an increase in the probability of voting of .140 and a decrease in $P(n,v)$ of only .010. This homeownership effect was offset by the increase in $P(y,v)$ of .151. Thus, homeownership in this case would increase $P(y,v)/P(n,v)$ to 1.717.

Employment in the government sector results in an increase in voter participation of .075, but leads to a decline in $P(v,y)$ of .193, and an increase in $P(n,v)$ of .268. As a result, $P(y,v)/P(n,v)$ falls to a value of .409.

If the household were in a community with a property tax rate less than 2½%, a further decrease in the tax rate of .005 led to an increase in $P(v)$ of .008. Also, $P(n,v)$ declines by .016 and $P(y,v)$ increases by .024. On the other hand, if the household were in an area with a property tax rate above 2½%, a higher value of the tax rate by .005 also leads to a slight increase in $P(v)$. There is a corresponding drop in $P(n,v)$ of .010 and an increase in $P(y,v)$ of .014. These results indicate that the farther a community is from a current property tax rate of 2½%, the greater the voter participation and the greater is the propensity to vote for passage of the property tax rate limitation proposition.

Concluding Comments

The results presented in this chapter indicate that voting behavior is usefully examined in terms of either the corresponding relative preference and expectation variables or demographic variables. We also find that significant differences exist between renters and owners in the effects of the independent variables on voting decisions. This finding suggests the need to examine more fully the differences in the effects of the proposition for these two groups.

Regardless of this distinction, a useful next step in the analysis is to consider voter participation decisions and the related voter choice by including the demographic as well as the preference/expectation variables together as explanatory variables. This would allow for analysis of the structural role of these variables in determining voting characteristics. In particular such an analysis would shed light on the manner in which the demographic characteristics serve as underlying determinants of the preferential and/or expectational responses.

References

Arrow, K. 1951. *Social Choice and Individual Values*. New York: John Wiley and Sons, Inc.

Attiyeh, R., and R. Engle. 1979. "Testing Some Propositions about Proposition 13." *National Tax Journal*.

Citron, J. 1979. "Do People Want Something for Nothing: Public Opinions on Taxes and Government Spending." *National Tax Journal*.

Courant, P., E. Gramlich, and D. Rubinfeld. 1980. "Why Voters Support Tax Limitation Amendments: The Michigan Case." *National Tax Journal*.

Davis, S. 1983. "A Brief History of Proposition 2½." In *Proposition 2½: Its Impact on Massachusetts* Ed. L. Susskind. Cambridge, Mass.: Oelgeschlager, Gunn and Hain.

Downs, A. 1957. *An Economic Theory of Democracy*. New York: Harper and Row.

Edel, M., and E. Sclar. 1974. "Taxes, Spending, and Property Values: Supply Adjustment in a Tiebout-Oates Model." *Journal of Political Economy*.

Epple, D., A. Zelenitz, and M. Visscher. 1978. "A Search for Testable Implications of the Tiebout Hypothesis." *Journal of Political Economy*.

Grieson, R. 1974. "The Economics of Property Taxes and Land Values: The Elasticity of Supply of Structures." *Journal of Urban Economics*.

Hamilton, B. 1976. "The Effects of Property Taxes and Local Public Spending on Property Values: A Theoretical Comment." *Journal of Political Economy*.

Haurin, D. 1978. "Property Taxation in an Urban Economy." Ph.D. diss., University of Chicago.

Ladd, H., and J. Wilson. 1982. "Why Voters Support Tax Limitations: Evidence from Massachusetts's Proposition 2½." *National Tax Journal*.

Oates, W. 1969. "The Effects of Property Taxes and Local Public Spending on Property Values: An Empirical Study of Tax Capitalization and the Tiebout Hypothesis." *Journal of Political Economy*.

———. 1973. "The Effects of Property Taxes and Local Public Spending on Property Values: A Reply and Yet Further Results." *Journal of Political Economy*.

Orr, L. 1968. "The Incidence of Differential Property Taxes on Urban Housing." *National Tax Journal*.

———. 1970. "The Incidence of Property Taxes: A Response." *National Tax Journal*.

———. 1972. "The Incidence of Differential Property Taxes on Urban Housing: A Reply." *National Tax Journal*.

Picus, L. 1984. "Predicting Voter Behavior in Tax Limitation Elections." Unpublished manuscript.

Sears, D., and J. Citron. 1982. *Tax Revolt: Something for Nothing in California.* Cambridge: Harvard University Press.

Tiebout, C. 1956. "A Pure Theory of Local Expenditures." *Journal of Political Economy.*

Tullock, G. 1970. *Private Wants, Public Means.* New York: Basic Books.

Tullock, G., and J. Buchanan. 1962. *The Calculus of Consent: Logical Foundations of Constitutional Democracy.* Ann Arbor: University of Michigan Press.

Wales, T., and E. Wiens. 1984. "Capitalization of Residential Property Taxes: An Empirical Study." *Review of Economics and Statistics.*

8
Financial Deregulation and the Cost of Mortgage Funds

Richard F. Muth

T he decade of the 1980s will almost certainly see the most significant changes in the structure of financial institutions in the United States in half a century. The Depository Institutions Deregulation and Monetary Control Act of 1980 took several significant steps. It allowed federally chartered Savings and Loan Associations (S&Ls) to invest up to 20% of their assets in corporate securities, commercial paper, and consumer loans. In addition, it permitted such S&Ls to accept transaction accounts and provided for the elimination by 1986 of deposit rate ceilings set by Regulation Q. More sweeping changes in the powers of S&Ls to acquire assets were granted by the Garn–St. Germaine Depository Institutions Act of 1982. As a colleague has characterized its provisions, thrifts are now virtually unregulated insofar as the assets they may acquire. Perhaps the most sweeping change of all occurred in the middle of 1978 when regulatory authorities first allowed depository institutions to issue money market certificates at interest rates comparable to Treasury bill rates.

It is widely believed that S&Ls, as dedicated or specialized mortgage lenders, have made homeownership less costly than it would otherwise have been. By allowing them to invest in a wider class of assets and by raising their borrowing costs as well as the borrowing cost of other depository mortgage lenders, it is also believed that deregulation will cause mortgage interest rates to be higher relative to other security yields than they would otherwise be. As is so often said, "After all, the homeowner cannot compete with General Motors!" Whether or not the homeowner can compete with General Motors depends, of course, upon the market for mortgage loans. Therefore, I will first consider the nature of this market. Next, I will examine the likely effects of a variety of deregulatory actions and tax issues on mortgage yields that operate through the quantity of funds supplied. In the final section, I will examine the question of whether removal of deposit rate ceilings on passbook accounts is likely to affect the cost of financing a home.

Nature of the Mortgage Market

Throughout the post-World War II period, roughly half of all mortgage loans have been made by S&Ls. During most of the period, S&Ls were permitted to hold only mortgages and related assets or government securities. Moreover, since 1962, S&Ls have received substantial tax benefits by holding 82% or more of their assets in mortgages or other qualifying assets. Many have argued as a result of these considerations that mortgage markets are segmented from other securities markets and that the supply of mortgage funds is a relatively inelastic one. Others have asserted that such was the case until the development of the secondary mortgage market by various federal agencies in the late 1960s.

While S&Ls have been the largest single source of mortgage funds in the post-war period, they are not the only source. Commercial banks have been important lenders throughout the period. In 1983, they held roughly 18% of outstanding mortgage debt. Unlike S&Ls, commercial banks have held a wide variety of securities. Mortgage yields may differ, of course, from, say, corporate bond yields for a variety of reasons, including differences in transactions costs, default risk, and characteristics such as call provisions. It is probably because of such differences that since 1952 the Federal Housing Administration market yield has averaged about one percentage point more than Moody's Aaa bond yield. There is no obvious reason, however, why the relative valuation that banks place upon mortgages and other securities should vary with their relative stocks outstanding or the relative number of new security issues. In particular, since mortgage yields fluctuate directly with other interest rates, the inclusion of mortgages along with other securities does not substantially affect the variability of the yield of a bank's portfolio. Thus, if commercial banks regard mortgages and other securities as perfect substitutes at a yield differential that compensates for differences such as were noted above, then mortgage relative to bond yields are fixed so long as banks make significant amounts of mortgage loans. The relative supply of mortgage loans under these conditions is perfectly elastic.

In addition to asserting that the relative supply of mortgage lending is relatively inelastic, many would appear to believe that the market for mortgage loans is characterized by a chronic excess of demand for loans. In consequence, it is often stated that the "availability" of funds for mortgages has an important effect upon the cost of financing the purchase of a home. Availability is presumed to mean the position of the supply schedule of mortgage funds. To the best of my knowledge, no one has ever offered a convincing explanation as to why mortgage markets are consistently out of equilibrium, however. It could well be the case, of course, that certain lenders may, at times, make fewer loans than borrowers might like to make with them at currently quoted interest rates, but this need not imply excess demand in the mortgage market as a whole. Indeed, if the supply of mortgage lending is a highly elastic one, the notion of excess demand at current interest rates is meaningless.

In a recent paper (Muth 1985), I have examined the nature of mortgage supply. Using mortgage minus bond yields as the left-hand variable, I find a supply elasticity of the order of 5. More convincingly, I find that neither purchases of mortgages by federal credit agencies and pools nor Treasury bill rates in excess of the ceiling for thrifts set by Regulation Q had a significant impact upon mortgage relative to total lending or upon mortgage minus bond yields. Federal agency purchases of mortgages, of course, would be expected to increase the quantity of mortgage loans supplied. The relative decline in inflows of funds into depository institutions when short-term interest rates rose above the maximum rates such institutions are allowed to pay would reduce the quantity supplied. The lack of observable market impact is most easily explained by a highly elastic supply schedule. With a perfectly elastic supply schedule, horizontal shifts would merely slide the supply schedule along itself with no effect upon rates or upon the volume of loans made.

In this same paper I have also examined whether availability of funds affects housing markets through other avenues. One such avenue is upon the real price of houses. A rise in the rate of interest would increase the rental value per dwelling given the price per dwelling, hence reducing the stock demand for housing. Given the stock of housing, housing prices would thus tend to fall as interest rates rise. Indeed, I find that house prices respond strongly to changes in interest rates; the long-run effect of a one percentage point increase in the rate of interest is to depress house prices by about 5% (Muth n.d.) A shortage of funds for mortgage lending should have similar effects. By making it more expensive to purchase units of housing stock, a shortage of funds would tend to depress the stock demand for housing and, hence, housing prices. Yet I find no impact either of federal agency purchases of mortgages, which would reduce shortages of mortgage funds, or of increases in Treasury bill rates in excess of passbook rate ceilings (which would increase shortages) upon house prices.

The other possible impact of a shortage of funds for mortgage lending is a direct effect upon new construction. Fair (1972), in particular, has argued that a shortage of funds for mortgage lending reduces the commitments home builders are able to obtain from lenders for mortgages. Alternatively, builders might expect a perceived shortage of mortgage funds to make it difficult for potential buyers of their houses to obtain their own financing. Either effect would make it more difficult for builders to sell their output and would lead them to reduce the number of houses that they build. In the comparisons I have made (Muth 1985), I find no direct effect upon construction either of federal agency purchases of mortgages or of increases in Treasury bill rates above the Regulation Q ceilings for thrifts. I do, however, find significant effects both of house prices and short-term interest rates upon new residential investment during the 1970s.

In summary, there are both theoretical and empirical grounds for believing that the supply of mortgage funds is a relatively elastic one. It does not appear, moreover, that housing markets are effected independently of the rate of interest by the availability of funds for mortgage lending. The effects of changes in market interest rates upon housing markets are strong, however. As was noted earlier, a one percentage point increase in interest rates ultimately reduces house prices by about 5%. Since the supply elasticity of new residential construction appears to be about 5 (Muth 1985), a one percentage point increase in interest rates can reduce new construction by about 25% through the effect on house prices. Furthermore, a one percentage point rise in short-term interest rates can reduce new construction directly by about 2.5%. Interest rates themselves, without any appeal to the availability of funds, thus seem capable of accounting for fluctuations in residential construction that have been observed since 1965.

Quantity of Funds Supplied

The effects of many deregulatory actions depend critically upon the nature of the market supply of mortgage funds. There is little doubt that many actions taken or contemplated to date would indeed affect the cost of financing a house purchase if, as is widely believed, mortgage markets were segmented from other securities markets and/or were characterized by a chronic excess demand for funds. As argued in the previous section, however, my perception of the situation is quite different. The cost of mortgage funds would appear to be fixed by the yields on other securities, and the availability of funds does not appear to exert an important impact apart from its effect upon mortgage interest rates. If I am correct, then many deregulatory measures will have little or no impact upon mortgage yields. Concern over housing and its finance, therefore, should not be a barrier to otherwise desirable deregulatory actions. The balance of this section is an elaboration of this position.

Broadening the powers of thrift institutions to acquire assets has been widely perceived as reducing the supply of mortgage loans. As any student of elementary economics is taught, a reduction in supply increases price. What many never learn, however, is that in the limit, as the elasticity of supply becomes infinite, the price increase approaches zero.

Suppose, for example, that over time S&Ls reduce the proportions of mortgages and mortgage-backed securities that they hold in their loan portfolios. As they do so, other things being the same, mortgage yields would tend to rise relative to the yields on other securities. If, as it would appear to me, commercial banks and/or some other lenders view mortgages and other securities as perfect substitutes, such lenders would reduce their purchases of other securities and increase their purchases of mortgages. Doing so would drive mortgage yields down to the same level relative to the yields on other securities as would have obtained had S&Ls not reduced their holdings of mortgages. Therefore, if the supply of mortgage lending is highly elastic, as I believe it is, allowing S&Ls wider powers to acquire assets will have negligible effects upon mortgage yields.

The situation is very similar with regard to actions taken to broaden sources of mortgage funds. Pension funds, whose assets now total over $500 billion (*Report of the President's Commission on Housing* 1982, 142; hereafter referred to as *Report*), are viewed hungrily by those seeking to broaden the sources of mortgage credit. In an effort to draw more funds into housing, President Reagan late in 1981 directed the Department of Labor to review regulations regarding pension fund investments. These regulations were perceived as needlessly limiting the investments of pension funds in mortgages. But even if pension funds were to increase their holdings of mortgages because of regulatory changes, it is by no means clear that there would be any appreciable effect upon mortgage yields. Mortgage yields would fall and other security yields would rise as pension funds increased their holdings of mortgages and reduced their holdings of other securities. Lenders other than pension funds would thus reduce their holdings of mortgages and increase their purchases of other securities. In the process, mortgage yields would rise again relative to the yields on other securities.

Conditions are similar with regard to privately issued mortgage-backed securities. There are a variety of tax and regulatory considerations that inhibit the development of private markets in mortgage-backed securities. (See *Report* 1982, 145–48). The most important, perhaps, is the fact that under the federal tax system, mortgage-backed securities may be taxed both at the pool and certificate holder levels, unlike tax provisions for mutual funds. It is doubtless desirable to remove conditions such as these that needlessly inhibit the growth of a private market in mortgage-backed securities. I find no reason to expect, however, that by doing so, mortgage yields would fall relative to the yields on, say, corporate bonds. If they were to fall initially, as investors who would otherwise have bought corporate bonds instead buy mortgage-backed securities, others would find corporate bonds more attractive than they would have been and would buy more of them.

Issues relating to the taxation of income from mortgage investments depend importantly upon the nature of mortgage markets. One important example is the bad-debt provisions for thrift institutions in the present federal tax law. Currently, S&Ls and Mutual Savings Banks are allowed to deduct up to 40% of their net income from taxable income, provided they hold at least 72 to 82% of their assets in mortgages or other qualifying assets. Doubtless, thrift institutions have held larger percentages in mortgages than they would have otherwise because of the tax advantage in doing so.

The effect upon mortgage rates, however, depends critically upon the elasticity of the market supply of mortgage funds. If the supply or mortgage lending were finitely elastic, then granting a tax-break to thrifts would shift the supply schedule to the right. Such a shift would, of course, reduce mortgage yields. However, if the market supply is highly elastic, increasing the quantity of funds supplied has no impact upon mortgage yields. Rather, the increased holdings of thrifts that are induced by the favorable tax provisions are counterbalanced by the reduced holdings of other mortgage lenders, leaving mortgage yields unchanged relative to the yields on other securities.

The nature of the conditions of supply of mortgage funds is also important for determining the effects of a mortgage interest tax credit. Such a credit was first proposed in 1970 by the Hunt Commission, included in legislation passed by the Senate but not by the House in 1975, and proposed again by the President's Commission on Housing in 1982 (*Report* 1982, 139). Unlike the bad-debt provisions for thrifts, all holders of mortgages or mortgage-backed securities would be eligible to receive the tax credit. This tax credit has generally been viewed as a replacement for the special tax deductions available only to thrift institutions. It is also seen as a means of broadening the sources of mortgage funds and, especially, inducing other lenders to substitute for thrifts as the latter make use of their new, broader asset powers.

The likely effects of the proposed mortgage interest tax credit are quite different from those foreseen by its supporters. Because the supply schedule of mortgage funds is highly elastic, any increases in quantity supplied at given yields would merely shift the supply function along itself with almost no market effects. However, the proposed tax credit does more. By reducing taxes paid on mortgage income earned, the before-tax yields would fall on mortgages that commercial banks and perhaps nondepository lenders view as equally attractive relative to the before-tax returns to other securities. The mortgage interest tax credit, therefore, would add to the substantial subsidies homeowners already enjoy because of the personal tax treatment of income from owner-occupied housing. Moreover, the mortgage interest tax credit would reduce borrowing costs to homeowners for virtually any purpose, for borrowed funds need not be spent for housing simply because a house is used as security for the loan.

Removal of Ceilings on Passbook Rates

One of the most interesting questions relating to financial deregulation is the effect of removing ceilings on rates paid to depositors upon mortgage yields. Most laymen, and even a surprising number of professional economists, react by saying, "Of course, if thrifts must pay more for deposits, they'll have to charge more for the money they loan out."

Those of us who believe that thrift institutions, like other firms, charge the market price for what they sell, regardless of what they must pay for raw materials, receive strong support from a recent study by Mayer and Nathan (1983). They regressed the mortgage rate separately for S&Ls and for Mutual Savings Banks on the mortgage rate charged by commercial banks and the respective deposit rate. The coefficients of the commercial bank mortgage rate were quite close to one and highly significant statistically. The deposit-rate coefficients were not significant and were negative in many of the regressions they show. These results give one little reason to believe that removing ceilings on rates paid to passbook account holders would cause thrift institutions to raise their rates on mortgage loans.

Indeed, one of the effects of ceilings on passbook rates may well have been to increase the costs of thrift institutions. The effect here is very similar to that of floors under fares that commercial airlines were permitted to charge prior to 1978. Just as airlines added additional flights and increased the quality of service provided over that which would have prevailed without regulation, so thrifts may have increased the number of offices and improved the service they offered to savers. In another recent study, Taggart (1978) suggests that the principal effect of rate ceilings on Massachusetts Savings Banks was to increase the number of their branches and the expenses they incurred.

Moreover, several writers (among them Mayer and Nathan 1983; and Gilbert and Holland 1984) have argued that ceilings on passbook account rates could actually increase mortgage interest rates. Suppose it were the case that the supply schedule of funds in passbook savings accounts was upward-sloping to depository institutions. The imposition of an interest ceiling below the market equilibrium rate on passbook accounts would reduce the funds available to depository institutions for mortgage lending. WIth a reduction in their lending, mortgage interest rates would tend to rise. On balance, then, just as rent control can actually increase the effective cost of rental accommodation, so the imposition of passbook rate ceilings could increase mortgage interest rates. Of course, if, as I have argued earlier, mortgage interest rates are fixed by the rates on other long-term securities, nondepository lenders would make up the shortfall in lending by depository institutions at unchanged mortgage yields.

The supply of mortgage funds might also be affected if eliminating rate ceilings alters the number of firms. If rate ceilings were to hold down the average cost of funds used for mortgage loans, then some firms might survive that otherwise would not have. Lifting rate ceilings on deposits might thus cause some firms to go out of business. The immediate impact of their doing so would of course be to reduce the quantity of mortgage loans supplied. Mortgage yields would then tend to rise, however. If other lenders view mortgages and other securities as perfect substitutes, as the evidence suggests to me, they would respond by increasing their mortgage holdings and driving yields back to the level at which they would otherwise have been. It is far from clear, then, that a reduction in the number of thrifts or even of small commercial banks would raise mortgage yields.

Actually, there is really no reason to speculate upon the effects of removing deposit rate ceilings. For, since the middle of 1978, when depository institutions were first permitted to offer money market certificates at market interest rates, deposit rates at these institutions have been removed at the margin. As was noted by the President's Commission on Housing, by the end of 1980, about 40% of deposits at S&Ls and Mutual Savings Banks were in accounts subject to market-determined ceilings; a year later 50% were (*Report* 1982, 124–25). If removing rate ceilings would raise mortgage rates relative to rates on other securities, rates should have been higher relative to those on other securities after the middle of 1978.

To estimate the effect of deregulation I examined three different mortgage yield series in relation to Moody's Aaa bond yield using quarterly data from 1971 through 1983. The three mortgage yield series examined are: the FHA secondary market yield, the conventional first mortgage yield on loans closed (the Federal Home Loan Bank Board series), and the GNMA secondary market yield. Data for the last of these is first available for 1971. Yield differences were examined primarily because expected inflationary rates are added to market interest rates. All rate or yield variables employed in this study are available monthly, and I used the observation for the middle month of the quarter as the value for the quarter.

In addition to a dummy variable, *DMMC*, which takes the value of 1 subsequent to the second quarter of 1978 and 0 otherwise, several other explanatory variables were included. One of these, designated *CPMAYL*, is the finance company six-month commercial paper rate minus Moody's Aaa bond yield. In my earlier paper (Muth 1985), I found this variable consistently associated with the spread of mortgage yields over long-term bond yields. My rationale for including it is that depository institutions, which are the principal mortgage lenders, raise funds for mortgage lending primarily in short-term markets. The higher the short-term/long-term yield differential, the higher relatively would be their cost of funds.

Now, it was suggested to me that the short-term/long-term differential might also serve as a proxy for the risk of call. Traditionally, mortgage loans in this country have not carried prepayment penalties. Thus, when mortgage rates fall, it may become desirable for some borrowers to refinance their homes with new mortgages. Typically, long-term interest rates that are below short-term rates are interpreted as indicating that the market expects falling short-term rates in the future. Long-term rates typically fall as well when short-term rates do, so high short-term rates relative to long-term rates may indicate a greater risk of loss through mortgage loans being called or prepaid more rapidly than usual.

Fortunately, there is another measure that can be used as a proxy for the risk of loss due to prepayment to distinguish between the two effects. A recent paper by Hendershott, Shilling, and Villani (1982) finds that mortgage rates vary directly with the spread of utility bond over industrial bond yields. They attribute this to the fact that utility bonds are protected against call for only five years, while industrial bonds are so protected for ten years. Therefore, as an alternative measure of the risk of call, I use the yield on recently offered Aaa-rated utility bonds over Moody's Aaa bond yield, designated as *UMAYLD*. This measure averaged about two-thirds of a percentage point over the period 1971–83, but was about four percentage points in the first three-quarters of 1982. Long-term corporate bond rates were falling sharply then, the Aaa rate having reached a level of almost 15% in the third quarter of 1981. I thus find it plausible to interpret *UMAYLD* as a measure of risk of loss through prepayment. I limited my comparisons to the period through 1983 because the Federal Reserve System, from whose publications all data were taken, began publishing the utility A yield instead of the Aaa yield for early 1984.

Another explanatory variable was included as a measure of default risk. Moody's Baa yield minus the Aaa yield, *BMAYLD,* was suggested to me by a paper by Black, Garbade, and Silver (1981). It too took exceptionally large values during the year 1982. FHA mortgages are insured against loss through default, but some loss may be incurred through delay in repayment. Losses through default are probably rare on conventional first mortgage loans, since these typically carry either loan-to-value ratios no greater than 80% or private mortgage insurance. GNMA securities are guaranteed for timely payment, even though payment on the underlying FHA or Veterans Administration securities is delayed. A final variable included is a linear time trend, equal to 1 in the first quarter of 1952. I included it to capture possible effects of variables that may work slowly over time, of which increased marketability of GNMA securities is an example.

Not only were three different mortgage interest rates series used, but three different models were fitted. The first merely states that the actual mortgage rate is the equilibrium rate, or that

$$\Delta_M = a_0 + a_1 CPMAYL + \cdots \qquad (8.1)$$

where $\Delta_M = i_M - i_B$, the i's referring to security yields, M to mortgages, and B to bonds. In the second, it is assumed that the change in the rate differential is proportional to the difference between the equilibrium differential and the actual differential, or

$$\Delta_M - \Delta_{M,-1} = \lambda(\Delta_e - \Delta_{M,-1})$$

Substituting for the equilibrium differential from (8.1) above,

$$\Delta_M = \lambda\alpha_0 + \lambda\alpha_1 CPMAYL + \cdots + (1 - \lambda)\Delta_{M,-1}$$

The final model fitted assumes that the change in the mortgage rate is proportional to the difference between the equilibrium mortgage rate and the actual rate,

$$i_M - i_{M,-1} = \lambda^*(i_e - i_{M,-1})$$

Again substituting from (8.1), this time for the equilibrium rate rather than differential,

$$i_M - i_{M,-1} = \lambda^*\alpha_0 + \lambda^*(i_B - i_{M,-1}) + \lambda^*\alpha_1 CPMAYL + \cdots$$

While the nine different equations run differed in some detail, the results are surprisingly uniform insofar as the principal question posed in this section is concerned. The coefficient of *DMMC*, the dummy for the time period for which depository institutions were allowed to offer market-determined rate accounts, is numerically smaller than its standard error in all nine equations. Indeed, in seven of the nine equations the coefficient is actually negative. The record since mid-1978, therefore, hardly gives any reason for believing that the removal of rate ceilings on passbook accounts will increase mortgage yields.

In other respects, the results using the FHA and GNMA yield differentials are quite similar, but differ from the regressions run using the conventional first mortgage yield to measure mortgage rates. In the former, the coefficients of the short-term/long-term yield differential, the utility bond differential as a proxy for call risk, and the time trend are all significantly positive. In only one instance is the Baa/Aaa Moody's yield differential, which I interpret as a proxy for default risk, significant. In two of the three regressions run using the conventional first mortgage yield to measure mortgage rates, however, the Baa/Aaa differential was significantly positive, but in none of the three is any of the coefficients of the other variables significant. The standard errors of the regression are typically much smaller (and are almost the same using the FHA and GNMA rates to measure mortgage yields) than when using the conventional first mortgage yield.

The best results, judging purely by statistical standards, are found using the GNMA yield to measure mortgage rates and assuming a lagged adjustment of the mortgage rate. The regression equation is as follows (all interest rates are in percent per year; standard errors are shown in parentheses below the coefficients to which they refer):

$$i_M - i_{M,-1} = -1.26 - .017DMMC + .824(i_B - i_{M,-1})$$
$$(.49) \quad (.166) \quad\quad\quad (.058)$$

$$+ .111CPMAYL + .704UMAYLD - .001BMAYLD$$
$$(.037) \quad\quad\quad (.128) \quad\quad\quad (.115)$$

$$+ .0131TREND, \quad\quad R^2 = .899, D\text{-}W = 1.52$$
$$(.0055)$$

In (8.2) above, mortgage rates adjust quite rapidly. (Adjustment was even more rapid when using FHA yields to measure mortgage rates, the coefficient of $i_B - i_{M,-1}$ being over .9). That the coefficient of $CPMAYL$ is small, though significant, probably reflects the fact that depository lenders do not expect short-term rates to remain high relative to long-term ones throughout the life of the loan. The fact that the coefficient of $UMAYLD$ is substantially smaller than 1 may reflect some measurement error. Yet, considering that the left-hand variable is in first difference form, the explanatory power of the regression equation is remarkably high. The equation implies that mortgage rates were high relative to bond yields in 1982 primarily because lenders perceived a high call risk, not because mortgages were thought to be especially prone to default at that time.

Concluding Observations

There are two sets of beliefs, or disbeliefs, among economists that I hope this chapter and my previous paper (Muth 1985) will help to dispel. The first is an even greater unwillingness to believe that mortgage markets work as do markets generally, since many have long believed that mortgage markets have been segmented from other security markets. Equally prevalent is the belief that mortgage markets are chronically in disequilibrium. For these reasons, a wide variety of special programs to enhance the flow of funds into financing residential real estate have been proposed and adopted. Yet the evidence suggests to me that mortgage funds are freely available at an interest rate that is largely determined by the rates yielded by other long-term securities. If such is the case, neither financial deregulation nor a variety of efforts designed to attract more funds to mortgage lending is likely to have any appreciable effect upon mortgage yields.

Economists have also seemed unwilling to admit that fluctuations in residential construction can be accounted for by fluctuations in market rates of interest. Rather, a variety of ad hoc explanations have been advanced to explain construction cycles. During the 1950s, such cycles were often attributed to rate ceilings on FHA and VA mortgages that lagged behind other long-term interest rates. The fact that mortgage yields were adjusted through charging "points" on loans was simply overlooked. More recently, in the 1960s and 1970s, the relative outflow of funds from depository lending institutions when short-term market rates exceeded ceilings set by Regulation Q was said to cause a shortage of funds for mortgages. That new construction reacted in a very similar way to increases in interest rates following mid-1978, during which time depository lenders have offered market-determined rates on money market certificates and other new accounts, is still not widely appreciated.

References

Black, Deborah, G., Kenneth D. Garbade, and William L. Silver. 1981. "The Impact of the GNMA Pass-through Program on FHA Mortgage Costs." *Journal of Finance* 36:457–69.

Fair, Ray C. 1972. "Disequilibrium in Housing Models." *Journal of Finance* 27: 207–21.

Gilbert, R. Alton, and A. Steven Holland. 1984. "Has the Deregulation of Deposit Interest Rates Raised Mortgage Rates?" *Review, Federal Reserve Bank of St. Louis* 66:5–15.

Hendershott, Patrick H., James D. Shilling, and Kevin E. Villani. 1982. "The Determination of Home Mortgage Rates." Paper presented at the meetings of the Financial Management Association, San Francisco.

Mayer, Thomas, and Harold Nathan. 1983. "Mortgage Rates and Regulation Q." *Journal of Money, Credit and Banking* 15:107–15.

Muth, Richard F. 1985. "The Supply of Mortgage Lending." *Journal of Urban Economics*.

Report of the President's Commission on Housing. 1982. Washington, Government Printing Office.

Taggart, Robert A., Jr. 1978. "Effect of Deposit Rate Ceilings: The Evidence from Massachusetts Savings Banks." *Journal of Money, Credit and Banking* 10: 134–57.

9

State Regulatory Responses to Competition and Divestiture in the Telecommunications Industry

Roger G. Noll

On February 24, 1983, the State of Michigan and its Public Service Commission asked the Federal Communications Commission to review the effects of procompetitive federal policies on the price and availability of local telephone service.[1] Michigan's public utility regulators, along with their counterparts in other states, suspect that federal policy in telecommunications has been persistently wrongheaded since the late 1960s, when the FCC began to open the telecommunications industry to competition, and that any serious confrontation of the facts by the FCC would force it at least to make public, if not so to see for itself, the error of its ways.

The essence of the state regulators' complaint, described in almost any order relating to telecommunications regulation that was issued by a state regulatory agency after divestiture, has three components. First, the FCC, desiring to substitute competition for rate and entry regulation wherever possible, adopted policies that shifted costs from the federal to the state jurisdiction. Second, diverstiture of the Bell Operating Companies (BOCs) in the settlement of the federal government's antitrust case against AT&T[2] exacerbated the problem. It cut the BOCs out of several lucrative lines of business, while loading them with money-losing services and a substantial amount of plant that formerly was paid for by services that went to AT&T in the divestiture. Third, in implementing divestiture, the FCC made matters worse by substituting customer access charges (for example, a fixed monthly subscription fee for access to the interstate network) for the old *de facto* excise tax on long distance telephone calls and customer end-use equipment, and by imposing faster depreciation rules for capital equipment used for intrastate services.

In most states, these policies are seen as causing substantial increases in

I gratefully acknowledge the useful comments of Nina Cornell, Patrick Power, and Michael Riorden on an earlier draft, and thank numerous staff members of state commissions for help in locating relevant documents.

the prices of intrastate services, including the basic monthly charge for local exchange service. Some states estimate that basic monthly rates will triple, reaching $25 to $30 for residential single-party service. Moreover, during the first eighteen months after the announcement of the Modified Final Judgment, the divested Bell Operating Companies confirmed their regulators' expectations by seeking approximately $7 billion in rate increases.[3]

The federal government's position is rooted in the belief that procompetitive policies will be more efficient. The FCC prefers competition because of the discipline that it forces on firms and because most FCC officials have come to believe that economic regulation cannot control telecommunications markets very effectively. Where regulation remains, the new FCC policy is to emulate the competitive price structure by tying prices to the cost of service and eliminating cross-subsidies. "Cost-causative" prices are favored for conventional economic reasons: they eliminate deadweight losses, give telecommunications firms the right signals for making decisions about entry, R&D, and innovation, and send customers the right messages about which services to drop or to find substitutes for. The changes in prices, services, and the distribution of business among companies are seen as causing relatively uninteresting rearrangements of customer's bills while permitting greater efficiency and so providing net economic benefits.

The reason state regulators give for rejecting the view of regulation promulgated by the FCC, Judge Greene, and the Antitrust Division is its distributional consequence. In the words of the literary giant among regulators, Hearings Examiner Mary Ross McDonald of Texas, "The contention that the impact of increased monthly flat rates will be 'offset' by the predicted lower toll rates is from the Marie Antoinette School of Rate Design: . . . 'Let them make toll calls!' "[4] The basis for this characterization is found in the testimony of a Southwest Bell witness who stated that a customer needed to average more than four toll calls a month in order to benefit from cost-causative pricing. Approximately 80% of Southwest's residential customers average fewer than four toll calls per month.[5] Of course, this is a crude measure of the distributional effect of a change in the rate structure: it ignores additional toll calling due to price elasticity effects, and it neglects "pass throughs" of business cost savings. Nevertheless, these figures illuminate the dispute between state and federal officials: the former see themselves as shouldering the burden of politically unpopular and, arguably, socially unwise redistributive effects, while the feds take credit for reductions in interstate toll and customer equipment prices owing to deregulation, divestiture, and competition.

The interesting questions surrounding this dispute are legion and cannot be addressed in a single chapter. The principal question is whether economic efficiency or distributional equity are really in conflict and, if so, which will win out. Subsidiary questions involve where the battle will be waged and how policy is constrained by the underlying engineering, economic and political forces. These issues are beginning to be faced in state proceedings. One set of state regulatory battles is over access charges for AT&T and the other common carriers (OCCs) and the prices of related competitive services offered by local exchange companies. The second is over the structure of the Bell Operating Companies, the battles' implications for the financial viability of local exchange service and for possible antitrust litigation against the BOCs for following the policies of state regulators. The third, already recognized as important but still largely a theoretical threat to BOCs and state regulators, is over policies concerning new technology that threatens the local monopoly in telecommunications access services.

In this chapter I attempt to describe these issues and apply economic and political analysis to them. Owing to lack of information, however, I can only guess at the central issue—how things are likely to work out in five to ten years. Relevant information is almost totally absent from public sources and, I suspect, from private ones as well. A major problem of state and federal regulators is the low reliability of information about costs and demand. The Texas proceedings state the issue well:

> As for Texas, this Commission has in the past neglected to force SWB [Southwest Bell] to come forward with cost studies which could have formed a proper basis for setting cost-based telephone rates in Texas. A concerted effort years ago on the part of the Commission to force SWB to present such studies may have prevented many of the serious problems we face in this docket.

> The rate design portions of the case this year can be frustratingly summed up by the simple statement that there is much more that is *not* known about telecommunications costs in Texas (intraLATA, InterLATA, etc.) than what is known. To say this record is chock-full of "imponderables" is to understate the obvious.[6]

The absence of comprehensive, accurate data on costs and demand has several important implications that go beyond the difficulties it creates for regulators and research scholars who would study telecommunications policy. First, it greatly enhances the stability of the regulatory status quo with regard to industry structure and pricing policy. Poor information makes the likely consequences of policy change more uncertain and makes it especially difficult to rebut those who claim that change will produce chaos and unmentionable horrors. In this milieu, the advocates of change cannot fully bear a burden of proof. Hence, rational regulatory behavior probably requires assigning some probability to the worst-case scenarios.

Second, the absence of information undermines the case for adopting methods derived from welfare economics for setting prices and making decisions about entry and competition. Economists' methods are based on cost and demand parameters that regulators know only vaguely at best. Traditional rate-making practice, especially in state commissions, requires much less knowledge, as discussed more completely below.

Third, poor information introduces a strategic consideration to the development of interim regulatory rules. The idea is to smoke out better information by assuming that facts not in evidence are contrary to the interests of the person best able to provide the facts. The proposition is quite analogous to the "least-cost avoider" principle in torts.[7] The tools available to regulators are assignments of burdens of proof and decisions about cost principles and pricing rules. In a state of poor information, the best transitional strategy for rationalizing prices and the structure of the industry may *not* be to undertake the best interim guess at these decisions on the basis of existing information, but consciously to depart from such policies in ways that enhance the incentives of regulated entities to provide better information the next time around.[8] Real-world regulators are constrained in their ability to implement such a strategy. Legally, they are required to enable the regulated firm to recover its true costs, including a reasonable profit. Nevertheless, some states are becoming more stringent with telephone utilities, even to the point of disallowing entire categories of costs, some part of which is undoubtedly legitimate, but these instances have been poorly documented.

With these preliminaries aside, we turn to the central focus of the chapter: the sources and nature of the conflict between federal and state regulators, how this conflict is manifested in regulatory policy-making, and where it all might end, given technical and political forces.

The Regulatory Environment of 1984

To understand the current dilemma of state regulators, we must begin our story around 1960. At that time, state and federal regulators shared much the same vision of the telecommunications industry and pursued mutually compatible policies. Both believed that the industry was a natural monopoly at all levels, including the vertical integration of companies such as AT&T and GTE. The job of the regulators was to determine the costs incurred by the telephone company, assure that total revenues were in line with these costs (including the cost of capital), and serve the "universal service objective" by keeping the consumer's entry prices to the network—the installment charge, the basic monthly flat rate, and the price of a local call on a pay telephone—as low as possible. This job was made relatively easy by the rapid rate of technological development in both telecommunications and the technologies that use communications facilities (such as broadcasting and computers). Technology was reducing the nominal as well as the real cost of service, while simultaneously stimulating demand. All components of telephone usage exhibited rapid growth: from 1960 to 1970, the number of telephones in service increased by more than 50%, the number of local telephone calls grew by nearly 70%, and the number of toll calls rose by 275%.[9]

To the extent that there was a problem in this otherwise glowing picture, it was the local loop and first switch in the network. Technological progress and user demands were pushing the system to become more complex and hence more costly (as well as more valuable) per customer. Moreover, in large urban areas, expansion began to face increasing real costs per customer for reasons other than enhanced capability. Switching generally faces mild diseconomies of scale because the number of possible interconnections rises faster than linearly with respect to the number of connections. Only because technology and switching algorithms have advanced rapidly have potentially great diseconomies of scale been avoided. In addition, technology progressed less rapidly in basic access—the wiring between a telephone and the first switch—than anywhere else in the network.

For these reasons, the price that regulators and telephone companies expressed most policy concern about, the basic monthly rate, was tied to the service that was performing least well in terms of average and marginal cost. Added to this was the realization that if further advances toward the universal service objective were to be achieved, new subscribers would have to be found in rural areas. The costs of local connection are highest in areas with low population density because of the length of the wires needed to connect a subscriber to the first switch. In urban areas, the average length of this connection is a little over two miles, whereas in rural areas the distance can be ten times as great.

The solution to the problem of rising local service costs was to capture the rapidly expanding revenue potential in toll service and in sophisticated customer equipment. The only difficulty in implementing such a policy was institutional: the feds regulated the interstate network and had to agree to a process that transferred federal revenues to state jurisdictions. The solution was "separations and settlements," an agreement for sharing the revenues from interstate toll calls between local telephone companies and the interstate carrier—at the time, exclusively AT&T Long Lines. The revenue sharing plan in place at the time of divestiture was the Ozark Plan, which had been adopted in 1971.

Interjurisdictional Revenue Sharing Arrangements

The postdivestiture debate is strongly shaped by the Ozark Plan. This plan's purpose was to allocate the costs of local operating companies between the interstate and intrastate jurisdictions. Such a sharing arrangement has two components: a method for deciding which costs are attributed to local exchange service, and a formula for dividing these costs.

Throughout most of the history of regulation, interjurisdictional cost allocation was not based on cost causation, but was viewed as an equity issue: what division of cost responsibility is "fair" to the various forms of users. Telephone accounting practices and cost allocation procedures, therefore, were not constructed for the purpose of estimating the cost parameters that would be of interest to a regulatory process that tried to implement economically efficient pricing. This unfortunate fact of life makes the state of knowledge about actual service costs very poor. It also makes determination of the actual magnitude of the interstate subsidy of local service little more than a guessing game, and causes the profound difficulties that states are experiencing in adjusting to the new market and regulatory environment.

The Ozark Plan contains a simple but almost incomprehensible formula for determining the fraction of local exchange plant that will be assigned to the interstate jurisdiction:

$$SPF = .85\,SLU + 2\,SLU \cdot CSR$$

where: *SPF* (Subscriber Plant Factor) is the proportion of local exchange; *SLU* (Subscriber Line Usage) is the fraction of telephone usage minutes in the local area that are interstate; and *CSR* (Composite Station Rate) is "the ratio of (1) the nationwide, industrywide average interstate initial 3 minute station charge at the study area average interstate length of haul to (2) the nationwide, industrywide average total toll initial 3 minute station charge at the nationwide average length of haul for all toll traffic for the total telephone industry."[10]

CSR adjusts *SPF* to take account of the fact that interstate tolls are over greater distances than intrastate tolls, and that on a per mile basis toll rates generally decline as distance increases. The latter effect does not offset the former, so the net effect of the *CSR* term in the formula is to cause the cost allocation to interstate tolls to be substantially larger than the fraction of calls that are interstate. Generally, *SPF* is about three times *SLU*.

In most cases, the "area" referenced in the definition is all of a state that is served by a single company. The *SPF* from the formula is then used to allocate the costs of the "nontraffic-sensitive" (*NTS*) portion of the local exchange—that is, the investment in lines and equipment that does not vary with use. In addition, traffic-sensitive portions of the local exchange (switching and interexchange trunks in the local calling area) are assigned to the interstate jurisdiction on the basis of minutes of use.

After the local exchange costs are allocated and revenues are collected from the federal jurisdiction, they must be distributed back to operating companies. Inexplicably, this process ignores *SPF*. Local companies are reimbursed solely on the basis of the minutes of use of the local exchange for interstate tolls. Because costs and disbursements are based on different formulas, the process causes very large and apparently pointless further redistributions among the states.

Once each jurisdiction has its allocation of local costs, it decides how to incorporate them in ratemaking. The job at the federal level was the easiest; until the mid-1970s, it amounted to approving an excise tax on toll calls, the structure of which was designed by AT&T Long Lines. The state problem was more difficult, because states set rental prices for telecommunications equipment provided by the telephone company, as well as rates for toll, basic service, installation, and pay phones. Again, the general strategy was a *de facto* excise tax on toll and equipment. The overall strategy of the states was called "residual pricing": let basic service rates (the flat monthly fee for local service, the installation charge, and pay-phone prices) be set to recover whatever revenue is still needed after other prices have been determined. These other prices were based primarily on the intensity of demand ("value of service"), and to a first approximation were set to maximize gross revenue. Of course, for some services revenue maximization meant prices that made no contribution to local exchange costs or that did not cover attributable costs. Several states have determined that private line rates were so priced. But owing to the fact that economic efficiency was not a criterion in ratemaking, the existence of such services was never really questioned until competitors charged that local operating companies were engaged in predatory pricing. Overall, intrastate tariffs, taken together, paid for roughly as large a share of the local exchange costs as did interstate tolls.

The Local Service Subsidy

Whether or not the cost allocations from the Ozark Plan actually measured real costs of service for local exchange service, the system transferred massive and growing subsidies to local exchange. When the FCC finally put a lid on the process, interstate toll was absorbing approximately 26% of local *NTS* costs (the FCC capped this percentage at 25% in December 1983). When Ozark was implemented in 1971, interstate contributions amounted to only 16% of *NTS* costs; thus, from 1971 to 1981, 1% of the nation's expanding *NTS* plant was being shifted to the federal jurisdiction each year.

The states, too, engage in reallocation of estimated *NTS* costs. Some states parallel the federal cost-sharing formulas, allocating a share of *NTS* costs to other intrastate services by the same formulas that are used to calculate the federal shares. Others adopt their own allocation methods, or make no formal allocation at all, but in nearly every case the end result is that intrastate tariffs (other than the basic monthly rate) cover a fraction of *NTS* costs that are comparable to the fraction covered by interstate services.[11]

At this point, a digression is in order to examine critically whether this subsidy is "real," that is, whether the economically attributable costs of local exchange access are truly greater than the basic exchange price. Of course, because of the paucity of relevant hard data on costs, no proposition about the magnitude of the subsidy can be difinitively proved. But there are several reasons to believe that the cost allocation practices of regulators and telephone companies overstate the subsidy, at least as it applies to the majority of residential subscribers.[12]

First, one must take into account the distinction between rural and urban subscribers. Existing cost data indicates that if we disaggregated residential subscribers according to the kind of community they live in, we would discover that quite a large fraction receive little or no subsidy, but a small fraction (in rural areas) capture a very large subsidy.

Second, the methods for allocating costs other than *NTS* subscriber plant probably overstate local service costs. Fully allocated cost methods for allocating switching and trunking equipment allocate too much cost to residential users because they are more likely to place off-peak calls than are businesses. The license fees paid formerly to AT&T and Bell Labs, and now to Bell Core (the part of Bell Labs owned by the operating companies) and to management service subsidiaries of the regional holding companies, are allocated as common costs. But relatively little research at Bell Labs/Bell Core is directed at reducing costs for *NTS* components of the network. Almost all of the research and development (R&D) has been oriented toward reducing trunk transmission costs, developing new services, and improving equipment (either switches or sophisticated customer devices).

Third, the treatment of installation charges also overstates the costs of local service. Until the FCC ordered an end to the practice in 1983, local operating companies would capitalize rather than expense some fraction of the costs of installing telephone service. These costs are the additional ones of connecting a subscriber to the system, given that all of the capital is in place to provide service. Roughly speaking, customer *NTS* costs are around $400, and the costs of installation are between $40 and $50 (according to various estimates in regulatory proceedings).[13] The rationale for capitalizing part of the installation cost was that it was priced below cost, like basic exchange rates, and that it was a permanent investment. In fact, about three-fourths of this account is the cost associated with a change of residence and involves no capital investment at all. Approximately 30% of *NTS* costs are accounted for by this fictitious asset.

Fourth, existing data do not measure the stand-alone cost of residential network access for exclusively local service. The existing telecommunications network is designed to accommodate under one system a variety of users and uses. The decision about the size of exchange (10,000 telephones) and the average length of the copper wires that connect residences to central stations has been made by a franchised monopolist facing an arbitrary set of service prices and serving everyone. The design of the local exchange may not reflect any optimization calculation because regulators have never closely scrutinized it, and until recently, competitors have never threatened it. But if it is optimized, it is most assuredly not single-mindedly with respect to the local residential subscriber. Local exchange service might be less expensive if local exchanges were smaller (and hence *NTS* costs were lower), but more calls were toll calls. The system optimized for local users, connected through a toll-bearing switch to the rest of the network, is the stand-alone cost of residential basic exchange service and is the relevant benchmark for calculating the subsidy.

In some rural areas, traditional copper wires strung to a central office are probably not the least-cost technology. Instead, an over-the-air transmission system should substitute for at least part of the local network.[14] For systems that cost more than $1,000 per line, these technologies look good, and such costs are common in the rural West. In these areas, part of the subsidy is the excess of the book value of the telephone company's capital over its replacement value. In this sense, it is a subsidy of stockholders, not customers, and arises from the necessity of regulators to let companies recover used and useful capital investments once they have been permitted into the rate base.

The most important implications of this discussion are as follows. First, the subsidy is an accounting and cost-allocation phenomenon that bears no necessary relationship to economically meaningful concepts of cost causation. Second, optimal pricing rules that are calculated on the basis of these cost data are constructed on a foundation of sand. Third, whatever we as economists might think of regulatory accounting practices, they are all that regulators have to work with, for several years at least. Hence, the subsidy is real to state regulators not because it makes sense economically, but because it makes sense legally: regulators are bound by law to adopt pricing rules that let utilities recover these costs. Fourth, whatever the true magnitude of the subsidy, most of what is interesting about it is lost by expressing it in terms of statewide or nationwide averages. Indeed, it is so expressed because of the tradition of rate averaging, which in turn has produced a regulatory information system that is incapable of revealing the structure of the subsidy among categories of users: rural versus urban, by age of neighborhood, and so on.

The Competitive Threat to Ozark

A principal source of state-federal conflict centers on the causes of threats to interjurisdictional revenue flows. This problem arose from a series of events that were roughly contemporaneous with the adoption of the Ozark Plan. As the FCC was negotiating a heavy excise tax on interstate tolls to transfer to the states, it was adopting policies that undermined the source of the funds. The relevant decisions are *Carterfone, MCI, Specialized Common Carriers,* and the *Computer Inquiry* (now called *Computer I*).[15] Each of these decisions opened the door to limited competition with regulated telecommunications monopolies. Richard Wiley, former chairman of the FCC and a participant in many of the key decisions, has argued that, starting in the mid-1960s, the FCC embarked on a grand procompetitive plan that led naturally to today's situation.[16] My own view, elaborated more completely elsewhere, is that the FCC began with an entirely different concept: that there would be competition, but not with AT&T—only among entrants that wanted to provide services that AT&T did not, and probably would not, offer.[17] In any case, these decisions marked the beginning of a new regulatory environment that let in largely unregulated competitors for both interstate telecommunications services and telecommunications equipment for customers of the network. These entrants did not have to pay the excise tax to local operating companies. Both AT&T and state regulators claimed foul, the former because regulated tariffs forced them to pay a cost their competitors did not have to bear and the latter because every inroad by competitors reduced the proportion of interstate and equipment sales that generated revenues for the state regulated utilities.

By 1978, the FCC *was* the procompetitive enthusiast described by Wiley. The key decision was *Execunet.* The courts reversed an FCC decision that denied MCI the authority to offer interstate toll service over its "specialized" common-carrier network, allegedly built for private-line service. The reversal did not bar the FCC from declaring interstate toll to be a regulated AT&T monopoly, but merely found that the agency had not advanced substantial evidence in support of that policy. The FCC elected not to hold a hearing to develop the evidence and then go back to the court with its proof, but instead let the reversal stand. This meant that interstate toll service was open to entry, was likely to evolve into a competitive business, and was likely eventually to be entirely deregulated.

Since the decision not to persist with the *Execunet* case, nearly all FCC decisions have reflected a commitment to expand the domain of competition. Probably the most important exception to this generality is the decision regarding cellular radio. This decision gave Bell Operating Companies the right to be one of two firms in the business and a first-in advantage. The importance of this is that cellular radio is the biggest single competitive threat at this time to the local telephone network: its costs are now above but within striking distance of the costs of local loops as a means to interconnect with the switched network, and it has the obvious service advantage of mobility.

Generally, though, the FCC has been procompetitive regarding even local service. For example, cable television systems are also a significant potential source of competition to local telephone monopolies, and here the FCC prohibited combined cable and telephone companies. The downside risk of this decision is that fiber-optic technology will make the joint local distribution of telecommunications and cable television a distinct natural monopoly in a few years. As yet, however, the costs of fiber optics for local distribution have not fallen enough to make them a serious contender, and, indeed, the technology has not progressed as rapidly as was predicted a decade ago.

FCC Preemption of State Actions

In the immediate future, the most important FCC decisions are not with respect to competitive technology. From the standpoint of the state regulator, some of the most important decisions are as follows.

Detariffing CPE. The FCC deregulated telecommunications equipment owned or used by customers (Customer Premises Equipment, or CPE) by asserting jurisdiction and then declaring the market to be competitive. This precludes state use of CPE tariffs to the FCC and also eliminated federal subsidy of CPE in the rate-base of operating companies.[18] This is not a major cost item; in Texas, for example, it accounted for about 3% of the last rate increase.[19]

Cap on Interstate Transfers. As discussed above, the FCC has capped the transfer of interstate revenues to local companies for the purposes of contributing to *NTS* costs at 25%.[20] Because this is roughly where the magnitude of the subsidy was when the cap was applied, its major implications are in the future: interstate transfers will no longer be a rapidly growing source of revenues for local operating companies.

Accelerated Depreciation. The FCC asserted jurisdiction over the depreciation rules adopted by the states for local plant.[21] The reasons were that services in the federal jurisdiction paid part of these costs, creating a federal interest, and that the FCC's overall procompetitive policy for equipment and interexchange services required realistic depreciation rules. The states fought the decision in courts, but lost.[22] Thus, over a six-year period they must amortize the remaining book value of a significant amount of very old equipment. In the short run, the revenue impact of this decision is significant and positive; its long-run effects depend on the intelligence of the operating companies' reinvestment practices and on the distributional effects of technological innovations among categories of services. The FCC believes that these changes will speed the introduction of cost-reducing and service-enhancing innovation, and so benefit customers within a few years. But from the standpoint of the states, the immediate effect is higher revenue requirements: in Texas, about 9% of the rate increase; in Vermont, about 13%; and in Kansas, over 25%.

Expensing of Station Connections. As discussed above, the FCC has required that the costs of connecting the customer to the network (not counting the physical investment in lines and switching capacity) be expensed rather than capitalized, regardless of whether states elect to equate installation charges with costs.[23] This will introduce accounting homogeneity across states regarding the meaning of *NTS* capital recovery costs, and in the view of the FCC, add to the meaning of the jurisdictional allocations of *NTS* costs. The immediate significance of this change is roughly equivalent to the importance of the change in depreciation rules; however, in the long run, after the adjustment period, it will lower revenue requirements by eliminating the allowed profits on capitalized installation costs.

Interstate Access Charges. Perhaps the most profound change in FCC policy does not actually affect the states, but politics is not necessarily affected by technicalities. The FCC has decided to replace surcharges on toll rates with access charges as a means of generating the interstate contribution to state revenue requirements of *NTS* costs.[24] An access charge is a flat monthly charge for the use of a line that connects a customer to the network. The theory of access charges is that, because *NTS* costs are determined independently of use, it distorts the price system to recover them by taxes on use charges (such as the minutes-of-use and time-of-day format of toll calls).[25] One can imagine either of two approaches to access charges: adding a component to the basic flat monthly rate of subscribers to pay the interstate portion of *NTS* costs, or imposing costs on companies that provide toll services in proportion to the number of customers (for example, subscriber's lines) that they serve. Judge Greene endorsed the idea of access charges in the Modified Final Judgment, anticipated that the proper solution was the latter, and indeed, as we will examine below, his view has considerable sympathy in the states. But the FCC has proposed the former—a flat monthly rate of $6 for business and, for residences, $2 that may eventually become $6.

The federal jurisdiction is imposing this new tariff, but the political reality is that it will appear on the customer's monthly bill as a net, bottom-line increase to the basic flat monthly rate. States are generally quite disaffected by this policy for a number of reasons. First, they expect that most subscribers will pay little attention to the state-federal distinction regarding the source of the increase. State regulators expect to suffer most of the outrage at what will be approximately a 50% rate hike for most residential subscribers. Second, they are concerned that the rate hike will reduce telephone penetration, especially by people who make few toll calls and therefore receive no offsetting benefits in reduced toll prices. Universal service objectives aside, this eliminates customers that account for little revenue in the federal jurisdiction, but $9 a month in basic exchange tariff in the state jurisdiction. Hence, the proposal, to the extent that it does cause service cancellations, imposes all the costs on the states. Third, by moving first and capturing the initial, politically least costly, rate hikes, the feds have preempted the room for movement in the rate structure. They have raised the political stakes to the states of shifting to the flat monthly charge as a source of revenues.

To the states, then, the FCC is a major culprit. Simultaneously, it has cut state regulators (and local telephone companies) out of some revenue sources while requiring actions that raise revenue requirements. All this would be bad enough, but in addition, the Department of Justice and Judge Greene have made matters worse by breaking up AT&T in a way that forecloses still more options.

The Consequences of Divestiture. From the state perspective, the most important part of divestiture is the formation of LATAs (Local Access and Transportation Areas). LATAs define the boundaries between AT&T and the divested operating companies. In principle, they represent localities and form a natural definition of a local service area. In reality, they were drawn to conform to area codes and Standard Metropolitian Statistical Areas. A few state regulatory commissions, learning that LATA creation was in the wind, undertook proceedings to draw their own. This gave them the opportunity to make non-AT&T service areas consistent with those served by AT&T (the LATA separation in the MFJ between local and toll service applies only to AT&Ts former component parts) and to infuse their own policy objectives through their knowledge of state communities of interest in drawing the boundaries. Illinois and Florida appear to have taken this responsibility most seriously and drew boundaries that created the smallest LATAs in the country. For example, larger and more populous California has eleven LATAs, whereas Illinois has nineteen. But with these exceptions, the states passively watched AT&T, the Department of Justice, and Judge Greene negotiate the boundaries between local service and interexchange toll. One of the important aspects of the MFJ is that the BOCs are barred from inter-LATA service. Consequently, inter-LATA toll is provided by national companies such as AT&T, MCI, GTE Sprint, and IBM's Satellite Business Systems (SBS), even when it is between two points in a single state.

Except in the few small or sparsely populated states which have only one LATA, the creation of LATAs effectively cut a large chunk of intrastate toll from the revenues of the Bell Operating Companies. Even in states with relatively large service areas covered by GTE, Continental, and other non-AT&T local operations companies, virtually all intrastate toll was provided by the Bell System prior to divestiture. Moreover, intrastate toll rates were regulated by state regulatory commissions following the spirit, if not the exact formulas, of the Ozark Plan. That is, in most states intrastate toll did its job of covering *NTS* costs through surcharges on toll rates.

Because these surcharges were within the Bell Companies, states did not have to adopt a formal policy of revenue transfer from toll to NTS. Indeed, instead of a formal policy, nearly all states used "residual pricing," as discussed above. States did put in place methods for passing through revenues from intrastate toll to independent operating companies, usually following the advice of NARUC.

After the creation of the LATAs, the BOCs lost a large part of their intrastate toll business. The magnitude, of course, depends on how the LATAs were drawn and the pattern of demand in the intrastate toll business. States with many small SMSAs could end up with many LATAs and hence almost total decimation of the BOCs' intrastate toll business. States with only a few very large SMSAs could end up with a few quite large LATAs containing a substantial amount of toll service within the LATA boundaries.

Another factor affecting the loss of BOC toll revenues was the policy of the state concerning the size of the local calling area—that is, the number of exchanges that a subscriber could call without charge as part of the service purchased by the basic monthly rate. States with large local calling areas found their BOCs stripped of more toll revenue than states that had adopted message toll service for relatively long-distance calls within the same metropolitan area.

In 1982, the cumulative effect of these changes began to have a substantial impact on the life of the state regulator; by late 1983, the state regulator's world could reasonably be described as having come unravelled. The federal government had once proved a trustworthy, sympathetic partner by adopting a revenue-sharing plan that caused a rapidly growing flood of funds to flow into the state jurisdiction. Indeed, so big was the increase that the basic monthly flat rate for telephone service was largely missed by the high inflation of the 1970s: in 1967 prices, 1982 basic exchange rates were something like $3! But the feds were now scheming for the undoing of state regulation. First, they introduced competition into equipment and interconnection markets. The entrants, being for the most part unregulated, escaped the contribution to state funds. Of course, the entrants were pretty tiny as a share of the market, even by 1982, so that their presence was hardly noticed in the tidal wave of revenues flowing into the regulated companies. But not satisfied with this, the feds then broke up Ma Bell in a way that shrank the regulatory domain of the states. And to implement this strategy and the concomitant plan to make telecommunications as competitive as possible, they imposed changes in regulatory policy that created still more rate pressure on state services.

Patterns of State Response: Early Reactions and the Likely Future

As a participant in the development of the despised FCC policies and the dreaded antitrust case against AT&T, I confess never to have doubted the ultimate outcome of the process—a competitive, largely unregulated telecommunications sector. But this view was not shared by state regulators. Judging from the tone of state regulatory decisions since the middle of 1982, state regulators appear not to have considered seriously the possibility that precompetitive policies would become sufficiently far-reaching so as to affect their activities. Because of the absence of contingency planning, the states have found themselves more poorly placed than they had to be. Moreover, the number of problems facing unprepared states greatly exceeds the short-run capability of most commissions. Combine this with the fact that states differ substantially in the magnitude and nature of problems created by changing federal policies, and the stage has been set for diverse responses.

This case hardly constitutes the textbook example of the federalist "laboratory of the states"—the idea that it made sense to have significant policy discretion residing in the states in order to provide a means for experimenting with policy adaptations to new circumstances. In regulatory affairs, the manifestation of the concept was the notion of "benchmark competition," whereby state regulation would provide the opportunity to compare the performance of regulated monopolies across jurisdictional boundaries, thereby giving regulators information that would enhance the feasibility of effective regulation. The early responses to divestiture and competition are surely more chaotic than considered, more a response to fire-fighting demands than reasoned policy differences based upon different perceptions of the problems and theories of regulation. They may well not indicate serious long-run strategic differences that will be narrowed on the basis of the relative performance of intrastate telephone companies over the next few years. But they are interesting nevertheless for two reasons: they reveal a great deal about how regulators currently think about state regulation and hence about what next moves they are likely to make, and they are socio-economic artifacts that themselves are candidates for explanation—that is to say, what are the economic and political causes of different policy responses among the states?

Before dealing with the differences, however, it first makes sense to outline the similarities.

Residual Pricing and Universal Service

States uniformly made their current situations worse by ignoring the implications of events in Washington. It was not ordained that the FCC would get in the first, most politically palatable increase in basic exchange charges. States did not have to engage in residual pricing of basic service, raising every other price for which demand was inelastic before increasing the flat monthly rate.

The rationale for residual pricing has been universal service.

In the stormy, turbulent circumstances of divestiture, there is one beacon that guides us—universal service, the notion that everyone, regardless of income, should have access to at least a minimum level of telephone service. Although not readily confirmed statistically, the consensus . . . is that we have attained universal service. . . . Our objective then is to maintain universal service. If a single phone is disconnected on account of divestiture, then we are all the poorer for it.[26]

The Board has a deep commitment to insuring universal service. Universal service is important not only so that all who desire to have access to the entire telecommunications network may do so, but also so that all Vermonters can share in the substantial economic externalities that are inherent in a system that reaches virtually every residence and business.[27]

State regulators usually assume that the universal-service objective rates be kept as low as possible. This reasoning depends on a series of empirical hypotheses, beginning with an implicit assumption about the elasticity of demand for telephone service. If the elasticity of demand for basic service is very low, and much lower than demand elasticities for other telecommunications service, then the universal-service objective has little policy significance. First, relatively few subscribers would be lost if the basic rate were raised, and second, if one used optimal pricing rules to raise funds to subsidize local service, the basic rate would bear most of the burden.

One would think that with decades of rate-making based upon the premise that significant loss of service would result from an increase in basic exchange rates, state regulators would have ordered substantial study by regulated firms and commission staffs of the elasticity of subscriptions to changes in the monthly rate. In fact, no really serious study of this issue has been undertaken.[28] The elasticity estimates that have been made generally find values between .01 and .10, or about an order of magnitude below the elasticities for most other services. This is consistent with the experience of the last two decades. Because of the pricing methods used in telecommunications, the real basic monthly rate has been cut in half since the late 1960s, yet telephone penetration has risen from 92% to 95%. Considering that during this period the uses of the telephone network increased, incomes rose, and toll charges fell, it is hard to imagine exactly where an elasticity above .01 or .02 is going to be found. Put another way, if the FCC immediately reallocated the entire federal portion of the *NTS* contribution from interstate services to customer access charges, residential phone rates would not be as high in constant dollars as they were in 1970, when telephone penetration was estimated by the census to be 92%.

There are even deeper reasons than this, however, to doubt the assertion that state rate-making is driven primarily by the universal-service objective and a belief in the high externality value of adding a subscriber to the network. The reason is that areawide rate averaging is a highly inefficient form of subsidy. One could relatively easily use census data to ascertain not just which cities but which blocks had atypically low telephone penetration, provide discount service to these areas, and finance it with increases elsewhere. In California, which engages in statewide rate averaging and has absolutely no information about the incidence of the subsidy or the geographic distribution of subscriber penetration, these very same census data were used for legislative reapportionment. Indeed, a model was developed for estimating the effect on votes for incumbent legislators of shifting district boundaries one precinct at a time—and then visually displaying the results at a computer terminal for the worried potential victim of a gerrymander. It is very difficult to believe that if universal service were such a priority for state regulatory policy, information about group-specific elasticities would be totally unavailable and longstanding practices with respect to rate averaging would be so sacrosanct.

The question that remains is why states unanimously subscribe to this tired and empty principle. One possible explanation is that it is the fault of AT&T: it *is* the telephone giant everywhere, and surely it has influenced the content of every rate proceeding since the dawn of state regulation. But this comfortable explanation does not really hold up either. As a regulated firm subject to some form of "cost plus" unit pricing, AT&T would have had a self-interest in maximizing telephone penetration and hence in proposing more effective subsidy schemes. While one can think of reasons that AT&T might have behaved against the self-interest of the company—monopoly sloppiness, a desire to avoid collecting detailed data, and so forth—such arguments are rather weak.

My hypothesis is that the explanation lies in the politics of the states. Recall the earlier discussion of the distributional impact of the subsidy: that it may not exist at all in urban areas, but that in any case it is much higher in rural areas. Obviously, this will be the case with rate averaging combined with large geographic differences in the cost of service. But why would states want to engage in such a heavy subsidization of rural areas?

Only in the 1960s did the Supreme Court develop the "one man—one vote" doctrine.[29] The universal-service objective, whatever its intellectual merits in the theory of economic externalities, was born long before *Baker* v. *Carr,* and long before toll services and sophisticated CPE made any significant contribution to revenues. Quite likely, the real political content of universal service is a euphemism for yet another form of rural subsidy. What happened since the mid-1960s is a gradual shift of the burden of the subsidy from urban basic service to toll, equipment, and other services. The current debate over the subsidy, therefore, misses the central issue. It focuses on whether all, or only part, of the rural subsidy has been transferred from urban local service to other things, rather than on the true nature of the policy.

If this account is correct, we need to explain why the policy did not change earlier than the 1980s. After all, the agricultural program shifted from commodity price support programs to food stamps, while several land-grant colleges changed their names from "A & M" to "State University" and started emphasizing engineering! But in telephones, basic exchange prices kept on being averaged to the benefit of rural subscribers. Why did the urban legislators not put an end to this before now?

The answer would seem to be the fortuitous happenstance of explosive growth in telecommunications technology and in the demand for services. With *all* prices falling, even during inflation, and new technologies coming on-line at a rapid rate, this particular rural subsidy was not a salient political issue—at least, not until the mid-1980s.[30] Meanwhile, a new generation of regulators replaced those who had developed the original pricing policies, and so might easily be unaware of the initial purpose of those policies, possibly even believing the public rationale.

Just as agricultural subsidies have not disappeared, rural telephone subsidies are not going to go away just because the underlying political conditions have changed. But this account does provide two predictions. First, the commitment to the existing system of rate making (rate averaging, especially) is likely to erode as the political process reawakens to the distributional content of current state policy. Second, the details of state regulatory reform ought to differ, in general, according to the strength of rural interests in the state. One would expect a pattern of rate making in the most urbanized states (New Jersey, New York, Massachusetts, California, Texas) different from that in the most rural (Vermont, West Virginia, the Dakotas, the Carolinas, Mississippi). The timing of the divergence in response will depend on how long it takes for urbanites to recognize that they are not being subsidized. In a few years, this proposition should be ready for testing. No state has yet indicated that existing pricing principles are about to be abandoned, but there are some faintly visible signs of change that will be discussed below.

Attacks on License Fees

Many states have adopted a generally hostile attitude toward the structure of the new Regional Holding Companies (RHC). The divested system contains seven multistate corporations, each of which owns the Bell Operating Company in each of several states. All have similar structures that closely parallel the parent AT&T, except that the RHCs lack a manufacturing division. The seven are equal partners in Bell Communications Research, and in Bell Core, the parts of Bell Labs that were spun off to serve the operating companies. Each has adopted essentially the same corporate structure. In each state, a subsidiary has been set up to provide regulated telecommunications services. Subsidiaries have also been set up (1) to market yellow pages, (2) to provide management services, and (3) to act as purchasing assistant and coordinator for the component companies. Finally, competitive activities that the companies might enter will also be undertaken through separate subsidiaries to maintain consistency with FCC regulation of AT&T and to protect against antitrust liability.

In regulatory proceedings, the payments to affiliates providing services (and, in the past, equipment) were called license contracts. With a few exceptions regarding prices set by Western Electric for telecommunications equipment, these have rarely been controversial. Before divestiture, the few percent of revenues paid for various services from affiliates were rather automatically entered as allowable costs.

Divestiture has changed all this. Although all aspects of the license fees have been attacked and scoffed at by regulatory commissions, the main assault has been on the treatment of yellow pages and of Bell Core.

The common arrangement is for a regulated BOC to sign an agreement with its yellow pages affiliate that permanently transfers the rights to yellow pages in return for a multiyear (normally five years) license payment. Regulators are concerned that after five years the revenue will stop or will turn out to be less than what the rights to yellow pages might fetch on a competitive market. Given the policy to use net revenues from yellow pages to offset local exchange costs, regulators fear that this will become yet another factor pushing up the basic monthly rate.

> In prior rate cases, this Commission has required net revenues from yellow page advertising to be used as an offset to the costs of local service. Judge Greene, in granting the yellow page operations to the seven Bell regional companies, did so with the clear intent that yellow page revenues would be used to support local service. However, the evidence shows that although applicant contemplates yellow pages will offset the costs of basic telephone service in the near future, it has failed to make a commitment that this will continue in the long-term. This is of great concern to the Commission, especially since yellow pages are separately incorporated, and there is no readily apparent substantial reason for doing so, if it is assumed that the profits from those operations will continue to support basic service. Indeed, based upon present circumstances, a case could be made that applicant has incorporated yellow pages as a first step toward an attempt to sever the yellow page tie to local service.[31]

After making similar arguments, Minnesota's Public Utility Commission concluded that the spin-off of yellow pages was not in the public interest and voided the license contract.[32] Vermont made the same arguments and said that it would like to void the contract, but concluded that it lacked the jurisdiction to do so. Instead, it promised to impute a reasonable value for yellow pages to New England Bell's revenues regardless of the actual revenues obtained.[33] In this case, the regulators are correct on economic theoretical grounds. First, yellow pages can be expected to return supercompetitive profits indefinitely. The BOCs have a natural cost advantage in yellow pages since subscriber names, addresses, and phone numbers are already part of their billing records. Thus, all forms of directories are a joint product for a BOC, but not for anyone else. Second, the value of yellow page advertising derives from the externality value of subscribers, an externality that, it happens, can be internalized in part by selling phone listings. When a potential customer of a firm subscribes to telephone service, the value of the firm's telephone increases by at least the derivative of advertising rates with respect to the number of subscribers. (By similar argument, it makes sense for telephone companies to charge customers extra for having an unlisted number.) Of course, the quantitative connection between the externality of subscription and these revenues is not robust, but the yellow page advertising rate surely cannot exceed it. Thus, it makes sense to use profits from directories to offset basic exchange costs.

A bigger surprise is the attack of state regulators on Bell Core. Some states have disallowed the contribution altogether, while other have given the BOC one last chance to prove the case. Three arguments have been advanced to support rejection of the Bell Core license fee.

First, regulators claim that no evidence has been presented that the costs of Bell Core's R&D projects are reasonable. This argument, while true, is not very powerful, for hardly any costs in rate hearings are shown to be reasonable in the sense that costs are minimized. In Vermont, for example, the Board found "reasonable" a new corporate headquarters that cost more per square foot than any other building in the same area (but, to be fair, only a few dollars above the upper range), that a contractor had testified was "gold-plated," and that was to be built on land that had somehow doubled in value during the few months before New England Bell acquired it (though the price increase was disallowed). At the same time, the Board found the costs of Bell Core R&D projects unreasonable.[34]

The second complaint is that the vast majority of Bell Core projects are for activities that are unregulated or competitive, and hence should not be financed by monopoly services. This case is quite persuasive. Several commissions have developed long lists of projects that in title and description seem to have nothing to do with regulated services and certainly nothing to do with basic access.

The third argument has to do with Bell Core's decision-making and budgeting process. The seven coequal companies vote on projects. If five approve, all seven must share equally in the costs. If four approve, those four can finance it voluntarily, with no requirements on the others and without the necessity of equal sharing. Because of the last wrinkle, RHCs know that a project will be supported before they know exactly what their own costs will be. Regulators have termed this a blank check policy. Here again they are not very persuasive, for their argument seems fundamentally inconsistent with their standard method of estimating revenue requirements, which is to examine a historical test year. Obviously, one knows how much one has spent retrospectively; one can tally up the expenditures on acceptable projects and use this sum as the basis for beginning negotiations about the next year's allowances. Regulators have used the change in the nameplate on the research labs serving the BOCs as an excuse to abandon historical cost estimation, and then have punished the companies for not knowing very accurately what future projects are likely to cost.

More generally, all three arguments were probably equally valid before divestiture. Yet state regulators did not generally go to the trouble of examining individual research projects to find titles that did not seem appropriate or to determine whether costs were reasonable. If they had, how could Bell Labs have employed so many excellent economic theorists? Instead, the more plausible view is that the changed circumstances caused state regulators to alter their beliefs about the appropriateness of the license contract for research.

We do not have to look very hard for reasons for this. Obviously, pressures on rates are high. Research is an easy target—it does not have an effect on anyone's service today, and the long-run effects will be conjectural in any case. Moreover, each state has an incentive to free-ride on the overall research contributions from all states, although this incentive has always been present.[35] In addition, the incentive structure has changed. State regulators should not have cared as much in the past about where the R&D was going to be spent. All of AT&T was a monopoly, so wherever the productivity and product advances arose, the revenues so gained were appropriated by the system. Moreover, pricing policy gave local service revenues from increased profits anywhere else in the system, so that states stood to gain from any R&D project. But now that the subsidy system is crumbling, the purpose of an R&D effort matters, for only a subset of possible advances will make life easier for state regulators.

None of this bodes well for Bell Core. The signs are that it will shrink dramatically, becoming closer in scale to the Electric Power Research Institute. R&D activities will then migrate to the entities that manufacture the equipment that the BOCs purchase, just as has long been the case in the electric utilities business. (This suggests that Bell Labs has much better long-term prospects.) Whether this is good or bad is probably a pure guess, but one likely consequence is more R&D on local exchange services.

Intrastate Competition

The difference among the states thus far are primarily in their general posture toward competitors. States have allowed other common carriers and resellers to compete with AT&T for intrastate inter-LATA toll traffic. The differences have to do with policies regarding competition within the LATAs and the prices that interconnect companies will have to pay for access.

The states' policies are to be found literally everywhere on the spectrum with respect to intra-LATA competition for toll service. Here the BOCs have a big stake, for intra-LATA is their one remaining toll service, and it usually is highly profitable. For example, Pacific Bell estimates that the average cost to the company of a five-minute daytime intra-LATA call of thirty-one to forty miles distance is 29¢, but the average price is $1.24.[36]

The easy option for regulators would be to deny OCCs and AT&T the right to serve intra-LATA markets, leaving it to the BOCs. A few states have adopted this policy, even though it is not very practical. First, nearly all of the connections of OCCs to the local exchange system are of a type that makes it technically impossible to identify the origin of the call. OCC measuring and billing systems were developed to satisfy the requirements of the OCCs, which are quite different from those of the integrated Bell System. Moreover, the Bell System was designed so that the methods of measuring calls and use were accessible to only one toll company. The OCCs gained access to customers by simply being one of the local subscribers to a BOC exchange. When an OCC is used, a call is first made as a local call to an OCC headquarters, and then is connected to the OCC toll network. Especially in eastern cities where metropolitan areas often cross state lines or are closely adjacent, the connection to the OCC network is often by a private line that crosses a state or LATA boundary. OCCs typically measure the origin and destination of calls at the point of connection to their network. Thus, the existing system has no direct, natural way to know whether a toll call actually crossed LATA boundaries. To require that OCCs not undertake service within a LATA is to require them to reengineer their systems, making substantial expenditures to reduce the quality of their service. Most regulators have hesitated to force people to pay more for less.

A second problem with the blocking strategy is that there are other, relatively cheap ways for major phone users to avoid it. A large user can rent a private line across the nearest LATA boundary and then place calls back to the home LATA using an OCC. In most states short-distance tolls are priced so far out of line that this can be a cost-reducing strategy for a large-scale customer. This, too, can be banned, but policing the use of private lines is virtually impossible at anything approaching a reasonable cost. Because states must have at least one inter-LATA service company that can supply private lines, it does no good to keep the OCCs out of the inter-LATA intrastate market, for even AT&T can be the vehicle for undermining the protection of intra-LATA toll.

Despite all this, some states are trying to ban intra-LATA competition altogether. Some, like California, have proposed that OCCs actually install the equipment to prevent their customers from making intra-LATA calls. Others, like Indiana, have hit upon the idea of giving the OCCs the choice of blocking or paying the BOCs the latter's loss of revenue for all calls that *might* have been intra-LATA. Because BOCs charge more than OCCs and because some of the *suspected* intra-LATA calls actually would be inter-LATA, the effect of this policy is to impose a massive penalty on OCCs.

A few states have thrown up their hands and permitted intra-LATA competition. Indeed, Texas never has regulated intrastate toll by OCCs and does not plan to start now. Some states have opted for symbolism. They let OCCs provide intra-LATA service, but the OCCs must never advertise that their system can be used for that nefarious purpose! To enforce this requirement, states insist that OCCs file copies of their promotional material with the regulators.

The intellectual basis for keeping out the competitors runs deeper than simply the desire to protect old friends, the BOCs, and to retain cross-subsidies. The rationale is that Judge Greene's LATAs really demarcate the boundary between natural monopoly and competition.

> In recognition of the increasingly competitive nature of telecommunications service, an industry model has been suggested which redraws the boundaries of what was historically considered the telephone "natural monopoly." The model—and the boundaries so essential to its conclusions—has been the foundation for recent federal legislative attempts, an implicit determinant in the FCC's access charge investigation, and the support for the antitrust remedy pursued by the DOJ.
>
> The model suggests that the cost structure associated with the provision of telecommunications service within some specified geographic area exhibits natural monopoly characteristics. Geographic areas thus defined have either been labeled—depending upon the source—as "exchange areas," LATA's or as MSA's.[37]

In fact, the LATAs were not intended to be such boundaries, as the MFJ states: "Thus, contrary to much popular and even industry understanding, the purpose of the establishment of the LATAs is only to delineate the areas in which the various telecommunications companies will operate; it is not to distinguish the area in which a telephone call will be 'local' from that in which it becomes a 'toll' or long distance call."[38] What the LATAs do is define the divestiture of AT&T. They are where they are because they provided the most natural places to divide the capital equipment of the company. They have nothing whatsoever to do with natural monopoly.

The economic theory of the AT&T case, including the relief, was that AT&T's anticompetitive position in equipment and toll derived from the "bottleneck" monopoly that it had in local service. Divestiture was the required relief in order to prevent effective anticompetitive behavior (principally exclusionary practices, not monopoly pricing) in potentially competitive markets.[39] The practicalities required something less than this, however, because of the technical configuration of the Bell System. In large cities, the number of interexchange calls between two exchanges is sometimes so voluminous that the two are connected by a trunk that is not integrated into the hierarchy of the toll network. Hence, had the BOCs been divested at the first switch (central office), AT&T would have become the proud owner of a large number of stranded trunks between two large exchanges.

Judge Greene also said that it was up to the states to decide where the boundary between toll and local service really was. States have generally wanted to use intra-LATA traffic to generate subsidies for basic exchange service, and so are prone to develop an instinctive fear of allowing competition anywhere inside the LATAs. Competition, they rightly perceive, will erode the ability of regulators to cross-subsidize.

Nevertheless, the meat-axe approach (blocking the OCCs from service inside LATAs) is not the most effective strategy to keep generating the subsidies. Indeed, doing this and nothing else actually guarantees that the subsidy will eventually be dissipated. Competitors, who do not pay it, will have a cost advantage, and states cannot effectively eliminate them because they cannot control all of the viable bypass options. Most states have clearly understood this, and have focused on access charges for interexchange carriers as the most promising means for maintaining the status quo.

State Access Charges

The FCC's access charges cover only the federal allocation of local exchange costs. The states are free to cover the intrastate portion however they please. States all recover traffic-sensitive costs by charges on use. Controversy arises concerning *NTS* costs. The states could recover these through another subscriber access charge, like the FCC's, but this seems politically unattractive and violates the principles and myths of rate making.

States have thus far exhibited considerable diversity in their early attempts to develop access charges for *NTS* costs. Given the decision to levy access charges on toll companies, there are two general approaches that can be taken. The first is to charge a company a fixed monthly rate for each customer it serves. Although this approach has the advantage of avoiding excise taxes on calls, it faces two major problems. One is that customers may subscribe to several tool companies, generating several access charges even though they cause only one access cost. The other rises from the differences between AT&T and its competitors. AT&T can claim that it has access cost responsibility only for inter-LATA tolls. The system is designed so that calls dialed only by number go through the BOCs (the calls inside LATAs), while calls beginning with a "1" and an area code are now nearly everywhere in the county switched only to AT&T.[40] Because of this arrangement, AT&T is blocked by the design of the system from providing intra-LATA service until it rebuilds its network. Thus, states adopting a per line access charge have a twofold problem: how much to charge AT&T for inter-LATA access, and how much to charge the OCCs for inter-LATA access. Meanwhile, the BOC does not charge itself "access," although it continues to price intra-LATA toll substantially above its costs.

The second approach to access charges for interconnect companies is to base them on use. Usage can be based either on the number of calls that are placed or on the minutes of use for toll calls. States typically opt for the latter. Traffic-sensitive costs of switching and transmission are already recovered in this way, so that tacking on a few cents more to cover some NTS costs is an easy action.

Regardless of the method that is used, access charges can generate some revenues to subsidize other services, but there are costs and limits. The costs occur because any system will cause efficiency losses by suppressing some economically warranted toll service and by encouraging uneconomic bypass. The limits are imposed by the bypass alternatives and by other factors affecting the elasticity of demand for toll using the BOC network. Due to residual pricing theory, states are probably already fairly close to these limits, so that they are not likely to find effective ways to increase even further the net revenues from intrastate toll. Indeed, technical progress may well reduce this net revenue limit by making bypass cheaper.

An interesting and potentially important difference among states is the size of the minutes-of-use access charge. At one extreme, several southern states, California, and Oregon have set access charges at 9.5¢ or more per minute. Illinois, Maryland, Iowa, Georgia, and New Jersey have all set the price at under 7¢; the difference between New Jersey (lowest) and Alabama (highest) is 7¢.[41] These differences seem unlikely to persist, for if bypass does not undermine the high charges, the lower charges are likely sources of new revenues for the states at the bottom of the list.

Access charge policies also affect the viability of the OCCs. A state commission can deceptively rule that OCCs are welcome everywhere in the state and then keep them out entirely by the way it sets access charges. All that it needs to do is adopt an access charge method that makes the OCCS unable to compete with the BOC intra-LATA or AT&T inter-LATA. For example, charging per subscriber line disadvantages OCCs, for their customers are likely to want to subscribe to more than one carrier.

A related issue is the "discount" for inter-LATA access for the OCCs because they have inferior access to AT&T. The nature of the interconnections of OCCs to central stations causes OCC circuits to have lower transmission quality and forces the OCCs to require customers to dial an access code before dialing the number they wish to reach. Most states have chosen to discount state access for OCCs in essentially the same way that the FCC does for federal-carrier access charges, but some use greater or lesser discounts, and so provide varying degrees of encouragement to OCCs, and to BOCs to install equal access equipment.

Local Measured Service

States have revealed quite different attitudes about local measured service. Approximately 40% of the costs attributed to local service are usage related. If these were unbundled from basic access charges, they would just offset the parts of *NTS* costs that are charged to toll. An obvious strategy for holding down the basic monthly rate is to charge for local calls.

Many states have instituted some form of voluntary measured service, at least as an experiment, although in some cases it is invidiously called "Lifeline" with the understanding that it is for the poor, and the elderly. Very few people opt for the service, largely because of the way it is priced. It is designed as a cheap way for people who not use the phone to get access. For the most part, states have been very reluctant to take the extreme step of making measured service mandatory.

Mandatory measured service makes a great deal of sense. First, it encourages conversation of resources that are consumed in use and so is efficient. Second, a substantial element of the costs of implementing it are fixed costs associated with installing measuring equipment in local exchanges. This is not prohibitively expensive in modern electronic switches, but is not likely to be worth doing in old mechanical switches. Third, to the extent that service to some people is threatened by higher basic exchange rates and that this constitutes a valid social problem, the people using this service are likely to place a low value on the telephone and presumably, to use it less. Thus, measured service seems to be consistent with the universal-service objective.

Vermont was the first state to incorporate these specific arguments into a rate hearing and to annouce its predisposition to adopt mandatory measured service in areas served by electronic switches.[42] Why Vermont? The circumstances in Vermont are unusual. It is a big net gainer from the *NTS* subsidy, being highly rural. It also is one of the few states in which competition from OCCs and resellers has not yet emerged. As of last summer, Vermont's regulators believed that no OCC had an office in the state! Thus, Vermont faces the tough task of generating a lot of revenue to pay for local service but under the favorable circumstance that the decision can be made outside the charged context of a battle for survival between OCCs and AT&T. Measured service probably appears to a Vermont regulator as a way to add some new toll service to replace the lost revenues from interstate toll and CPE. If so, local measured service will not be efficient; it will have too high a price per call, but too low a basic monthly rate. Constraining this behavior, however, will be the parallel policy of subsidizing pay phones (they are still a dime a call in Vermont). An outrageous measured service plan will see a boom in pay phones, especially since Vermont does not impose a minimum monthly revenue requirement on pay phones that are accessible to the public.

It appears that in a decade or so local measured service will be a clear winner. It is the one move that serves two otherwise competing principles: making the system more efficient by tying prices more closely to cost causation, but keeping down the basic monthly rate. Even if measured service is now regarded skeptically, it is likely to appear increasingly attractive as regulators come to realize that current policies are simply not viable in the long run.

Assessment of State Policies

An end to piling up more and more surcharges on intrastate toll and other services is in sight. Federal policy has created a handful of vigorous competitors that will continue to charge very low rates. Heavy users of the system, the tiny fraction of customers that generates half the revenues of telephone companies, have available to them cheap alternatives to use of the intrastate part of the network if intrastate surcharges are too high. They probably will not bypass the local exchange in sufficient numbers to bankrupt it, but they can put great pressure on the regulators. One result of regulation is that once capital is made part of the rate base, it stays there, even if customers stop using it. The circuits abandoned by bypassers will still figure into revenue requirements and put pressure on residential rates.[43] The more that regulators try to recover these revenues in usage-based rates on toll, the greater will be the extent of bypass and hence the upward pressure on the basic monthly rate.

Proponents of the view that bypass presents a serious problem have often overstated the case, warning of a never-ending spiral of rate hikes and customer defections. This "doomsday scenario" is probably incorrect, but is unnecessary to the argument.[44] The more germane question is whether toll prices are above the level that maximizes net revenue because of the magnitude of bypass that they induce. All agree that such a situation is bad policy. But obviously, the monopoly price for toll would induce some bypass. The extent of bypass can be controlled by clever forms of price discrimination, but the very fact that bypass is taking place does not mean that state regulators are not maximizing the flow of subsidies from toll.

The real issue in state commissions for the next few years is not about either the existence of bypass or the never-ending spiral. It is whether toll should be priced more efficiently, or more like a monopoly, to generate revenues for rural telephones. Excessive rhetoric on both sides has clouded the issue, as is evident in the rather confused way it is dealt with in state rate findings.

The interesting analytical question is how much monopoly rent us available for squeezing several years from now. To my knowledge, this question has not been addressed. But given that roughly half the capacity is used by less than 1% of the users, it seems highly unlikely that a lot of revenue can be squeezed out. Small users can continue to be charged monopoly rates, forcing urban residential and small business customers to foot the rural telephone bill. But big users cannot. Given also that revenues are probably close to maximal now, in the long run, the rents from intrastate toll as a fraction of costs and revenues must decline. And, if bypass costs fall faster than toll demand grows, the absolute size of the rent could fall. Most bypass technologies are very young and just beginning to slide down the electronics-learning curve, so this possibility is by no means remote.

The bottom line is that looking ahead to the early 1990s, the existing system of state regulation of telephones is neither economically nor politically viable. It is a transfer of too much from too many to too few in too inefficient a manner. Moreover, it appears to be founded upon a subsidy base that will erode relatively quickly.

There is no panacea, but local measured service would soften the blow. So, too, would rate deaveraging to concentrate subsidies, assuming that this practice is politically viable once people discover that it is neither middle-class suburbanites nor the urban poor who are receiving subsidies.

Meanwhile, state regulators had better learn more economics. Sadly, we are not doing much of a job teaching them. As one regulator put it.

> The proposals in this docket which are grounded in what is purported to be pure economic theory are nothing more than a best case scenario—speculation in common parlance. Real people frequently do *not* behave as economists would have them do, that is according to the principles of economic efficiency. . . .[45]

This is not an isolated example; it is simply one among those that most clearly reveal a lack of understanding of economics. Almost all state regulators have generally rejected the concept that prices ought to bear some relationship to costs and ought to be used as a means to ration the use of various services.

The reason regulators have so concluded is that they have been given the impression that economics is fundamentally inconsistent with the social and distributional goals that the political process demands that they pursue. The problem with this position, of course, lies in the misperception of what economics is about: using regularities in the behavior of economic agents—firms and their customers—to estimate the economic consequences (costs, benefits, and distribution) of ways to organize a market. Obviously, there are more and less costly ways to achieve distributional and other objectives, and economic analysis is useful in identifying these differences.

The regulators' misperception is not their fault. It arises, I conjecture, from the adversarial context in which economic analysis is presented, and as a result, some regulators believe that economists are venal and/or that economics has no meaningful content. As one judge put it:

> [W]e directed the parties to respond to the natural monopoly question in analytic terms. Their responses, offered as highly technical economic theory, present a wide range of positions from the proposition that the entire telecommunications network is a natural monopoly (Pacific) to the observation that no part of the network is a natural monopoly (AT&T). Considering that the facts underlying these opinions are not in dispute, the status of economics as an art rather than a science is well-founded.[46]

Of course, this quotation is technically incorrect, in that the issue in dispute is essentially an unresolved question of fact. But its deeper significance lies in the reasons why an administrative judge would have such a cynical view of economics and economists, especially *this* judge, who, elsewhere in the same opinion, was one of the few state regulators to espouse competition and to favor economic costs as a basis for pricing. My hypothesis is that the problem is to be found in the way economists frame the issues.

Economic testimony is inevitably designed to defend a policy conclusion, and therefore it is usually an incomplete analysis of the issue that is at stake. Moreover, it so thoroughly blends the positive and normative aspects of the analysis that, to a noneconomist, the utility of the former is obscured. Not surprisingly, none of the testimony represents the "adversarial economics" document that would be prepared to reflect the objective of regulators, for lawyers make sure it reflects instead the purposes of the participants in the process that they represent. In this milieu, regulators are sure to find the normative aspects of all testimony at best incomplete and quite likely unacceptable. And because the normative and positive aspects are blended, rejecting the former leads to undervaluing the latter.

The consequences of this state of affairs reach beyond telephone services that are, on average, more costly than they need to be to include the data collection problems that confound regulators and economic analysts alike. Because regulators are skeptical of economics, they are not likely to listen to economists' advice on how they ought to collect and to analyze cost and demand information. But lacking the theoretical structure of economics to guide them to the solution to their information problems, the regulators are unlikely to write data requirements that will enable them to avoid hasty decisions, with unintended consequences that they will ultimately regret, such as the promotion of uneconomic bypass and the construction of disincentives to adopt better, more efficient technology.

Jurisdiction Wars: The FCC as Death Star

State regulatory actions that ignore questions of economic efficiency may temporarily satisfy state political demands and be economically viable. The longer-run problems of economic and political viability, however serious they are, may not be the most important force working to restructure state policy. The more immediate threat could prove to be the irreconcilable conflict between state and federal policy.

Federal policy is built on the premise that most if not all of the telecommunications industry can and ought to be competitive. State policy cannot easily be characterized, for it differs substantially among jurisdictions, but for the most part it is built on the premise that competition ought to end at the boundary of federal jurisdiction, for example, inside the LATAs for technologies and services that have been left to states to regulate.

Federal policy also accepts the principle of cost-causation as highly relevant, if not determinative, in setting prices. Although states are heterogeneous here as well, they generally subscribe to quite different principles and many have explicitly rejected cost-causative pricing principles.

These substantial policy differences cannot exist side-by-side for more than a few years. The reason is more than just ideological imperialism—the desire of each jurisdiction to have its right-thinking principles adopted by others—although this is surely an element of the interjurisdictional conflicts. The deeper cause is that decisions by one jurisdiction affect the ability of the other to carry out its policies. This is most obvious in interexchange toll service. The viability of competitive common carriers, and hence the procompetitive policy of the FCC, is enhanced if the OCCs are given access to all or most of the intrastate toll market and face state regulatory policies that do not impose substantial costs on them in comparison to AT&T and the BOC toll services. The viability of state policies to use intrastate toll charges as a source of subsidy for basic exchange service depends on the FCC's pricing policies with respect to interstate services, for in many areas (especially the small eastern states) the costs to users of chaining interstate toll calls to reach an intrastate destination can place a binding ceiling on intrastate toll subsidies.

The interaction between state and federal regulation occurs in a slightly more subtle fashion in equipment. Technological developments in communications and computer equipment are permitting ever greater substitution possibilities between terminal equipment and the use of lines and switches. One example is the choice between a PBX and Centrex as a means of communicating between terminal devices at the same location. A PBX is essentially a switch on the customer's premises that allows one of the customer's terminals to connect to another without touching the external telecommunications network. Centrex is a means of providing the same capability through the local exchange network. A local operating company has a franchised monopoly to provide Centrex, but a PBX can be purchased or rented in a competitive market that is (de)regulated by the FCC. If state regulators set Centrex prices below cost to preserve this business for the operating company, the FCC's procompetitive policy is undermined; however, if the state sets Centrex prices substantially above costs to raise revenue to subsidize something else, the FCC's procompetitive policy on equipment will undermine the state policy.

The result of policy conflict in an interdependent environment is a jurisdiction war: a battle in which state and federal authorities adopt policies and practices for the purpose of inhibiting or thwarting the policies of the other. The telecommunications jurisdiction war has three kinds of battlefields. The first includes the examples cited above; within the recognized domain of each authority are activities that can seriously impinge on activities in the enemy's jurisdiction. In the second, one authority will assert jurisdiction in new territory that is either unclaimed or staked out by the opposition. The third battlefield is in the political realm, and the tactic used is the political pincer move: one authority will attack the other through the political bodies that exercise control over it. In the wake of AT&T divestiture and widespread federal deregulation, bodies are strewn over each type of battlefield.

In two of the three arenas of conflict, the FCC clearly has the upper hand. The FCC is advantaged in "competitive regulation" in two ways. It has jurisdiction over several bypass technologies that can be used to provide local service and interexchange competition without state asset. By virtue of its authority to regulate the use of the electromagnetic spectrum, it controls non-wire bypass technologies. These are likely to become relatively cheaper as production experience increases and technology advances, so that the FCC can use them to put pressure on the states to reduce toll prices. In addition, the FCC has the advantage that it adheres more closely to principles of economic efficiency in making policy decisions. Even for services that are regulated, an agency that uses cost-causative pricing will win a jurisdiction war against an agency that does not, since the latter will see its subsidizing services shrink in sales while it retains all of its subsidized ones.

The FCC is also advantaged in asserting jurisdiction if it wants to acquire turf from the states. One example is the FCC's depreciation rules; another is its cable television policy. The FCC first asserted jurisdiction over cable television regulation in the 1960s on the grounds that cable activities affected its policies in regulating over-the-air broadcasting. The FCC was upheld in *U.S. v. Southwestern Cable Company.*[47] Subsequent regulatory decisions by the FCC, including cable deregulation in 1980, have reasserted this jurisdiction and placed constraints on franchising activities by state and local governments.

It is plausible that the courts would allow similar assertion of jurisdiction over additional parts of state telecommunications activity if the FCC thought that it had to take jurisdiction in order to implement national policy objectives. This could mean eventual FCC regulation of local exchange service, removing the state entirely from telecommunications regulation.

The immediate issue that could give rise to expanded federal jurisdiction is the access charge problem facing state regulators. Because states are reluctant to establish access charges on customers as part of the basic exchange rate, they continue to seek ways to cover *NTS* (access) costs through excise charges. This inevitably leads the states to use access charges to slow the gains of competitive suppliers of toll and other services. One plausible counterattack by the FCC is to parallel the depreciation decision by requiring that states mirror federal policies in setting access charges.

In the final arena, that of the political process, the FCC is not so clearly advantaged. Superficially, the FCC would appear to be strong because FCC pricing and competitive policies have the effect of transferring responsibility for some relatively visible and potentially unpopular consequences to the states. Members of Congress and the Executive Office of the President, therefore, should be favorably disposed to such a move. But working in the other direction are the realities of the hierarchy of government office. The principal source of challengers to incumbent federal legislators is state and local government. Governors and big-city mayors run for the Senate, and state legislators and other local officials run for the House. To the extent that the basic exchange rate becomes a salient political issue at the state and local level, incumbent legislators could become vulnerable to challenges based in part on their association with the big increases in telephone prices. Consequently, a preemptive legislative strike to cushion some of the short-term rate shock could have potential political value to federal legislators.

That telephone rates can become salient politically is exemplified by the story of Hickory Telephone.[48] This small, rural phone company in Hickory Corners, Michigan, serving about nine-hundred residences, tried to raise its basic monthly rate by about $6 in 1975. The local citizenry banded together to boycott the company, to fight the rate increase at the Public Service Commission, and to sue the state regulators. Before the dust cleared four years later, when some rate relief was granted, the plight of Hickory Corners had become a state political issue and was picked up and championed by the state attorney general.

The congressional response to the FCC's initial access charge decision seems to bear out the preceding argument. In February 1984, just before that primary election season got underway, the FCC agreed to delay adoption of its residential access charge decision until the spring of 1985, well after the elections of 1984.

The ultimate resolution of the jurisdictional war will be decided by Congress, probably in a highly invisible way. The crucial issue is whether to try to undo legislatively some of the actions of the FCC and Judge Greene. If positive congressional action is not taken, the war will be fought on grounds that favor the procompetitive policies now in vogue within the federal government. Under this scenario, the relevant choice facing state regulators is whether to accommodate FCC policies gradually over the next few years, or to battle the FCC and eventually lose the jurisdiction war. The former choice is the less costly to society, but it will involve tackling some distributional issues that are politically difficult to manage. The latter course, however, is politically attractive in the short run, for it enables regulators to go down fighting as defenders of low telephone rates. For a while, at least, regulators probably will prefer to play the role of the martyred hero.

Notes

1. The FCC granted the petition, undertook a formal inquiry, and published its findings in CC Docket 83–788. Not surprisingly, the FCC did not find the impact of its policies to be all that distressing.

2. U.S. v. AT&T, U.S. District Court for the District of Columbia, CA No. 74–1698.

3. Of course, not all of this will be granted, and not all is due to federal policy interventions. In CC 83–788, the FCC estimated that the BOCs had been getting about 40% of what they asked for, and that in pending cases about 40% of the proposed increase was due to procompetitive federal policy decisions.

4. Examiners' Report, Docket No. 5113, Public Utility Commission of Texas, April 2, 1984, p. 35.

5. Examiners' Report, Docket No. 4545, Public Utility Commission of Texas, December 15, 1982, p. 52.

6. Examiners' Report, Docket No. 5220, Public Utility Commission of Texas, April 2, 1984, p. 92.

7. Guido Calabresi, *The Cost of Accidents* (New Haven: Yale University Press, 1970).

8. The literature on policies for inducing truthful revelation of costs is providing increasingly better insight into this problem. Thus far, the policy of setting marginal price equal to marginal cost (with a two-part tariff, cost uncertainty, and strategic responses to rules regarding the use of information in setting prices) can be shown to be optimal only under a set of rather restrictive conditions, among which are the independence of cost uncertainties from period to period and the ability of a regulator to make credible commitments about future pricing rules. See David Baron and David Besanko, "Regulation and Information in a Continuing Relationship," in *Information Economics and Policy* (forthcoming).

9. Federal Communications Commission *Statistics of Communications Common Carriers, 1981* (Washington, D.C.: GPO, 1983), 18.

10. National Association of Regulatory Utility Commissioners, "Separations and Settlements in the Telephone Industry," June 1979, p. 48. NARUC obviously could use the skills of Ms. McDonald of Texas.

11. In Texas, interstate accounts for 23% of *NTS* costs, while intrastate toll contributes another 21%. See Examiners' Report, Docket 5113, p. 12–13. In Kansas, however, state regulators have concluded that intrastate toll contributes very little subsidy. See Order, Docket No. 137, 534–U, State of Kansas Corporation Commission, p. 90.

12. For a more complete analysis of the so-called local service subsidy, see Nina W. Cornell and Roger G. Noll, "Local Telephone Prices and the Subsidy Question," *Stanford Studies in Industrial Economics,* January 1985.

13. See, for example, Order, State of Vermont Public Service Board, Docket No.s 4751/4752 and 4762, August 11, 1983, p. 65–70 for a rather extensive discussion of installation charges.

14. Some of the candidate systems are discussed in Alan Baughcum and Gerald Faulhaber (editors), *Telecommunications Access and Public Policy* (Norwood, N.J.: Ablex, 1984.

15. 13FCC2d 420 (1968), 18FCC2d 953 (1970), 29FCC2d 871 (1971) and 28FCC2d 267 (1971).

16. Richard E. Wiley, "The End of Monopoly: Regulatory Change and the Promotion of Competition," in *Disconnecting Bell,* ed. Harry M. Shooshan III (New York: Pergamon Press, 1984).

17. Roger G. Noll, "Regulation and Computer Services," in *The Computer Age,* ed. Michael L. Dertouzos and Joel Moses (Cambridge: MIT Press, 1979).

18. 77FCC3d 384 (1980), 89FCC2d 1 (1980).

19. Examiners' Report, Docket No. 5220.

20. FCC83–564 (1983).

21. 89FCC2d 1094 (1982).

22. Virginia State Corporation Commission v. FCC, 4th circuit, No. 83–166, 1984.

23. 85FCC2d 818 (1981).

24. 48 *Federal Register* 10319 (March 11, 1983).

25. For a thorough treatment of the use of access charges, see Robert D. Willig, "The Theory of Network Access Pricing," in *Issues in Public Utility Regulation,* ed. Harry M. Trebing (East Lansing: Michigan State University, 1982).

26. Proposed Decision of Administrative Law Judge Patrick Power 83–06–91, State of California Public Utilities Commission, 1984, p. 190–91. Unlike most state regulators, Judge Power did not find competition a serious threat to unusual service.

27. Order, Dockets No. 4751/4752 and 4762, p. 82–83.

28. Those that have been made are reviewed in Order, CC Docket No. 83–788, Federal Communications Commission, December 1, 1983, FCC 83–567.

29. In Baker v. Carr, the Court held that federal courts could review legislative redistributing. This was followed by numerous cases that challenged the structure of legislative districts. In Reynolds v. Sims, the Court stated: "Legislators represent people, not trees or acres." These decisions were made in 1962 and 1964, respectively, and were followed by legislative redistricting on a massive scale. See Mathew D. McCubbins and Thomas Schwartz, "The Politics of Derustication: Court-Ordered Redistricting and Its Policy Effects," CEPR Publication No. 30, Stanford University.

30. The view of the politics of regulatory pricing expressed here is similar to that of Joskow, who first examined the plausibility of an assymetric response to upward

and downward price movements by regulators. See Paul Joskow, "Inflation and Environmental Concern," *Journal of Law and Economics* 17 (1974):291–328.

31. Order, Docket No. 137, 534–U, p. 16 (Kansas).

32. Order, Docket No. P–421/GR–83–600, Minnesota Public Utility Commission, July 27, 1984.

33. Order, Docket No. 4874/4875, State of Vermont Public Service Board, October 5, 1984, p. 78–82.

34. Ibid., pp. 86–92, 116–21.

35. Gunter Knieps and Pablo Spiller, "Regulation by Partial Deregulation: The Case of Telecommunications," *Administrative Law Review*, 35 (Fall 1983):391–421, use a similar free-ride argument to support their hypothesis that states will not be as prone as the FCC to deregulate for the purpose of gaining information about costs and new technology.

36. "Statement of Pacific Bell," Public Hearings on the Regulation of Telecommunications, California Public Utilities Commission, November 8, 1984, Appendix D.

37. Order, Docket No. 82–0268, Illinois Commerce Commission, February 9, 1983, p. 3.

38. U.S. v. AT&T (1983) 569 F. Supp. 994–5.

39. The economic theory of the Antitrust Division's case is obviously an elusive concept. Many people were involved in the case, and those who finished it were not those who began it. Here I speak of the case as it was developed at the beginning. Relevant documents are: Robert Reynolds, "Bell"; and Roger Noll and Bruce Owen, "The Economic Theory of the AT&T Case." Both are internal DOJ memoranda that are now in the public domain.

40. The MFJ requires customer choice of the "dial one" company by 1986, which is probably optimistic because it requires substantial investment in central office equipment. But in some places—Charleston, West Virginia, was the first—customers already have the choice.

41. AT&T Communications, "Comments on Regulation of Telecommunications in California," Hearing on the Regulation of Telecommunications, California Public Utilities Commission, November 8, 1984, p. B–4.

42. Order, Dockets No. 4611, 4746 and 4805, State of Vermont Public Service Board, January 20, 1984. Procedurally, the board could not order the service because no one had proposed it. Instead, the issue was a set of proposals to make alterations in voluntary measured service, which the board denied because, in the course of the investigation, it became convinced the service should be mandatory.

43. For a comprehensive review of the effect of bypass possibilities, or local telephone companies, see Gerald W. Brock, "Bypass of the Local Exchange: A Quantitative Assessment," OPP Working Paper 12, Federal Communications Commission, September 1984.

44. This is the finding of Brock, "Bypass." Ms. McDonald of Texas concluded that the "doomsday scenario was not supported with any substantial evidence." She did note that 77 of Southwest Bell's 320 largest customers currently use bypass technology. Nevertheless, she found comfort in the fact that SWB had failed to prove that this caused them any loss of revenues. Order, Docket No. 5113, p. 30.

45. Docket No. 5113, Texas, p. 35. On the preceding page, the examiners dis-

missed the believability of Alfred Kahn's testimony about the economics of utility pricing as follows: "Furthermore, it is difficult for the examiners not to be somewhat skeptical of the economic bliss promised—if only we would price telephone service according to cost causation principles—by the economist who deregulated the airlines for us."

46. Proposed Decision of Administrative Law, Judge Patrick Power, p. 191.
47. 392 U.S. 157 (1968).
48. CC Docket No. 83–788, Appendix 17.

10
Perspectives on Mergers and World Competition

Janusz A. Ordover
Robert D. Willig

There is growing awareness among antitrust policymakers, scholars, and judges of the increasing importance of foreign firms, products, and technology in maintaining competition in U.S. markets. This changing perception is dramatically reflected in the Merger Guidelines promulgated by the Justice Department. Whereas the 1968 Merger Guidelines barely even mentioned the importance of foreign firms and imports in assessing the economic consequences of a merger, the 1982 Merger Guidelines acknowledge that, "depending on the nature of the product, the geographic market may be as small as a part of a city or as large as the entire world."[1] Yet in 1982, distinct caution remained:

> The Department [of Justice], however, will be somewhat more cautious, both in expanding market boundaries beyond the United States and in assessing the likely supply response of specific foreign firms.[2]

In contrast, the latest revision of the Guidelines issued in June of 1984 specifically renounced distinction between domestic and foreign competition in merger analysis:

> . . . the Guidelines' standards relating to the definition of markets and the calculation of market shares will apply equally to foreign and domestic firms. Moreover, no foreign firm will be excluded from the market solely because its sales in the United States are subject to a quota.[3]

The argument for including in market share calculations firms domiciled in countries subject to a quota rests implicitly on models of international trade that have been recently formulated.[4] In general, only recently has the

An earlier version of this paper was presented at an NBER Conference on Strategic Behavior in International Trade. The authors would like to thank the National Science Foundation for support in the preparation of this article.

work of international trade theorists become relevant to the formulation of antitrust policy in a transnational context. In contrast, other areas of antitrust have long been subjects of focus and contribution for economic analyses.

The reason for this discrepancy is easily identified. As Avinash Dixit noted in his survey lecture:

> Almost all of the received theory of international trade, positive or normative, is based on the model of atomistic competition. . . . It is recognized that a country may have monopoly power in trade, but this is supposed to be exercised by its government through the use of tariffs.[5]

Such a model cannot capture the basic issues that underlie American antitrust policy or what Europeans more aptly term "competition policy." Antitrust policy issues do not arise without concentration of market power in the hands of sellers or buyers, the possibility of dangerous creation of market power through mergers or anticompetitive practices, or entry barriers that protect the incumbent firms from the competitive constraints of prospective entrants. A number of excellent, recently published papers in international trade theory explicitly focus on the efforts of imperfect competition, both intra-and internationally, and these papers thus constitute a new foundation on which antitrust policy for transnational industries can be built.[6] Our aim in this chapter is less to break new analytical ground than to derive some lessons for antitrust policy from this new learning on international trade among imperfectly competitive economies.

We conduct our analysis using what has become a familiar model of international trade in identical commodities. The model can, however, be easily extended to allow for trade in differentiated variants of the same product. We employ this model to explore formally two issues: first, the extent to which foreign competition can be relied upon to ameliorate the adverse effects of mergers in the home country; and, second, the extent to which enhanced foreign competition improves home welfare. Our analysis suggests that whereas foreign competition can frequently be a potent constraint on the ability of domestic firms to elevate price, therefore benefitting *consumers* in the home country, it can nevertheless reduce producers' profits to an extent that outweighs the consumer gains. As a rule, we find that producers' losses from enhanced competition relative to consumers' gains therefrom are large when imports compose a small portion of total consumption in the home country.

Regardless of its net impact on domestic welfare, we find that import competition can be a potent substitute for domestic competition in eliminating adverse effects of domestic mergers. However, this conclusion is tempered by our findings that this effect is sensitive both to the level and the variability of the exchange rate. In the context of our model, we show that when import competition is more important than domestic competition, potentially adverse effects of a domestic merger are more significant the more volatile is the relevant exchange rate. Thus, while transnational markets may be appropriate for merger analysis, attention should be paid to the special features of the flows of international trade that occur within them.

The Basic Model

So as to address concisely a wide range of policy issues, we work with an extremely simple model. The model represents the markets for a traded homogeneous product in two nations: the home country and the foreign country. In each nation, the commodity in question can be produced by means of a technology with constant unit variable costs, m_1 at home and m_2 abroad. The technology is deployed by N_1 firms at home and N_2 firms abroad, each of which may incur some fixed costs in addition to its variable costs. Insurmountable entry barriers are assumed to constrain the population of active firms. In country i, the demand for the good is characterized by a linear inverse demand function: $p_i = A_i - B_i \bar{x}_i$, where p_i is the consumers' price prevailing, and $\bar{x}_i$ is the total quantity supplied to the country's market. All supply to each market is controlled by the producing firms, so that there is no explicit arbitrage activity between the countries.

Firms choose their levels of sales in each country so as to maximize individual profits. The profit net or fixed cost for firm ℓ domiciled in country i is

$$\Pi_i^\ell = x_{i1}^\ell (p_1 - m_i - t_{i1}) + x_{i2}^\ell (p_2 - m_i - t_{i2}),$$

where x_{ij}^ℓ = sales in country j of firm ℓ domiciled in country i and t_{ij} per unit costs of international transportation from country i to j. Firms are aware of their possible influence over prices, both directly through the markets' inverse demand functions and indirectly through other firms' conjectured reactions to their own supply decisions. Define v_{ij}^k to be the conjecture held by a firm located in country j regarding the response to a change in its shipments to country k on the part of other firms located in country i. Thus,

$$v_{ij}^k = \sum_\ell \frac{dx_{ik}^\ell}{dx_{jk}^m}, \text{ where the summation excludes } \ell = m \text{ when } i = j.$$

We assume that conjectured responses to supply variation are limited to the market that is directly affected. (This is rational here in view of the constant returns to scale in variable costs.) We term as Cournot the case in which the conjectures are all zero, and generally assume that $v^k_{1i} + v^k_{2i} \geq -1$.

Given this pattern of conjectures,

$$\partial \Pi^\ell_i / \partial x^\ell_{i1} = p_1 - m_i - t_{i1} - B_1 x^\ell_{i1}(1 + v^1_{1i} + v^1_{2i}),$$

$$\partial \Pi^\ell_i / \partial x^\ell_{i2} = p_2 - m_i - t_{i2} - B_2 x^\ell_{i2}(1 + v^2_{1i} + v^2_{2i}),$$

As a result of the linearities and symmetries of the model, the equilibrium is unique and entails like behavior by all the firms located in a given country. The equilibrium level of supply to country j by a firm located in country i is denoted by x^*_{ij}. If $x^*_{ij} > 0$ then $\partial \Pi^\ell_i / \partial x^\ell_{ii} = 0$ in equilibrium, and if $\partial \Pi^\ell_i / \partial x^\ell_{ij} = <$ equilibrium, then $x^*_{ij} = 0$. Depending on the relative values of the parameters, the model's equilibrium may entail all production effected in one country, or production in each country but no trade, or two-country production with one-way trade, or two-country production with two-way trade.

For the case of two-country production with two-way trade, the first-order conditions in matrix form are:

$$\begin{bmatrix} B_1(N_1 + 1 + v^1_{11} + v^1_{21}) & B_1 N_2 & 0 & 0 \\ 0 & 0 & B_2(N_1 + 1 + v^2_{11} + v^2_{21}) & B_2 N_2 \\ 0 & 0 & B_2 N_1 & B_2(N_2 + 1 + v^2_{12} + v^2_{22}) \\ B_1 N_1 & B_1(N_2 + 1 + v^1_{12} + v^1_{22}) & 0 & 0 \end{bmatrix} \times \begin{bmatrix} x_{11} \\ x_{21} \\ x_{12} \\ x_{22} \end{bmatrix}$$

$$= \begin{bmatrix} A_1 - m_1 \\ A_2 - (m_1 + t_{12}) \\ A_2 - m_2 \\ A_1 - (m_2 + t_{21}) \end{bmatrix} \quad (10.1)$$

Then, application of Cramer's rule gives:

$$x^*_{11} = \frac{(A_1 - m_1)[N_2 + 1 + v^1_{12} + v^1_{22}] - [A_1 - (m_2 + t_{21})]N_2}{B_1[N_2 + 1 + v^1_{12} + v^2_{22})(N_1 + 1 + v^1_{11} + v^1_{21}) - N_1 N_2]} ; \quad (10.2)$$

$$x_{21}^* = \frac{[A_1 - (m_2 + t_{21})][(N_1 + 1 + v_{11}^1 + v_{21}^1)] - (A_1 - m_1)N_1}{B_1[N_2 + 1 + v_{12}^1 + v_{22}^1)(N_1 + 1 + v_{11}^1 + v_{21}^1) - N_1 N_2]} \; ; \quad (10.3)$$

$$x_{12}^* = \frac{[A_2 - (m_1 + t_{12})][N_2 + 1 + v_{12}^1 + v_{22}^2)] - (A_2 - m_2)N_2}{B_2[N_2 + 1 + v_{12}^2 + v_{22}^2)(N_1 + 1 + v_{11}^2 + v_{21}^2) - N_1 N_2]} \; ; \quad (10.4)$$

$$x_{22}^* = \frac{(A_2 - m_2)[N_1 + 1 + v_{11}^1 + v_{21}^1] - [A_2 - (m_1 + t_{12})]N_1}{B_2[N_2 + 1 + v_{12}^2 + v_{22}^2)(N_1 + 1 + v_{11}^2 + v_{21}^2) - N_1 N_2]} \; ; \quad (10.5)$$

In fact, if the parameters of the model render these expressions nonnegative, then it follows that two-way trade between two producing countries is the relevant case. This is more likely the less competitive in the domestic market of a country where home production costs are less than the delivered costs of imports. For example, (10.4) shows that x_{12}^* is more likely to be positive, given that $m_2 < m_1 + t_{12}$, the smaller is N_2 and the more collusive are country two's firms, as indicated by larger value of v_{12}^2 and v_{22}^2.

The equilibrium levels of prices in the two countries can be found from the inverse demand functions and the relationships,

$$\bar{x}_i = N_1 x_{1i}^* + N_2 x_{2i}^*, \qquad i = 1,2.$$

Then, for the case of two-country production with two-way trade, (10.2)–(10.5) imply these levels of equilibrium prices:

$$p_1^* = A_1 - \left(\frac{B_1}{D_1}\right)[N_1(A_1 - m_1)(1 + cv_2^1)]$$

$$+ N_2(A_1 - (m_2 + t_{21}))(1 + cv_1^1)) \qquad (10.6)$$

and

$$p_2^* = A_2 - \left(\frac{B_2}{D_2}\right)[N_1(A_2 - (m_1 + t_{12})](1 + cv_2^2)$$

$$+ N_2(A_2 - m_2)(1 + cv_1^2)). \qquad (10.7)$$

Here, D_1 denotes the denominator of equation (10.2) and D_2 denotes that of (10.4). Also,

$$cv_1^1 = v_{11}^1 + v_{21}^1, \qquad cv_1^2 = v_{11}^2 + v_{21}^2$$

$$cv_2^1 = v_{12}^1 + v_{22}^1 \text{ and } cv_2^2 = v_{12}^2 + v_{22}^2.$$

Thus far, there is little in this formulation other than notation that is special to the international context. For example, the home price given by equation (10.6) would obtain if there were no trade, but instead the home country had two types of firms: N_1 firms with a marginal cost of m_1, and n_2 firms with a marginal cost of $m_2 + t_{21}$, where each of the firms holds the specified conjectural variations. However, one feature that is fundamental to international markets is the incentive for each of the nations involved to make policy on the basis of its own welfare, rather than the welfare of all market participants. Then it will be critical below to assess home welfare as the sum of home consumer surplus, profits of home firms on home sales, and profits of home firms on foreign sales. In equilibrium, these components of home welfare are the three terms respectively, on the right-hand side of:

$$W_1 = \left(\frac{1}{2}\right) B_1 x_1^{-2} + N_1 B_1 (x_{11}^*)^2 (1 + cv_1^1) + N_1 B_2 (x_{12}^*)^2 (1 + cv_1^2) \quad (10.8)$$

It is important to note that this formulation, for the sake of simplicity, excludes consideration of possibly important additional welfare effects. These could include impacts on rents earned by domestic input factors, on domestic tax revenues, and on operational inefficiencies within domestic firms. Instead, it is assumed that domestic firms are neither taxed nor subsidized, that they operate efficiently, and that they purchase their inputs in competitive markets.

Analysis

The Number of Foreign Competitors

One possible index of the strength of the foreign competition is the sheer number of the foreign firms, N_2. Indeed, as the number of foreign firms increases, *ceteris paribus,* the price-cost margins ought to fall, both at home and abroad. Reference to (10.6) and (10.7) shows that as the number of foreign firms grows very large, the home price, p_1, approaches $m_2 + t_{21}$ from above, and the foreign price, p_2, approaches m_2 from above.

The effects on home welfare of increased international competition are, however, ambiguous. True, as N_2 grows larger, home consumers benefit because of lower prices. Home producers, however, lose profits both at home and abroad. The net impact depends on the share of imports in home consumption, $s_{21} \equiv N_2 x_{21}^* / \bar{x}_1$.

PROPOSITION 1. A small increase in the number of foreign firms lowers home welfare if

$$s_{21} < \frac{1}{2}, \tag{10.9}$$

provided that the change in N_2 does not affect the conjectural variations.

To prove this proposition, we first note that an increase in N_2 surely lowers the profits earned by home firms from their foreign operations, provided that these firms export anything. These earnings are represented by the last term in (10.8). Differentiating the rest of (10.8) with respect to N_2 yields an expression proportional to

$$(1 + cv_1^1)(1 + cv_2^1)[1 - 2(1 - s_{21})]. \tag{10.10}$$

Thus, if $s_{21} < 1/2$, the sum of home consumers' surplus and the profits of home firms from their domestic sales declines as N_2 increases.

While the conjectural variations do not have a direct influence on this conclusion, they do have an indirect influence through their impact on the shares of home and foreign firms in home consumption.

PROPOSITION 2. The share of imports in home consumption is a declining function of the conjectural variation held by foreign firms, and an increasing function of the conjectural variation held by home firms. That is,

$$ds_{21} / d(1 + cv_2^1) < 0 \text{ and } ds_{21} / d(1 + cv_1^1) > 0.$$

This follows directly by differentiating equations (10.2) and (10.4).

Of course, the import share is also sensitive to the degree of foreign competition as measured by N_2. Equations (10.2) and (10.3) reveal that $\partial s_{21} / \partial N_2 > 0$, so long as $0 < s_{21} < 1$. Notwithstanding this fact, $\lim_{N_2 \to \infty} s_{21} < 1/2$ if and only if $2N_1[m_2 + t_{21} - m_1] = (1 + v_{11}^1 + v_{21}^1)(A_1 - m_2 - t_{21})$. Thus, if home production costs are low relative to the cost of delivered imports, and if N_1 is sufficiently large, then s_{21} remains below

1/2 no matter how numerous are the foreign firms. In this case, by proposition 1, home welfare is larger the fewer are the importing firms.

Obversely, if the delivered cost of imports is less than home production costs, then for large N_2, foreign firms entirely replace home firms both at home and abroad. Here, domestic welfare is diminished by the loss of profit on home firms' foreign sales, but is increased by the replacement of home production for the domestic market by low-priced imports. This is illustrated by figure 10–1, where p^* is the autarky home oligopoly price, and the associated operating profits of home firms are given by the shaded area. With trade opened, N_2 large, and $m_2 + t_{21} < m_1$, the home price falls below m_1 and the gain in home consumers' surplus exceeds the lost profits to home firms from their domestic sales.

Avinash Dixit generalized the result of proposition 1 by allowing nonlinear demand schedules.[7] As one would expect, with general demand schedules, the welfare effect of an increase in the number of foreign firms does depend on the curvature of the demand schedule, as well as on the import shares if $(p' + x_{11}p'') - s_{21}(1 - s_{21})^{-1}p' < 0$ then $\partial W/\partial N_2 < 0$. Since stability of a Cournot equilibrium requires that $p' + x_{11}p'' < 0$, our proposition 1 follows, provided that $p'' \leq 0$.

We conclude that there is an international stake in the structure of industries. In particular, changes in the degree of concentration abroad affect home welfare. As foreign supply becomes less concentrated and more competitive, home welfare may be diminished.

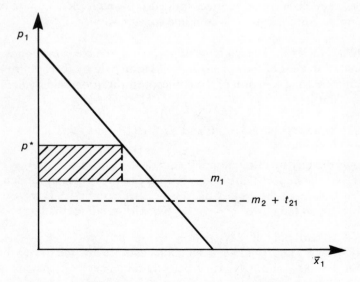

Figure 10–1. Domestic Welfare as a Function of International Competition

There is less ambiguity in assessing the constraining effects of foreign competition on the ability of home firms to elevate price as a result of a merger. Working from equation (10.6) we have that

$$\frac{\partial p_1}{\partial N_1} = \frac{B_1(1 + cv_1^1)(1 + cv_2^1)}{D_1} x_{11}^*.$$

Differentiating this expression with respect to N_2, we obtain

$$\frac{\partial p_1^2}{\partial N_1 \partial N_2} = -\frac{B_1(1 + cv_1^1)(1 + cv_2^1)}{(D_1)^2} \cdot \frac{\partial x_{11}^*}{\partial N_2} D_1 + (1 + cv_1^1)x_{11}^* > 0,$$

since $\partial x_{11}^* / \partial N_2 < 0$, and $cv_1^1 \geq -1$.

> **PROPOSITION 3.** The smaller the number of foreign firms, the greater the loss to home consumers from a merger between two home firms. (See figure 10–2.) In fact, at the point at which $x_{11}^* = x_{21}^*$, home firms and foreign firms are perfect substitutes in constraining price increases in the home country.

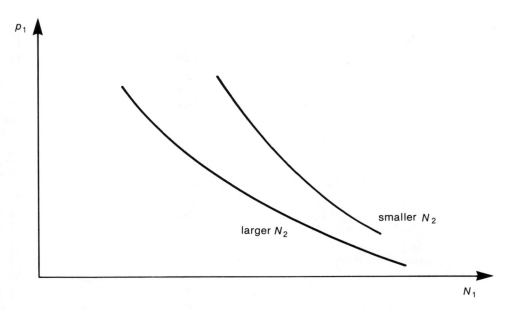

Figure 10–2. Home Consumers' Losses from Two Firm Mergers: N_1 and N_2 Variable.

We have conducted our analysis of mergers without paying attention to the question of profitability of mergers at home or abroad. Yet, in an industry in which conjectures do not increase as the number of firms falls (for example, in a "Cournot" industry), mergers are generally unprofitable, absent cost savings.[8] In order to model private merger incentives, one could postulate that a merger saves the merging partner a fixed cost of F. Then a merger can be profitable if the saving in fixed cost is sufficiently high to outweigh the loss due to the erosion in the combined market share. However, when a merger saves fixed costs, it can also benefit social welfare. In particular,

> **PROPOSITION 4.** The larger the number of firms, the more likely it is that a profitable cost-saving merger of two firms benefits social welfare. For example, in the no-trade situation, but given all the other assumptions of the model, a merger that is just profitable is welfare improving if $N^2 > 3/2 (1 + 2N)$, when $cv_1^1 = 0$.

To prove this proposition, we calculate and compare the values of profits and social welfare in situations in which the number of firms are N_1 and $N_1 - 1$. Then algebra yields the requisite inequality.

We have seen, however, that foreign firms are a substitute for home firms in restraining the upward effects on price of a domestic merger. Hence,

> **PROPOSITION 5.** The larger the number of foreign firms, the more likely it is that a profitable domestic merger elevates social welfare.

In other words, the more intensive is foreign competition, the more likely it is, within the confines of this model, that a domestic merger is motivated by cost efficiencies.

Export Subsidies

Export subsidies are often perceived as a powerful policy instrument for advantaging a domestic industry in its rivalry with foreign producers for profits and share in the world market. As was noted by Brander and Spencer,[9] an export subsidy improves the relative position of domestic firms *vis-á-vis* their foreign rivals and enables them to capture some of the rents that accrue to oligopolistic firms in the noncooperative market equilibrium. For the policy to generate added profits that exceed the subsidy payments, it must induce the foreign rivals to contract their output at a greater rate than the domestic firms themselves perceived that they could accomplish without government intervention.

We now consider the effects of export subsidies in the context of our model of constant conjectural variations. First, we examine the effect on the welfare of country one of a change in the subsidy, τ, that is applied to the export sales of firms in country two by their government. Differentiating equation (10.8) with respect to τ, we obtain

$$\frac{\partial W_1}{\partial \tau} = 2B_1 x_1 \cdot N_2 (1 + cv_1^1) D_1^{-1} - N_1 B_1 x_{11}^*(1 + cv_1^1) N_2 \qquad (10.11)$$

Rearrangement of (10.11) demonstrates the following:

PROPOSITION 6. The home country's welfare declines as a result of an increase in the export subsidy if the share of imports is less than 50% and it increases if that share is greater than 50%. That is, $\partial w_1/\partial \tau \gtrless 0$ as $s_{21} \gtrless 1/2$.

Here the intuition is clear: when imports are small relative to the home market, a small expansion in imports diverts rents (that is, monopoly profits) to the foreign country without inducing a substantial gain in consumers' surplus. When imports are large relative to the market, the subsidy benefits from home consumers more than it hurts home firms.[10]

It is important to note that the home country can exactly offset the effects of the subsidy by imposing a countervailing duty equal to τ. From the viewpoint of political economy, it appears to be more likely that such a duty will be imposed when the share of imports is large. Ironically, it is when s_{21} is large that the home country as a whole would benefit from the subsidy.

The incentives of the home country to receive subsidies can be compared with the incentives of the foreign country to apply them to its exports. We differentiate the welfare of country two with respect to the size of its export subsidy, τ:

$$\frac{\partial W_2}{\partial \tau} = \frac{N_2}{D_1} \{[p_1 - (m_2 + t_{21})](1 + N_1 + cv_1^1) \qquad (10.12)$$

$$- N_2 B_1 x_{21}(1 + cv_1^1)\}$$

Equating (10.12) to zero permits the following inferences concerning the subsidy level, τ^*, that is optimal for the welfare of country two.

PROPOSITION 7.

(i) If $cv_1^1 = -1$, so that home firms act as perfect competitors, then $\tau^* > 0$ iff $m_1 > m_2 + t_{21}$.

(ii) If $cv_1^1 = cv_2^1 = 0$, then $\tau^* > 0$ iff $N_2 < N_1 + 1$.

(iii) If $cv_1^1 \neq -1$, $\tau^* > 0$ iff

$$N_2 < \frac{(1 + cv_2^1)(1 + N_1 + cv_1^1)}{(1 + cv_1^1)}. \qquad (10.13)$$

Proposition 7 (iii) follows from (10.12) by rewriting $\partial W_2/\partial \tau = 0$ as

$$-\tau(1 + N_1 + cv_1^1) + [B_1 x_{21}(1 + cv_2^1)(1 + N_1 + cv_1^1)$$
$$- N_2(1 + cv_1^1)] = 0,$$

after using the first-order conditions for the optimum choice of x_{21} by an individual firm. The implications of (10.13) are summarized in proposition 8.

PROPOSITION 8. Positive export subsidization by the foreign government is less likely (1) the smaller is the home industry (N_1 small); (2) the larger is the foreign industry (N_2 larger); (3) the more collusive are the conjectural variations (cv_2^1) held by foreign firms (4) the more collusive are the conjectural variations (cv_1^1) held by home firms.

These results are quite intuitive. Where the foreign industry behaves competitively (because N_2 is large or cv_2^1 is close to -1), the foreign firms are already exporting too much, from the perspective of their total profit. Hence, a subsidy that further stimulates exports would only compound their problem. Also, when the home industry is behaving collusively, it already has restricted its market share and ceded share to foreign firms in the interest of home profits.

We conclude from proposition 8 that domestic mergers would reduce the incentives for subsidization of exports to the home market. To that extent, domestic mergers have additional negative effects on home consumers. On the other hand, export subsidies received by foreign firms increase their competitiveness and make domestic mergers less undesirable. Of course, the opposite is true of tariffs imposed on imports to the domestic market. To show this, we work from equation (10.6) to obtain

$$\frac{\partial p_1^2}{\partial N_1 \partial \tau} = \frac{B_1 N_2(1 + cv_2^1)(1 + cv_1^1)}{D^2} > 0.$$

Thus,

PROPOSITION 9. The more subsidized are foreign imports, the less adverse are the effects of a merger on consumers' welfare. However a merger may induce import subsidies to be curtailed, to the detriment of consumers' welfare.

Reliability of Foreign Competitive Constraint: Exhange Rate Fluctuations

It is generally recognized that foreign competition is an imperfect substitute for competition among domestic producers because the flow of imports is subject to vicissitudes which do not affect home supply. For example, the home country may impose import tariffs or quotas for political-economic reasons. Of, for macroeconomic reasons, the home currency may depreciate *vis-á-vis* foreign currency and make imports more costly.

In this section, we show how exchange rate fluctuations affect the ability of foreign firms to constrain the exercise of market power by home firms. We also investigate the importance of these fluctuations as a function of the size of the foreign and home industries. We introduce the role of exchange rate variability in the simplest possible way. We posit that production and transportation costs do not depend on the value of the exchange rate, only revenues do. This means that in either country there is no import content in the production and transportation of the commodity under consideration. Then, the profit in its own currency of a foreign firm from its exports to the home country (country one) is given by

$$(ep_1 - m_2 - t_{21})x_{21} = e[p_1 - m_2']x_{21}$$

where e is the exchange rate measured in terms of the units of foreign currency per unit of home currency, say (D.M./\$U.S.), and $m_2' = (m_2 + t_{21})/e$. With this formulation, exchange rate fluctuations translate into fluctuations in the full marginal costs of exports, for the purpose of analyzing the impact on x_{21}^*.

It follows that exchange rate fluctuations have real effects similar to those induced by changes in levels of export subsidy, which we have analyzed above. In particular, a devaluation of a foreign currency increases the value of e, lowers the full marginal cost of exports, and thereby stimulates exports. It is important to note here also that exchange rate fluctuations affect the volume of domestic firms' home sales only because they affect the flows of competing imports. The assumed constant returns to scale of variable production costs means that the volume of exports does not depend on the volume of output for domestic consumption.

For the sake of further simplicity, we here assume that all conjectural variations are zero, and differentiate p_1 with respect to m_2':

$$\frac{\partial p_1}{\partial m_2'} = \frac{N_2}{N_2 + N_2 + 1}.$$

Further,

$$\frac{\partial p_1^2}{\partial m_2' \partial N_1} = \frac{N_2}{(N_2 + N_1 + 1)^2} < 0,$$

Thus, $\partial p_1 / \partial e < 0$ and $\partial p_1^2 / \partial e \partial N_1 > 0$. Figure 10.3 depicts the effects of exchange rate fluctuations on the relationship between home price and home concentration. As shown, devaluation of the home currency (that is, a decrease in e), has especially adverse effects on price when N_1 is low. On the other hand, appreciation in the value of the foreign currency is especially stimulative of competition at low values of N_1. For merger policy, the implication is that the impact of devaluation on rivalry at home increases with the concentration of home industry. Another way to capture this insight is

> **PROPOSITION 10.** The absolute value of the elasticity of the home price with respect to the value of the foreign exchange rate decreases with the size of the home industry; that is
>
> $$\frac{\partial \dfrac{\partial p_1}{\partial e} \cdot \dfrac{e}{p_2}}{\partial N_1} > 0.$$

There is another significant way to investigate the effects of exchange rate fluctuations on the competitiveness of the home market and on domestic welfare. This is to focus on mean-preserving spreads in the value of the full marginal cost of foreign exports. If we restrict our attention to home welfare realized from home consumption and domestic profits, we see that its expected value is given by

$$E \tilde{W}_1 = + \tfrac{1}{2} B_1 N_2^2 (N_2 + N_1 + 1)^{-2} \sigma_{m_2'}^2 \tag{10.14}$$

$$+ B_1 N_1 N_2^2 (N_2 + N_1 + 1)^{-2} \sigma_{m_2'}^2.$$

In equation (10.14), C is a term that involves only the unchanging mean values of the relevant variables. Differentiating with respect to $\sigma_{m_2'}^2$, the variance of the full marginal cost of exports, shows that the domestic portion of the home country's welfare increases with the variance of m_2. This variance is positively related, in turn, to the underlying variance in the foreign exchange rate. Differentiating equation (10.14) with respect to N_1 and $\sigma_{m_2'}^2$ yields

$$\frac{\partial^2 E \tilde{W}_1}{\partial N_1 \partial \sigma_{m_2'}^2} = B_1 N_2^2 (N_1 + N_2 + 1)^{-3} (N_2 - N_1) \gtreqless 0 \tag{10.15}$$

as $N_2 \gtreqless N_1$.

This leads to

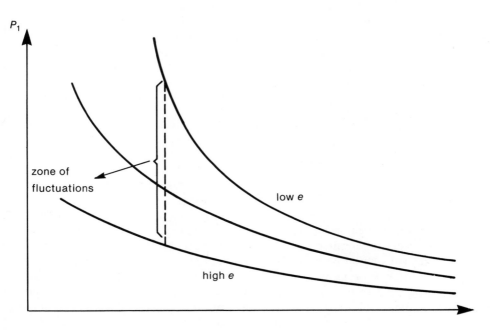

Figure 10–3. Exchange Rates and the Home Price-Concentration Relationship

PROPOSITION 12. The decrease in expected home welfare caused by a domestic merger is greater the larger is $\sigma^2_{m_2}$, for $N_2 > N_1$, and the smaller is $\sigma^2_{m_2}$, for $N_2 < N_1$.

Thus, if the principal restraint on doemstic market power arises from competition with imports ($N_2 > N_1$), then exchange rate volatility undermines protection against adverse welfare effects of domestic mergers. Obversely, if imports offer only secondary contribution to competition in the home market ($N_2 < N_1$), then exchange rate volatility magnifies the protection against the adverse effects of domestic mergers that is afforded by imports.

Finally, we can investigate how the number of foreign competitors affects the importance of the fluctuations in the rate of exchange for the home price. Not unexpectedly, the zone of home price fluctuations induced by exchange rate variability is wider the more competitive is the foreign industry (that is, the greater is N_2).

We have shown that the effect of a reduction in the number of domestic producers on home price is very sensitive not only to the number of foreign producers, but also to the value and variability of the exchange rate. This confirms to some extent the view that, *ceteris paribus,* foreign competition is a less reliable constraint on the market power of domestic firms than is domestic competition. Consequently, in merger analysis, while transnational market definition may certainly be appropriate, it should be used with due regard for its possible fragility.

Export Cartels and Transnational Mergers

U.S. antitrust law views export cartels with less disapproval than it does cartels whose main purpose is to elevate home price.

The model utilized in this paper suggests that export cartels are in general unprofitable, unless foreign and domestic firms that are not members of the export cartel cannot quickly expand their output, or if the cost savings from a cartel are substantial because, for example, the cartel obviates the need for parallel distribution networks. Those export cartels which constrict exports for the purpose of price elevation may in a variety of scenarios prove to be unprofitable. In addition, under some assumptions regarding home cost functions (for example, marginal costs fall as total output increases), a constriction in exports may increase home price even if the export cartel is not used as a vehicle for facilitating collusion over domestic price. Thus, preliminary analysis of export cartels based on the model developed here does not suggest any obvious or overwhelming welfare gains from export cartels. This does not mean that such gains cannot occur. It only means that different descriptions of the transnational marketplace may be necessary to capture these gains formally.

Transnational mergers combine the productive capacities of firms that are domiciled in two different countries. In the presence of cross-shipping, such mergers should be profitable because, at the very least, they permit rationalization of production and the avoidance of some or all transportation costs. Calculations reveal, however, that Cournot firms tend to squander some of these gains with noncooperative adjustments to the changed set of players. In particular, the merged firm is likely to produce less than the combined pre-merger output of the two firms that merged. The remaining firms expand their pre-merger outputs, but not enough to compensate for the removal of the active international trader. Thus, in models of this kind, we find that:

PROPOSITION 12. A transnational merger raises prices at home and abroad.

It is difficult to provide an easily interpretable expression that would enable us to assess the profitability of a transnational merger. Sample numerical calculations suggest, however, that a transnational merger is likely to be profitable if pre-merger transportation costs are high. In such circumstances, the cost savings might outweigh the price increases in their efforts on welfare.

This brief discussion suggests that our knowledge of merger incentives in the international context is still quite rudimentary. More sopisticated models of international competition must be developed before the full implications of such mergers can be assessed.

Concluding Remarks

We have attempted in this chapter to develop some implications of the new learning in international trade theory for antitrust policy in open economies. The discussion suggests that reconsiderations of this policy are necessary. First of all, a more activist competition policy in the home country may be undesirable from the narrow perspective of home welfare if it causes a reduction in rents that home firms extract from foreign consumers. Second, the efficacy of antitrust policy is intimately related to trade policy, through tariffs and quotas, and to macroeconomic policy, through the movements in rates of exchange and differential rates of cost and price inflation. This suggests that, in open economies, a coordination of industrial and macroeconomic policies becomes even more crucial than in (mostly) closed economies. Third, the efficacy of domestic antitrust policy is much influenced by industrial, trade, and macroeconomic policies abroad. Finally, analyses of trade and competition policy based on narrow domestic concerns, like the ones contained in this chapter, should be broadened to consider the perspective of international agreements among governments. These analyses have the potential for internalizing the negative externalities of policies that serve the interests of individual nations, so as to raise the welfare of all.

Notes

1. U.S. Department of Justice, Antitrust Division, Merger Guidelines 47 Fed. Reg. 28, 493, 28, 494 (1982.
2. Ibid.
3. U.S. Department of Justice, statement accompanying release of Review *Merger Guidelines (June 14, 1984), sec. 3, p. 12. See also Merger Guidelines* §K2.34, 2.4, and 3.23.
4. See, for example, J.S. Brander and P.R. Krugman, "A Reciprocal Dumping Model of International Trade," *Institute for Economic Research,* Queens University

(November 1980); J.A. Brander, "Intra Industry Trade in Identical Commodities," *Journal of International Economics,* 11 (1981).

5. A. Dixit, "International Trade Policy for Oligopolistic Industries," *Economic Journal* (Supplement), 84 (1984):5–16.

6. For reviews of this new research in international trade, see A. Dixit, 1984; G. Grossman and J.D. Richardson, "Strategic U.S. Trade Policy: A Survey of Issues and Early Analysis," NBER Research Progress Report (1984).

7. See A. Dixit 1984, 13–14.

8. See S.W. Salant, S. Switzer, and R.J. Reynolds, "Losses from Horizontal Merger: The Effects of an Exogenous Change in Industry Structure on Cournot-Nash Equilibrium," *Quarterly Journal of Economics,* 98 (May 1983):185–99; N.K. Perry and R.H. Porter, "Oligopoly and the Incentive for Horizontal Merger" (August 1983); mimeographed.

9. J.A. Brander and B.J. Spencer, "Export Subsidies and International Market Share Rivalry," NBER Research Paper No. 1464 (September 1984).

10. This result was generalized by Dixit (1984) to cover the case of nonlinear demand curves; see equation (10.14).

11
Capital Adjustment Costs, Monopoly Power, and the Regulated Firm

Robert S. Pindyck

I t is generally understood that in almost any industry, capital is a quasi-fixed factor of production. That is, there are significant *adjustment costs* that must be incurred when changing a firm's capital stock, and the more rapidly the stock is changed, the larger those costs are likely to be. This chapter examines some of the antitrust and regulatory implications of capital adjustment costs by addressing the following two questions:

1. In what way and to what extent is the monopoly power of a firm or group of firms affected by the presence of adjustment costs?
2. How are the effects of rate-of-return regulation altered by adjustment costs, and, in particular, will the standard Averch-Johnson effect hold during periods of capital adjustment?

These questions are of interest because any application of antitrust or regulatory policy to a firm or industry must usually begin with a diagnosis and measurement of monopoly power and an evaluation of the likely effects of a regulatory constraint.

Adjustment costs can affect a firm's degree of monopoly power because they introduce intertemporal constraints into the firm's production and pricing decisions. The monopoly power of a firm depends in part on its *total* marginal cost, which in a dynamic setting includes any relevant "user costs"—that is, the sum of (discounted) future costs or benefits resulting from current production decisions. Such user costs are present when there are costs of adjustment and the firm's capital stock is not in equilibrium. Thus, the monopoly power of a firm will vary, perhaps considerably, depending on whether it is increasing or decreasing its capital stock in response to changes in demand or other variables.

Such user costs can likewise alter the effects of rate-of-return regulation.

This work was supported by the National Science Foundation under Grant No. SES–8318990, and that support is gratefully acknowledged.

Given a current capital stock that is not in equilibrium (but that nevertheless appears as in the rate base), the firm's full marginal cost (including user costs) will differ from its "accounting" marginal cost and in a way that depends on whether the firm is in the process of increasing or decreasing its capacity. This in turn affects the firm's demands for capital and labor. We will see that as a result, the Averch-Johnson effect is enhanced during periods of contraction, but during periods of expansion it is reduced or even reversed.

We will begin by examining the effects of adjustment costs on monopoly power. To do that, however, we need a measure of monopoly power that is applicable to a dynamic market in which firms face intertemporal production constraints. In a recent paper (1985), I suggested such a measure and showed how the presence of user costs will bias the standard Lerner index. In the next section of this chapter I briefly review that measure (which in essence simply incorporates any relevant user costs in the calculation of "full" marginal cost).

Section 2 of this chapter then examines the effects of adjustment costs on a firm's degree of monopoly power. We will see that monopoly power is *reduced* during periods of expansion and *increased* during periods of contraction. Section 3 examines the regulatory implications of adjustment costs and in particular shows how the standard Averch-Johnson effect is altered. Section 4 briefly summarizes the results and offers some concluding remarks.

1. A Relevant Index of Monopoly Power

How does the presence of adjustment costs affect the actual or potential monopoly power of a firm or group of firms? To answer this question, we need a measure of monopoly power applicable to situations in which firms face intertemporal constraints. The commonly used Lerner index, $L = 1 - (MC/P)$, is not appropriate for our purpose; it is based on an assumption of static profit maximization, so that the firm produces where marginal revenue equals current marginal production cost.

As I have shown elsewhere (1985), the following generalization of the Lerner index does provide an *instantaneous measure* of monopoly power that is consistent with firms' intertemporally maximizing the expected sum of their discounted profits, subject to intertemporal constraints on production or price:

$$L^*(t) = 1 - (FMC_t/P_t) \tag{11.1}$$

Here FMC_t is the *full* marginal social cost at time t of producing the monopoly output level, and P_t is the monopoly price. (I am using the word "monopoly" to refer to any firm that has nonzero monopoly power.)

In equation (11.1), full marginal cost, FMC_t, includes any "user costs" that result from the intertemporal nature of the firm's optimization problem. However, these user costs are to be calculated under the assumption that the firm is a *price taker* (that is, competitive), so that they reflect the change in the present value of future discounted consumer-plus-producer surplus resulting from an extra unit of production.[1] Finally, as with simple marginal cost in the Lerner index, those user costs are to be evaluated over the *monopoly* output path.[2] With FMC_t calculated in this way, $0 = L^*(t) = 1$ for all t, and $L^*(t) = 0$ in a perfectly competitive market.[3]

$L^*(t)$ only measures monopoly power at an instant of time. In a market where production is intertemporally determined, however, one needs a measure that applies to the entire trajectory of production. Such a measure is obtained by calculating $L^*(t)$ over the monopoly output trajectory and then aggregating over time.

That aggregation requires the choice of a weighting variable. As I have explained elsewhere (1985), the relative impact of monopoly power at different points in time can be approximated by multiplying $L^*(t)$ by expenditure at time t, so that expenditure (rather than price or quantity) is the appropriate weighting variable. Weighting $L^*(t)$ in this way yields the following time-aggregated index of monopoly power:

$$I_m(t) = 1 - \frac{\int_t^\infty FMC(\tau)Q(\tau)e^{-r(\tau-t)}d\tau}{\int_t^\infty P(\tau)Q(\tau)e^{-r(\tau-t)}d\tau} \tag{11.2}$$

Note that this index is itself time-dependent. Looking into the future at a particular point in time, it describes the monopoly power of a firm, and as conditions change, so will the firm's monopoly power.[4]

We can now use this measure to evaluate the effects of adjustment costs on monopoly power. To do this, we must next determine the signs and magnitudes of any user costs that arise during the adjustment process.

2. Costs of Adjustment

A firm's long-run cost structure differs from that in the short run because it takes time to alter the capital stock and change the firm's production capacity. As Lucas (1967) and Gould (1968) have shown, one way to capture the time phenomenon is by assuming that there are convex costs of adjustment associated with changes in the capital stock (and/or changes in other factor input levels). In this section, I show that when adjustment costs are present, a firm will experience an (internal) capital gain or loss when it adjusts to a new long-run equilibrium position, and those capital gains (which occur as capacity is reduced) or losses (occurring as capacity is increased) are part of full marginal cost. As we will see, these costs *reduce* monopoly power during periods of industry expansion and *increase* it during periods of contraction.

For simplicity, we will assume in this section that output is a function only of capital, K, that is, $q = F(K)$, with $F'(K) > 0$ and $F''(K) < 0$, so that there are diseconomies of scale. The capital stock is assumed to be "quasi-fixed," so that the purchase and installation of "usable" capital at rate I involves a cost $vI + C(I)$, where v is the purchase price of a unit of capital, and $C(I)$ is the full adjustment cost, with $C(0) = 0$, $C'(I) > (<) 0$ for $I > (<) 0$, and $C''(I) > 0$. Here $C(I)$ includes the cost of installing the capital, training workers to use it, and so forth. Since these activities take time, $C''(I) > 0$, that is, it is more costly to increase capacity quickly than slowly.[5] Thus, firms are assumed to maximize:

$$\operatorname*{Max}_{I(t)} \int_0^{\infty} [p(q)q - vI - C(I)]e^{-rt}dt \qquad (11.3)$$

subject to

$$\dot{K} = I - \delta K \qquad (11.4)$$

where δ is the depreciation rate, and a dot denotes a time derivative, that is, $\dot{K} = dK/dt$. Note that *competitive* firms perform this maximization with $p(q) = \bar{p}$ taken as given.

It is easily shown that the optimal level of investment satisfies:

$$\dot{I} = \frac{1}{C''(I)}\{(r + \delta)[v + C''(I)] - MR \cdot F_K\} \qquad (11.5)$$

where MR is marginal revenue. (In a competitive market, $MR = AR = 0$.) The behavior of investment and the capital stock in competitive and monopolistic markets is characterized by the phase diagram of figure 11–1. In that figure, $\dot{K}_m^*$ and $\dot{K}_c^*$ are the steady-state equilibrium capital stocks in monopolistic and competitive markets. Because there are diseconomies of scale, in both markets $\dot{I} < (>) 0$ if $K(t) < (>) \bar{K}^*$.

In steady-state equilibrium (found by setting $\dot{I} = \dot{K} = 0$),

$$MR \cdot F_K = (r + \delta)[v + C'(I)] \qquad (11.6)$$

where the right-hand side of (11.6) is the cost of a marginal unit of capital. The marginal cost of an additional unit of output is then

$$MC = (r + \delta)[v + C'(I)]/F_K \qquad (11.7)$$

In equilibrium, the use of this "direct" marginal cost in the standard Lerner index would give an unbiased measure of the degree of monopoly power.

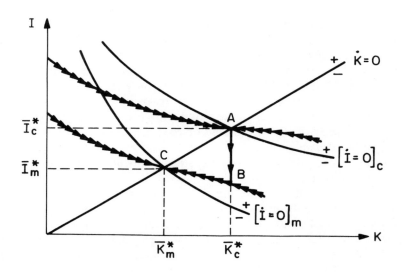

Figure 11–1. Phase Diagram

Furthermore, this "direct" marginal cost can itself be measured—it is simply the *amortized capital outlay* required to increase production capacity by one unit.

In disequilibrium, however, *full* marginal cost is not equal to direct marginal cost. Equating full marginal cost with marginal revenue, observe from equation (11.5) that

$$FMC = MC - C''(I)\dot{I}/F_K \qquad \qquad *(11.8)$$

The value to the firm of the marginal unit of capital is its total purchase and installation cost, $v + C'(I)$, so that $C''(I)\dot{I}$ is the *rate of capital gain* on the unit, and $C''(I)\dot{I}/F_K$ is the corresponding capital gain in terms of a marginal unit of production capacity.

Suppose the firm is growing so that $K(t) < \bar{K}^*$. Then we will have $\dot{I} < 0$ and $FMC > MC$. The reason is that as $K(t) \rightarrow \bar{K}^*$, the marginal profit rate is falling, so that the value to the firm of a marginal unit of capital is also falling. This capital loss *raises* the full marginal cost of additional production capacity. This in turn *reduces* the firm's monopoly power. Conversely, suppose that the firms in a competitive market cartelize and agree to reduce their aggregate production capacity to a monopoly level (path ABC in figure 11–1). As they do so, each incremental reduction in capacity raises the marginal profit rate and bestows a capital gain. As a result, during the adjustment process, $\dot{I} > 0$ and $FMC < MC$, and monopoly power is *increased*.

In periods of adjustment, the standard Lerner index is therefore a biased measure of monopoly power. The actual degree of monopoly power will depend on whether output is growing or contracting (and cannot be determined simply from an elasticity of demand). The bias in the Lerner index is positive during periods of industry expansion and negative when industry output is contracting.

The latter case is important, and the effect is often ignored in analyses of the potential monopoly power from collusion. If producers cartelize and replace output in an industry that had been competitive, the cartel's monopoly power will exceed the value that would be inferred from the market demand curve (even if that demand curve is static). The bias is largest in the early periods ($\dot{I} \to 0$ as $K \to \bar{K}_m^*$), but depending on the discount rate and the size of marginal adjustment costs $C'(I)$ relative to v, it may be sufficient to affect significantly the time-aggregated index of monopoly power, I_m.[6]

3. Regulatory Implications of Adjustment Costs

We now turn to the implications of capital adjustment costs for the theory of the regulated firm. In particular, should we expect the standard Averch-Johnson (1962) effect to hold when firms are in the process of adjusting their capital stock to changing demand or cost conditions?

As before, we assume that the purchase and installation of a unit of "usable" capital at the rate I involves a cost $vI + C(I)$. Now we also introduce labor as an aggregate *flexible* input. Thus, the firm's instantaneous profit is now given by:

$$\Pi(t) = p(q)q - wL - vI - c(I) \tag{11.9}$$

where w is the cost and L the quantity of the flexible input (for example, labor), and $q = F(K,L)$ is a strictly quasi-concave production function. The firm's capital stock again evolves according to:

$$\dot{K} = I - \delta K \tag{11.10}$$

where δ is the depreciation rate.

The regulatory agency sets a "fair" rate of return $s > (r + \delta)v$, but in practice the firm's actual rate of return may often exceed s, or be less than s, particularly over short periods of time. To capture this, we assume that the firm perceives a penalty function $\phi(x)$, with $\phi(x) = 0$ for $x \leq 0$, ϕ, ϕ', $\phi'' = 0$, for $x = 0$, and x is the difference between the firm's total return on its capital stock and the "fair return," that is,[7]

$$x = p(q)q - wL - C(I) - sK \tag{11.11}$$

It should be stressed that the introduction of this penalty function describes a *mode of behavior*. There is no actual cash flow corresponding to $\Pi(t) - \phi(x)$; the cash flow to the firm is just $\Pi(t)$. However, function constrains the behavior of the firm so that, although its price can vary, its return is on average close to the regulatory guideline, but can deviate from the guideline by larger amounts over short periods of time.

The use of this penalty function allows us to capture some basic behavioral constraints without having to introduce a complicated model of regulatory lag and regulatory review. Although there is no cash flow corresponding to $\Pi(t) - \phi(x)$, the firm will behave *as if* a process of regulatory lag and review gave it the opportunity to earn more than the fair rate, especially over short periods of time. Also, note that by the proper choice of $\phi(x)$, we can force the firm to keep its return arbitrarily close to the fair rate. This approach therefore provides a flexible but analytically convenient framework that lets us focus on the regulatory effects of dynamic adjustment.[8]

The firm's problem, then, is to maximize:

$$\underset{L,I}{\text{Max}} \int_0^\infty [\Pi(t) - \phi(x)]e^{-rt}dt \tag{11.12}$$

where r is a rate of time discount. The maximization is subject to equation (11.10) and to the conditions $L(t)$, $K(t) = 0$. Note that $[C(I) + vI]$ is strictly convex, so we need not impose a nonnegativity constraint on I (that is, the firm can sell off excess capital, but will incur an adjustment cost in doing so).

The solution of this problem is straightforward. Write the Hamiltonian as:

$$H = [\Pi(t) - \phi(x)]e^{-rt} + \lambda(I - \delta K) \tag{11.13}$$

Maximizing with respect to L gives $MR \cdot F_L = w$, where $MR = p + q(\partial p/\partial q)$ is marginal revenue. Maximizing with respect to I gives the undiscounted shadow price of a unit of capital:

$$\lambda e^{rt} = [1 - \phi'(x)]C'(I) + v \tag{11.14}$$

The right-hand side of (11.14) is the cost of a unit of capital in terms of the *firm's* objective function; the cost is reduced by an amount $\phi'(x)C'(I)$ because the adjustment cost associated with the unit reduces the firm's return, and therefore reduces the penalty associated with regulation.

Differentiating equation (11.14) with respect to time and substituting $-\partial H/\partial K$ for $\dot{\lambda}$ gives the equation for $\dot{I}$ describing the optimal investment trajectory. Setting $\dot{I} = 0$ in that equation gives the following equilibrium condition:

$$MR \cdot F_K = (r + \delta)[v + C'(I)] + \phi'(x)[MR \cdot F_K - (r + \delta)C'(I) - s] \quad (11.15)$$

This equation, together with the conditions $I = \delta K$ and $MR \cdot F_L = w$, gives the equilibrium values of K, I, and L. The equation just says that in equilibrium the marginal revenue product for the last unit of capital should equal the amortized "direct" marginal cost of the unit plus the marginal penalty cost (which may be negative) associated with the effect of the unit on the return on capital.

Now observe that equation (11.15) can be rewritten as:

$$MR \cdot F_K = (r + \delta)[v + C'(I)] + \frac{\phi'(x)[(r + \delta)v - s]}{1 - \phi'(x)} \quad (11.15')$$

Since $s > (r + \delta)v$ by assumption, the last term in (11.15'), and thus the last term in (11.15), is negative. Therefore one effect of regulation is to increase unambiguously the absolute size of the firm's equilibrium capital stock. (Note that this is not true in the static A-J model, for reasons that are spelled out clearly by Baumol and Klevorick 1970).

Dividing equation (11.15) by the equation $MR \cdot F_L = w$ gives the following for the marginal rate of technical substitution in equilibrium:

$$\frac{F_K}{F_L} = \frac{(r + \delta)[v + C'(I)]}{w} - \frac{\phi'(x)[s - (r + \delta)v]}{w[1 - \phi'(x)]} \quad (11.16)$$

Observe that the *efficient* marginal rate of technical substitution is given by the first term on the right-hand side of equation (11.16). We have $s > (r + \delta)v$ by assumption; and since[9] $0 < \phi'(x) < 1$, the firm's input choice is inefficient, that is, the capital-labor ratio is greater than that which minimizes cost. Thus, the standard A-J result holds in equilibrium.[10]

What happens during the adjustment to equilibrium? Regulation will still induce an inefficiency, but the direction of that inefficiency is no longer clear and will depend on the initial capital stock, production function, and so forth. Furthermore, it may change during the adjustment process. To see this, obtain an expression for $\dot{\lambda}$ from the condition $\dot{\lambda} = -\partial H/\partial K$, combine this with equation (11.14) and rearrange to give the following optimality condition:

$$MR \cdot F_K = (r + \delta)[v + C'(I)] + \phi'(x)[MR \cdot F_K - (r + \delta)C'(I) - s]$$
$$- (d/dt)(\lambda e^{rt}) \tag{11.17}$$

This differs from equation (11.15) only by the last term, which is the rate of capital gain (as perceived by the firm) on the marginal unit of capital. Now divide (11.17) by $MR \cdot F_L = w$ and rearrange to obtain:

$$\frac{F_K}{F_L} = \frac{(r + \delta)[v + C'(I)] - (d/dt)(\lambda e^{rt})}{w} - \frac{\phi'(x)[s - (r + \delta)v]}{w[1 - \phi'(x)]}$$

$$- \frac{\phi'(x)(d/dt)(\lambda e^{rt})}{w[1 - \phi'(x)]} \tag{11.18}$$

In the absence of regulation, $\phi'(x) = 0$ and the firm produces efficiently, with its marginal rate of technical substitution equal to the ratio of its factor costs. (Note that the cost of capital is now the amortized purchase plus adjustment cost, *less* the implicit rate of capital gain.) But with regulation effective, there are now two terms contributing to inefficiency in the factor mix. The second term on the right-hand side of (11.18) also applies in equilibrium, and as long as regulation is effective (that is, $x = 0$) leads to overcapitalization. However, the sign of the last term in (11.18) is ambiguous and depends on the initial capital stock and the trajectory to equilibrium. In particular, if the initial capital stock is too small (for example, if there is a sudden and unexpected increase in demand), the last term (after the minus sign) will be negative, and, if it is large enough in magnitude, it will imply *undercapitalization*. The opposite will be the case if the initial capital stock is too large.

To see that undercapitalization is possible, suppose demand unexpectedly increases by a large amount, and consider the firm's adjustment to a new equilibrium. Following the increase in demand, revenue will rise, x will be large, and both $MR \cdot F_K$ and $s\phi'(x)$ will be large relative to terms in $C'(I)$ and v. As can be seen from equation (11.17), the rate of change of λe^{rt} will therefore be negative. (As one would expect, the sudden increase in demand raises the value to the firm of a unit of capital, and that value falls to a new equilibrium level as the capital stock is increased.) The last term in equation (11.18) would then have the effect of *raising* F_K/F_L, and reducing—or even reversing—any A-J effect. Note that this result hinges on the fact that the firm incurs adjustment costs as it increases its capital stock in response to the demand shift, but these costs, while "embodied" in the added capital, are not part of the rate base.

Thus, the net effect of regulation depends on the particular path of adjustment. During periods following unanticipated *drops* in demand, the degree of regulation-induced overcapitalization will be greater, but during periods following unanticipated *increases* in demand, the effect will be smaller or even reversed.

4. Concluding Remarks

This chapter has examined the implications of capital adjustment costs for two related problems: the determination of a firm's or group of firms' actual or potential monopoly power, and the extent to which the Averch-Johnson effect can be expected to hold in a world of dynamic adjustment. In both cases, simple models have been used to isolate the effects of the adjustment process.

Using an index that is consistent with the presence of intertemporal production constraints, we have shown that monopoly power is increased or decreased, depending on whether the firm is (respectively) contracting or expanding its production capacity. The reason is that the presence of adjustment costs creates an internal capital gain or loss, that in turn reduces or increases the firm's full marginal cost of additional production. Note that this effect might help to explain the empirical work of others that shows little evidence of significant long-run monopoly power in the U.S. economy.[11] Given that on average industries are expanding, the existence of adjustment costs will reduce long-run monopoly power.

Using a model of rate-of-return regulation that allows the firm to deviate temporarily from the allowed rate, we found that the Averch-Johnson effect will hold in long-run static equilibrium, but that the effect is reduced or even reversed during periods of capacity expansion. Of course the model we have used is a simple one that ignores a number of issues that may be important. For example, for many firms, capital cannot be adjusted continuously, but instead is "lumpy." Also, we have assumed that any capital purchased by the firm is used in production, whereas in fact, firms can hold excess capacity, and thereby reduce adjustment costs. Finally, we have assumed that only capital inputs are costly to adjust, while in fact long-term contracts and union agreements might imply adjustment costs for labor as well.[12]

Nonetheless, our results might help to explain why empirical work has thrown doubt on the actual existence of an Averch-Johnson effect.[13] Again, on average regulated firms have been expanding their capacity, and depending on the magnitude of adjustment costs, this should reduce or reverse any A-J effect.

Notes

1. It is important to distinguish between monopoly and competitive user costs, as they are derived from different objective functions. The monopoly output path maximizes the sum of discounted profits, and monopoly user cost is the reduction in that sum resulting from one extra unit of cumulative production. The competitive output path maximizes the sum of discounted consumer-plus-producer surplus, and competitive user cost is the reduction in that sum from an extra unit of cumulative production. (Competitive user cost will exceed monopoly user cost because consumer-plus-producer surplus exceeds the monopolist's profit.) Since a measure of monopoly power should make a comparison with competitive conditions, or equivalently (in the absence of externalities) with the social welfare maximum, it is competitive user cost that should be added to marginal cost in calculating *FMC*.

2. Just as marginal cost is measured at the monopoly output level when calculating the standard Lerner index in a static model, competitive user cost must be calculated using the monopolist's output path. In this way FMC_t is the full marginal social cost of producing the monopoly output.

3. For applications of this measure to examples such as exhaustible resources and learning by doing, see Pindyck (1985).

4. This is important in the context of antitrust; $I_m(t)$ might be high initially so that antitrust action seems warranted, but such action will be of little value if it takes considerable time to implement and $I_m(t)$ falls rapidly over time.

5. For a general discussion of adjustment costs and their effects, see Nickell (1978). As in Nickell, I assume that adjustment costs are a function of *gross* investment. This means that the firm will have some positive cost even if it is not expanding its capital stock. This implies diseconomies of scale, so that the firm has a determinate size even if the production function is homogeneous of degree 1.

6. For empirical evidence on the size of marginal adjustment costs for U.S. manufacturing as a whole, see Pindyck and Rotemberg (1983).

7. Note that adjustment costs are treated as noncapital expenses and therefore are subtracted from revenue in calculating the firm's return. We are assuming here that the adjustment process requires additional labor costs, outside consulting services, and so forth, but does not require the purchase of additional capital. The simplest way to view this is to consider that outside consulting and engineering firms are employed to handle all adjustment problems.

8. A high rate of inflation combined with regulatory lag works against a regulated firm, and in recent years many regulated firms have earned *less* than the "fair" or "allowed" rate. With the proper choice of $\phi(x)$, that is, so that $\phi, \phi', \phi'' > 0$ for $x > x_0 < 0$, the model can be adapted so that the realized rate will be below the allowed rate.

9. If $\phi'(x) = 0$ regulation would be ineffective, so clearly $\phi'(x) > 0$. If $\phi'(x) = 1$, equation (11.16) becomes $s = (r + \delta)v$. Since $s > (r + \delta)v$ by assumption, $\phi'(x) \neq 1$. Finally, note that since $MR \cdot F_L = w$ always, for equation (11.16) to define a *maximum*, we must have

$$\frac{\partial}{\partial K}\{[(1 - \phi'(x)]MR \cdot F_K - (r + \delta)[v + C'(I)] + (r + \delta)\phi'(x)C'(I) + s\phi'(x)\} < 0$$

or, $[1 - \phi'(x)](\partial MR \cdot F_K/\partial K) < 0$. Since the marginal revenue product of K declines with K by assumption, we must have $\phi'(x) < 1$.

10. Note that regulation shifts the firm's output level. Equation (11.16) says the K/L is greater than that which minimizes cost at the new level of output.

11. See, for example, the recent paper by Salinger (1984). That paper suggests that any monopoly power that might exist is largely captured by unions. Our results here help (but do not fully) explain why that monopoly power might be small to begin with.

12. The results in Pindyck and Rotemberg (1983) indicate that this is *not* the case; adjustment costs on labor are small, both in absolute terms, and relative to capital adjustment costs.

13. For a survey of some of the evidence, see Joskow and Noll (1981). Of course there may be other reasons for a failure to observe an A-J effect. For example, Baumol and Klevorick (1970) show that the regulated firm will undercapitalize if its objective is the maximization of revenue rather than profit.

References

Averch, H., and L.L. Johnson. 1972. "Behavior of the Firm Under Regulatory Constraint." *American Economic Review* 52:1053–069.

Baumol, William J., and Alvin K. Klevorick. 1970. "Input Choices and Rate-of-Return Regulation: An Overview of the Discussion." *Bell Journal of Economics* 1:162–90.

Gould, John P. 1968. "Adjustment Costs in the Theory of Investment of the Firm." *Review of Economic Studies* 35:47–55.

Joskow, Paul L., and Roger N. Noll. 1981. "Regulation in Theory and Practice: An Overview." In *Studies in Public Regulation,* ed. G. Fromm, 1–65. Cambridge: The MIT Press.

Lucas, Robert E. 1967. "Adjustment Costs and the Theory of Supply." *Journal of Political Economy* 75:321–34.

Nickell, Stephen J. 1978. *The Investment Decisions of Firms.* Cambridge: Cambridge University Press.

Pindyck, Robert S., and Julio J. Rotemberg. 1983. "Dynamic Factor Demands under Rational Expectations." *Scandinavian Journal of Economics* 85:223–38.

Pindyck, Robert S. 1985. "The Measurement of Monopoly Power in Dynamic Markets." *Journal of Law and Economics.* Forthcoming.

Salinger, Michael A. 1984. "Tobin's q, Unionization, and the Concentration-Profits Relationship." *Rand Journal of Economics* 15:159–70.

12
Illogic and Unreality: The Odd Case of Ultra-Free Entry and Inert Markets

William G. Shepherd

T he peculiar notion of "contestability" was first published in 1982, amid fanfare led by William J. Baumol, its primary author.[1] Within a year, some influential economists had already set it aside as passé, an "uprising" that had sunk.[2] Yet the Baumol group continues to promote it as a momentous new system, and many young careers are being committed to it.[3] This notion of "contestability"—which actually is just an analysis of the special case of *ultra-free entry* into *inert markets*—may eventually contribute something to economic analysis. But it has already caused much confusion and, I believe, distraction from the mainstream issues in industrial organization.

Though I have noted its main defects elsewhere, there is a need to extend several of the points and to discuss real cases in more detail. Therefore, I will reassess its logical problems in section 1 and consider empirical patterns and cases in section 2. The conclusion will be that the idea has even less weight than I had noted previously, while there are substantial harms from treating it as a leading, new approach.

1. Conceptual and Logical Problems

The task is to define competition in accurate, meaningful concepts, so that it and its effects can be studied. Hundreds of scholars have done so for over fifty years, as the modern field of industrial organization has developed.[4] "Contestability," and important features of "sustainability," seek to replace that literature with eccentric cases labeled in odd jargon.

Before exploring the defects of the new theory, one needs to note that the term "contestability" is itself confusing and meaningless. Note how extreme its three key assumptions are:

I am indebted to Joe S. Bain, to members of the Five College Seminar on Industrial Organization and to participants in a Smith College seminar for further discussion of these ideas.

1. *Entry is free and without limit.* A new firm can do far more than gain a foothold quickly, as conventional free entry envisages. The entrant can immediately duplicate and entirely replace any existing firm, even a complete monopolist. There are no costs or significant lags in entry, and the entrant can match all dimensions of size, technology, costs, product array, brand loyalties, and other advantages of all existing firms. Entry is, in short, *ultra-free.*
2. *Entry is absolute.* The market is inert: the entrant can establish itself before an existing firm makes any price response. If the entrant obtains an advantage, even a tiny price difference, it will prevail absolutely and displace the existing firm, with no interaction or sequence of moves. This assumption of no response holds even if a pure monopolist faces elimination and would have to abandon its monopoly pricing entirely.
3. *Entry is perfectly reversible.* Exit is perfectly free, at no sacrifice of any cost. Sunk cost is zero. These conditions are pure, and the deductive results hold only when they hold. Under any departures from the pure conditions, the Baumol group's deductive analysis becomes merely speculative.

In markets where there are any departures from the pure assumption, the issues are part of the normal world where the familiar standards of market power still apply.

In the interests of clarity, the term "contestability" should be excluded in discussing all such realistic cases, because it adds no economic meaning and it causes confusion.[5] "Contest-able" seems to cover a range of complex, real conditions, and the Baumol group has often slipped into claiming that it does. But to do so is incorrect. The correct approach is to say the obvious: where degrees of competition and entry are in question, one must judge them by the established criteria in the literature.

To sum up, "contestability" is a vague term that has recently been applied to one extreme theoretical case. It implies degrees of variation that are not permissible for inert markets with ultra-free entry.

For the Baumol special case, I have proposed the expression "ultra-free entry"; one may also use the phrase "inert market," because it accurately reflects the lack of incumbent's response. Both phrases correctly apply just to the extreme case, with no confusion about degrees of "contestability."

Problems of Assumptions

The Model's Key Assumptions Contradict Each Other. The model assumes that any new competitor is so *small* that the existing firm will not bother to react to it at all (the Bertrand-Nash basis). This permits *assumption number 2* above, that no response occurs. It gives the entrant time to get fully established, so as to replace the incumbent before it can strike back. But to replace the incumbent totally and instantly (*assumption number 1* above), the newcomer must enter on a *large* scale, especially if it is replacing a full monopolist.[6]

The two assumptions are diametric opposites. Entry cannot be both trivial and total; to claim that it can is ridiculous! If entry is trivial, it has no force. If it is total (or even merely large), the incumbent will respond. Indeed, the incumbent's actions will be fiercest precisely when it is a monopolist facing total elimination.

This contradiction renders "contestability" illogical at its core.

Entrants Do Not Have Primacy over Existing Competitors. The theory of inert markets assumes that entry has supreme force, superseding existing rivals already in the market. Instead, as the literature has long held, the existing rivals in the market are the main force of competition. If competitors already exist (for example, trucks already competing with railroads), then "contestability" has nothing to say about that competition. The truckers who have not yet entered have less force than those already in. To focus on the possible entrants as if they were crucial is to misplace reality.

The Total Entry Assumption (Number 1 Above) Is Quite Silly in Any Event. In no significant real market could an established monopolist be totally replaced, instantly, by a bare newcomer. Such replacement is likely only for small firms in already competitive markets.

The absurdity of total entry unfortunately infects also the Baumol group's analysis of "sustainability," which focuses precisely upon complex established multiproduct monopolies (such as AT&T), which in turn are assumedly faced by instant total displacement. In that analysis, the Baumol group presents the regulated monopoly firm as being fragile and vulnerable to entry. The monopoly firm is likely to reach an optimal result, but only if it is protected from entry. Such a strange model departs sharply from the growing literature that utilities are strong and often wasteful under regulation and that competition can often improve their economic performance.[7]

The main assumptions of the Baumol group analysis are given in the left-hand side of table 12–1. Regulation is assumed by the Baumol group to be "ideal": omniscient and all-powerful. Optimal prices and outputs are known and enforced. This result holds even if the regulated firm is a multiproduct producer with complex joint-production and overhead costs.

Under natural monopoly conditions (assumption 2) and ideal regulation, the firm offers the ideal set of products at "Ramsey" prices which maximize consumer surplus.[8] Since there is unlimited reselling of products (assumption 3), the monopolist can set only one price for each product. The Baumol

Table 12–1
Assumptions for "Sustainability" Analysis

1. *Regulation is ideal.* Regulators' information and powers are complete, and their actions impose ideal results without any friction or delay. The monopolist produces the socially ideal set of products, under regulation. The monopoly earns zero excess profits.

1. Actual regulation is usually imperfect, incomplete, and lagged. The firm has wide discretion in product offerings. Profits are often well above zero.

2. *Costs.* For the single-product firm, there are large economies of scale. For multiple-product firms, there are high joint and overhead costs.

2. Cost conditions vary, in both scale economies and joint costs.

3. *Reselling.* All products can be freely resold among customers, so that only one price can be set by the monopolist for each product.

3. Reselling is usually not feasible, except for certain limited products. Price discrimination is usually possible.

4. *Nature of the products.* (1) No distinction is made between core goods (crucial to the firm's survival) and adjacent goods. All are treated as if they were core products. (2) The monopolist's and entrants' goods are identical items; no variation is permitted, either at the start or as events unfold. (3) The social value of goods is reflected only in demand conditions (including consumer surplus).

4. The products vary, both among core and adjacent services and between the established firm's products and entrants' products. Social values often go beyond demand conditions.

5. *Technology* is transparent (both the existing conditions and possible future choices). It is as completely known and and accessible to entrants as it is to the monopolist. The regulators also have complete knowledge of present and alternative future technologies.

5. Actual and alternative technologies are often complex and incompletely known to outsiders.

6. *Frictions in adjustments.* There are none. Changes are instantaneous.

6. Frictions and irreducible lags in adjustments are often large.

7. *Barriers to entry.* There are none (other than those created by scale economies or joint costs in the multiproduct case). Barriers to entry by low-cost firms can only be provided by actions of the regulators.

7. Barriers to entry are often large and have many sources.

8. *Competitive advantages of the monopolist (in knowledge, financial ties, customer loyalty, experience, etc.).* There are none.

8. The monopolist often has large advantages over entrants.

Table 12–1 (continued)

9. *Responses or preemptive actions by the monopolist.* There are none, and the entrant expects none to be made (by the "Cournot-Nash" assumptions).	9. The monopolist typically responds sharply to new entry, and entrants usually expect retaliation by price cutting or other actions.
10. *X-efficiency and innovation.* The monopolist is expected to optimize them under perfect regulation.	10. Monopoly effects on innovation often remain. Also, the side effects of regulation itself often raise costs and enlarge investment (the cost-plus and rate-base effects).

Source: Adapted from Shepherd 1982b.

group does not consider the nature or relative importance of these various products (core or adjacent; large or small volume). Nor does the Baumol group permit the firm or new entrants to vary the products as the action proceeds. By assumptions 5 through 8, the monopolist is completely exposed to entry, without advantages, frictions, or barriers. Nor by the Bertrand-Nash assumption (number 9) is the monopolist expected to retaliate at all against entrants, or even to threaten a response.

It seems obvious that these assumptions are self-defeating: they contradict the reality that the analysis is intended to clarify. The right side of table 12–1 summarizes actual conditions in regulated firms, based on the rich literature on these subjects (for example, Kahn 1971). Assumptions 2, 4, and 10 are doubtful in most cases. Assumptions 1, 3, and 5 through 9 are radically inaccurate.

The Baumol group has indicated at some points that its analysis is merely an "exercise," not pretending to deal with real sectors. Certain assumptions (especially number 9) are needed only to make the analysis "tractable" and to give "insights." Yet the results have been presented forcefully as if they have great relevance, and they are gaining acceptance as being important and conclusive. Therefore one must judge the relation of the Baumol group analysis to reality. As table 12–1 indicates, it is virtually nil.

The Static Context

The Baumol group theory is primarily *static,* analyzing the effects of ultra-free entry into inert markets only on consumer surplus.[9] The group admits that it omits questions of dynamic processes and innovation, equity, and other social criteria. Yet it still makes sweeping claims for the normative power of its theory.

Instead, the omitted values may swamp the niceties of the Baumol group's short-run static-efficiency results. As Schumpeter (1942) urged, the yields from innovation can quickly dominate the static effects of monopoly. The contrast between Schumpeter and the Baumol group is striking, because the Baumol group's theory of total displacement of a monopolist would be precisely Schumpeterian.[10] But its analysis wholly misses the Schumpeterian point and has nothing to say about innovation and true competitive *processes*.

Gradients

Even if entry could supersede all internal imperfections, actual entry-exit conditions will usually deviate from the perfect inert-market assumptions. Robustness is then crucial: what gradients apply? Do small deviations result in large departures from efficiency? Or *vice versa*?

The gradients on entry are known to be significant, though not large (as the next section shows). Here, in the context of inert markets, the only novel issue is the gradients on *exit*. Two contrasting possibilities are illustrated in figure 12–1, which relates exit (as embodied in sunk costs) to price-cost ratios. (Entry barriers are assumed to be smaller than exit barriers.) P_1 represents the ratio caused by internal market power and entry barriers, if exit is fully blocked (by sunk costs S_1). If inert-market theory is robust, then the "strong" exit-price function A might exist, close to a competitive price-cost ratio of 1.0 over a large range. Alternatively, the "weak" exit-price function B rises close to the monopoly price-cost ratio even when sunk costs are small, at S_2; there, the internal features of market power exert nearly full effects. Among other possibilities, the intermediate function C may be likely.[11]

Note that in both functions A and B, the slopes are equal between S_2 and S_3. Prices are largely invariant with sunk costs over that large range. In fact, any significant linear slope between the two variables over that range (such as along curves A, B or C) does not test for robustness in the crucial range where sunk costs are low.

Of course each industry with ultra-free entry may have a different exit-price function, lying anywhere in the space above 1.0. But it is the average function that matters here, for it governs the importance of exit as a general phenomenon. The Baumol group analysis implies that A is common. If instead B is typical, then the theory of inert markets itself is of little importance, even where its assumptions are fully met.

The Incorrect Analogy to Pure Competition

The Baumol group often likens its theory to that of pure competition, as an ideal case. All markets are imperfect in some degree, they say, and yet the theory of competition is a powerful guide for results when conditions are *partly* competitive. Why can't contestability theory be accepted as a guide for conditions which are partly, or nearly, "contestable" in the pure sense?

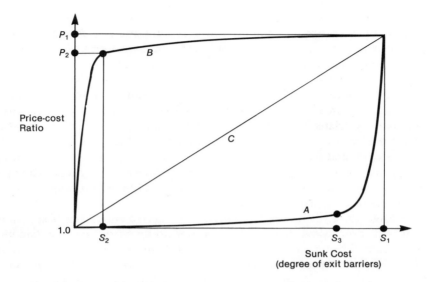

**Figure 12–1. Alternative Relationships between Sunk Cost and Price-Cost
Ratios**

The answer is that it can't be accepted for two reasons. One is that contestability theory has a fatal logical flaw at its core, in the clash between the
assumptions of total entry and trivial entry (as I have noted above). Pure
competition contains no such crucial flaw.

The other reason is that *contestability theory tries to draw lessons about
monopoly, at the opposite extreme from pure competition.* It concludes that
ultra-free entry will nullify a total monopolist. If entry is only "nearly" free or
"partly" free, the Baumol group would like to claim that the monopolist is
still strongly restrained.

But that is decidedly *not* similar to saying that nearly pure competition
gives close to pure-competitive results. As research since Bain's seminal work
in 1956 has shown, a monopolist can devise many ways to forestall "partly"
free entry. Therefore, the deductive conclusion about ultra-free entry, if it
holds at all, holds only for the pure case. There is no inductive basis for confidence that a "little" deviation from ultra-free entry in inert markets will
cause only a "little" departure from static-efficient results.

Internal and External Conditions are Correlated

As the literature has long recognized (see Shepherd 1972, 1979; and Bain
1956), there is a correlation between the internal degree of monopoly and the

238 • Antitrust and Regulation

height of entry and exit barriers. Consequently, there are likely to be few cases combining internal monopoly with free entry and exit. And conversely, ultra-free entry (or a close approximation to it) is most likely to occur where internal conditions are already fully competitive.

Past discussions have shown that complex forces are involved, and so the causation is not simple or precise. One cause is economies of scale, which can breed both high market shares and high barriers to entry and exit (sunk costs are usually associated with the costs involved in economies of scale). Another cause is the incentive structure. A dominant firm has high incentives to create entry barriers, and that can be done in many ways (for example, by adopting sales-promotion or strategic pricing policies). Conversely, firms already protected by entry barriers have incentives to raise their market shares (possibly by merger) so as to exploit the potential profits more fully.

In table 12–2, the range of internal and external conditions is shown in condensed form. Most markets are expected to lie on or near the diagonal from A to P. The field has focused on cells J–L and N–P; the Baumol group looks elsewhere, especially at cells C and D. Few cases are likely to be found in cells C, H, I and H, and scarcely any in the corner cells D and M.

Indeed, D and M are probably unstable cases, existing only briefly. A pure monopoly facing free (and strong) entry will probably either (1) undergo a decline in market share, as entry proceeds, thereby shifting the market to cells C, B, and perhaps A; or (2) create entry barriers to protect its position, thereby migrating to cells H, L, and possibly P; or (3) some mixed outcome. Rather than a static analysis of cases in cell D, as if they were stable, a dynamic analysis of adjustment may be needed. Equivalent lessons apply to cell M.

Table 12–2
A Matrix of Internal and External Structure

Entry and Exit Barriers	Degree of Internal Monopoly			
	Loose Oligopoly or Lower	Tight Oligopoly	Dominant Firm	Pure Monopoly
None (perfectly free entry and exit)	A 0	B 0	C 0	D 0
Low	E 16	F 2	G 0	H 0
Moderate	I 9	J 30	K 5	L 0
High	M 0	N 8	O 2	P 0
Shares in the U.S. Economy, 1980[a]	76%	18%	3%	3%

Sources: for the matrix, data from Shepherd 1983b; for shares in the U.S. economy, Shepherd 1982a.

[a]National income originating in industries with the specified degree of internal monopoly.

In fact, the expected correlation between internal structure and entry barriers has been repeatedly observed (see also Scherer 1980, ch. 3). The two conditions interact; high barriers breed high market shares and concentration; and *vice versa*. Also, potential entrants are numerous mainly when actual competitors are also numerous, in competitive industries with small economies of scale.

As a result, there are few significant markets in cells *D* and *M* of table 12–2. In 1972, for example, seventy-two major U.S. industries were distributed approximately as shown in table 12–2.[12] None were in *D* and *M;* indeed, there were none in any of the six cells above the *A–P* diagonal (cells containing industries are shaded). There is no reason to expect other sectors to add many cases for cells *D* and *M*.[13] Indeed, the total share of pure-monopoly and dominant-firm markets in the U.S. economy is only about 6%, as shown in the bottom line of table 12–2.[14] If cases of nullified high internal monopoly constitute in turn only a small share of those cases, they will be an insignificant share in the whole economy.

In sum, the theory of ultra-free entry into inert markets (that is, both "contestability" and "sustainability") is marked at its core by defects and contradictions. Its possible "insights" are gained only under bizarre assumptions; instead of a new, powerful general theory, we seem to have here only an odd special case. Moreover, it faces a steep uphill route to gain empirical relevance.

2. Empirical Evidence

The main difficulty in appraising the factual relevance of the Baumol group theory is that the weight and breadth of evidence is so overwhelmingly against the theory. Over five decades of statistical analysis, case studies, and intensive debate have established that internal structure is predominant. Conceivably, new research can up-end these extensive and consistent findings, but that will require an astounding reversal of a massive research literature.

Main Lines of Established Research

This literature, as summarized in Bain (1968), Scherer (1980), and Shepherd (1979), is too complex to rehearse here. It is of course well known to all serious scholars in the field, although the Baumol group gives it few references. One of the clearest contrasts of the Baumol group view with the literature can be found in my own econometric results in testing for the effects of structural elements upon profitability (Shepherd 1972, 1975, 1979). The essentials are shown in tables 12–3 and 12–4 and figure 12–2. Market shares have a substantial role, separate from that of entry conditions. Entry barriers

Table 12–3
Basic Analysis of Profitability of Large U.S. Industrial Firms, 1960–69

Dependent Variables	Constant Term	Independent Variables						
		Market Share M	Concentration C	Group G	Size (log of assets) S	Advertising Intensity A	Growth E	R^2
Profit rate, 1960–69	5.13 (5.92)[a]	.250 (12.19)		.028 (1.60)	-.182 (1.34)	.021 (4.39)	.792 (3.93)	.554
Profit rate, 1960–69	4.38 (4.22)		.105 (5.57)		-.175 (1.06)	.024 (4.04)	1.28 (5.31)	.344

Source: W.G. Shepherd, *The Treatment of Market Power* (New York: Columbia University Press, 1975).
[a]*t*-ratios are in parentheses.

Table 12–4
The Role of Entry Barriers as an Element of Structure

Dependent Variables	Constant Term	Independent Variables					
		Market Share	Group	High Barrier	Medium Barrier	Growth	R^2
All 245 large firms Profit rate, 1960–69	4.58 (4.60)[a]	.251 (11.81)	.001 (0.05)	2.45 (2.84)	1.55 (2.64)	.925 (4.36)	.528
202 firms with medium or low barriers Profit rate, 1960–69	4.49 (5.16)	.239 (10.65)	-.001 (0.03)		1.69 (3.03)	.881 (4.29)	.518
71 firms with low barriers Profit rate, 1960–69	5.39 (4.20)	.175 (5.14)	.019 (0.68)			.807 (3.80)	.461

Source: Shepherd, *Treatment of Market Power*.
[a]*t*-ratios are in parentheses.

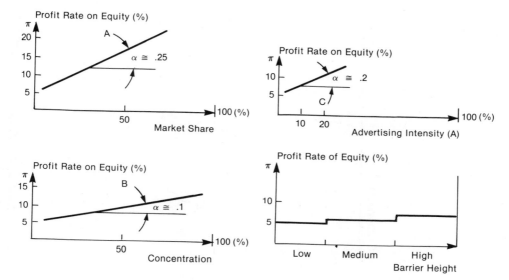

Source: Shepherd, *Treatment of Market Power.*

Figure 12–2. Estimated Relationships between Profitability and Market Share, Concentration, and Advertising Intensity

have at most a moderate, secondary influence; high barriers add only about 2.5 points to the profit rate, while market shares of 70% add about 17 points, which is seven times as much.

Moreover, in table 12–4, market share has a large role, even for firms which have low entry barriers (line 3). This directly contradicts the Baumol group theory. A more recent testing of the entire model, up to 1975, confirms the basic patterns (see table 12–5). Market share's role is even larger (the coefficient rises from .25 to .29), while size and advertising (two possible elements of barriers) have less of a role. Indeed, absolute size now has even a larger negative effect on profits: the coefficient is larger and now statistically significant.

New research by Leonard Weiss and colleagues (Brannman, Klein, and Weiss 1983) further reinforces the importance of market share. They show that the number of bidders (for bond underwriting, offshore oil leases, and national forest timber) strongly affects the price of the winning bid. Open bids involve free entry and exit, so the Baumol group theory would predict that no effect of market numbers and market shares occurs.

Figures 12–3 and 12–4 present the patterns graphically for two of those cases. Going from one monopolist bidder to two equal duopolists has a very big impact on price. It reduces the effect of the pure monopoly on price by

Table 12-5
Analysis of Elements of Structure, 1960–75 (182 Large U.S. Manufacturing Corporations)

Dependent Variable	Constant Term	Market Share	Rivals (C–M)	Size (Log of Assets)	Ad/Sales Ratio	Growth	R^2	F
(1)	(2)	(3)	(4)	(5)	(6)	(7)	(8)	(9)
Profit rate on equity 1968–75	+4.32 (2.25)	+.29 (10.89)	−.04 (1.96)	−.54 (2.13)	.00 (.01)	1.89 (5.87)	.50	35.4
Profit rate on equity 1960–69	+7.69 (5.16)	+.29 (12.49)	−.04 (2.02)	−.72 (3.66)	+.22 (4.25)	+.40 (1.88)	.63	60.2

Dependent Variable	Constant Term	4-Firm Concentration	Size (Log of Assets)	Ad/Sales Ratio	Growth	R^2	F
(1)	(2)	(3)	(4)	(5)	(6)	(7)	(8)
Profit rate on equity 1968–75	+3.28 (1.47)	+.14 (6.35)	−.51 (1.72)	+.01 (1.80)	+2.00 (5.33)	.32	20.8
Profit rate on equity 1960–69	+7.34 (3.94)	+.12 (6.01)	−.73 (2.97)	+.29 (4.48)	+1.03 (4.01)	.42	31.8

Source: further testing of my large-firm data bank.

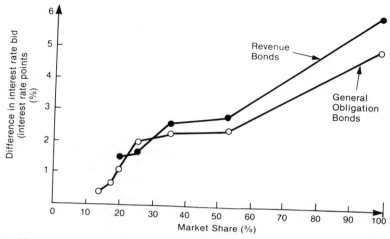

Source: "Comments by William G. Shepherd: Discussion of 'Concentration Winning Bids in Auctions'," *The Antitrust Bulletin,* vol. XXIX, no. 1, Spring 1984. Reprinted with permission of Federal Legal Publications, Inc.

Note: Low bids win, so high bids reflect monopoly effects.

Figure 12–3. Effects on Interest Rates in Winning Bids by Underwriters

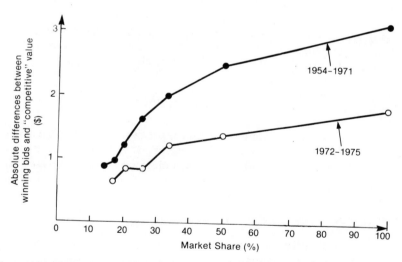

Source: "Comments by William G. Shepherd: Discussion of 'Concentration Winning Bids in Auctions'," *The Antitrust Bulletin,* vol. XXIX, no. 1, Spring 1984. Reprinted with permission of Federal Legal Publications, Inc.

Note: The predicted competitive bid is 7.4 for 1954–71 and 12.9 for 1972–75 (see the constants in table 4, Brannman, Klein, and Weiss). The absolute deviations shown on the vertical axis indicate the effect of monopoly.

Figure 12–4. Effects on Bid Prices for Offshore Oil Leases

about one third, on average (between one-half in bond bids to one-fourth in some oil and timber leases). This suggests that my own regressions would extend with a substantial (perhaps constant) slope in the range up to 100% market shares, if data were available for testing those high market shares. By extending research into this upper range of near and actual monopoly, the Weiss paper makes a large contribution.

The Baumol Group's Research Design

The Baumol group has offered virtually no factual research supporting its theory. The one statistical study (done as part of a proposed Ph.D. dissertation) has serious flaws of methods and data, which I have discussed elsewhere (Shepherd 1984). The research plans of the Baumol group deserve quoting; they come at the end of the book, after frequent earlier references to this research, which will validate their approach. They propose

> Determination of the structural contestability of a market requires evaluation of the costs of entry and exit and of the magnitude of unavoidable sunk costs. In particular, the availability of resale markets for durable inputs and their usability in other activities (fungibility) must be investigated since, clearly, the less the financial loss incurred in such a transfer, the lower will be the costs that are truly sunk and the smaller will be the costs of exit. It will also be essential to have a description of the sources of entry and exit costs as well as of the sunk costs to determine whether these costs can readily be reduced by appropriate policy measures. For example, if sunk costs are increased by legal inhibitions to the formation of resale markets, appropriate remedial measures may suggest themselves. Finally, it will be desirable to determine how entry costs are affected by the size of the potential entrant, that is, to estimate the $E(y)$ function roughly. (BPW, p. 469)

All of these are complex phenomena, needing precise, thorough discussion and tests. But here they are only vaguely mentioned, with no clear research design. This offers little likelihood of making a mark on established research, much less reversing its findings.

Possible Cases, Especially Airlines and Railroads

Important cases could give the ultra-free entry inert-markets theory valuable support. But they too are lacking.

There are no recognized actual cases of entry-dominated monopolists: that is, markets where incumbents hold large market shares but could be easily replaced, and where the firms do not respond quickly to competitive challenges. At first, the Baumol group presented airlines (after deregulation) as its leading case. Airline capital appears to be mobile and entry could be rapid. Yet the evidence shows that monopoly power is still exerted in the standard patterns: airlines with high market shares tend to set higher price-cost ratios. Airlines are mainly concerned with their *actual* rivals, not the possibility of new ones. They respond swiftly and sharply to price actions, in many cases within hours. They strongly defend their market positions, and nothing close to instant replacement of dominant positions has occurred.

Therefore, the contestability assumptions do not hold, and the supposed ultra-free entry has not restrained important areas of monopoly power which remain in the airline sector. The industry closely fits the established analysis of market structure. The Baumol group itself has now largely given up airlines as an example of contestability.[15]

Other possible instances might include long-distance telephone service. But entrants there were unable to gain more than 9% of that market during the four years, 1979–83, even though AT&T was prevented from matching their prices. And AT&T is now taking strong price actions. The newcomers, in any event, have had no conceivable chance to replace AT&T completely (in line with the first assumption), either instantly or in a matter of years. But contestability can be seen not to apply to this centerpiece Baumol group case.

Railroads are another of the few cases offered by the Baumol group, but as an example, they too are unsatisfactory. First, intermodal competition does exist in varying degree, but *that is not "contestability" and new entry*. It is simply a recognition that in some areas there is some degree of interaction between trains, trucks, barges, and other forms of transport. The task then is to define the markets carefully to include true overlaps and then consider the market shares of each of the carriers. The share held by a railroad in a given market will suggest whether or not it has market power.

Trying to fit these markets into a "contestability" model is arbitrary and wrong. Of the three assumptions for a "contestable" market, the first two are strongly violated.

1. *Instant replacement.* Could trucks instantly and totally replace railroads, such as the merged Santa Fe–Southern Pacific? No! In some geographic areas and with some classes of goods, trucks could not replace railroads effectively at all, because railway costs are lower.
2. *No response.* Are railroads strictly passive in response to truckers' tactics? No. They now respond vigorously in a variety of competitive settings.
3. *A zero sunk cost?* Not in this case. Although trucks can be moved quickly, a trucking firm's initial commitment in planning, warehousing, system support, and developing shipper's trust, usually involves some significant sunk cost.

Yet, in testimony before the ICC, we find Professor Baumol making sweeping claims about the merger of the Santa Fe and Southern Pacific railroads (Baumol 1984). These are the only railroads in the "southern corridor" between Los Angeles and Texas, and their joinder would create a rail monopoly in the corridor, subject to some degree of intermodal competition from trucks and barges. The complexity of this merger and its impacts poses major research issues. Many commodity classes are involved, some subject to intermodal competition, some not (because railroad costs are lower than costs of other modes).

Yet Professor Baumol testifies that this merger will cause no rise in market power whatever. His reasoning attempts to convert trucking and barge operations (which surely can have some effect on many classes of freight) into a limitless force because they involve ultra-free entry into inert markets. In the following representative quotations, note the peremptory tone and the absolute conclusions:

> The point in all this is that the contestability of trucking and barge operations precludes market power to both these transport modes even in geographic markets where the number of such transport firms currently in operation happens to be small. But the contestability of these modes—the ease of their exit from and entry into individual geographic markets—also denies market power to any merged railroad along any route and for any type of freight which is currently carried to any extent by either road or water transport. Indeed, the presence of one or the other in a geographic transport market contributes a type of constraint upon market power which even the presence of another railroad cannot. For if the two railroads were not to compete as vigorously as might be desired, in the absence of trucking or water carriers, the market mechanism could do nothing to force stronger rivalry upon the railroads. But in a market where trucks or water carriers can enter, excessive pricing or poor service by two railroads (or even one) becomes a lure and must attract incursions by the more mobile carriers, which will soon enough bring the hypothetical railroads' attempt at monopolistic behavior to an end.

> . . .Thus, the availability of just one type of close competitive option, particularly if that role is played by contestable barges or trucks, is all that is needed for tight constraint of pricing by the merged railroad, and for effective preclusion of all exercise of market power.

> . . . there is only a small proportion of the expected traffic of the combined railroad which will not continue to be subject to substantial intramodal rail competition. That traffic, and most of the remainder, moreover, will face competition from road or water transportation. If this is true, it is simply not possible for a merger to serve as a source of market power, for any attempt to exercise such power will elicit a competitive response that must undermine it.

> On these grounds alone, I am led to conclude that any argument for a rejection of this merger is untenable. For as was explained earlier, once it is shown that no anticompetitive consequences are to be feared from a merger, public interest grounds for its rejection evaporate.[16]

I have quoted Professor Baumol at length to indicate how far the "suggestions" and "insights" of the theory are being stretched in other contexts. The key terms here are deductive and strict: "precludes," "denies," "must," "simply not possible," and "any argument . . . is untenable." The distinction between "might" have an effect, "will often" have some effect, and "must have a total effect," has been forgotten. In this theorist's checkerboard world, conditions are entirely one way or the opposite. Gradations of probability and strength of effects are assumed away and ignored.

The Santa Fe–Southern Pacific railroad merger is a "mega-merger," the largest one pending in the United States in 1984. Every experienced specialist knows that it will raise market power in at least some substantial transport markets. Yet "contestability" is urged here in flat, definitive terms, as if it were some sort of magic wand that can make reality irrelevant. The certitude displayed here by Professor Baumol contrasts with the greater balance and care shown in his recent published discussion of railroads and trucking (Bailey and Baumol 1984), a paper that was subject to professional standards of publication.

The railroad testimony suggests that the dangers of the Baumol group's theory constitute more than just a source of confusion and diversion of professional research, especially for impressionistic young scholars. The theory's ideas also encourage extravagant claims in the advice given on important policy issues.

3. Conclusions

The Baumol group's handling of the theory of ultra-free entry and inert markets raises disturbing questions of scientific method and responsibility. Of course, the creation of ideas must always precede the testing and validation of ideas, and so one would never wish to oppose imaginative thinking, per se. But that creative action may verge on irresponsibility if it ignores much of the literature and makes repeated exaggerated claims for normative lessons.

This disproportion between large real-world claims and the absence of a real-world basis for the theory's premises would not be acceptable in graduate-level papers, much less in published work. Here the eminence of the authors has had a large impact. Also, their notions about ultra-free entry and inert markets have been packaged with other issues, in their analysis of multi-product cost questions. These two special advantages have imparted to the contestability notion a glamour which it could not gain on its own merits.

The usual pruning of bright new ideas to a proper place in the literature must be quite severe in this case. It would be better had the Baumol group done the trimming itself, by testing its ideas in some degree before rushing them out with incautious claims. It would also be wise for the group to avoid further exaggerations about the normative lessons, until a significant research basis has been prepared.

In the meantime, the burden has been placed on others to do the pruning, by pointing out the flaws and limits of these notions. This negative role is not a comfortable one, and so I look forward to the day when ultra-free entry and inert markets are placed in their proper small niches in the literature. The mainstreams of concepts and evidence in the field of industrial organization are broad and deep. They can accommodate the Baumol group ideas nicely, as long as the evaluation is careful and balanced.

Notes

1. The main source is Baumol, Panzar, and Willig (1982; cited as BPW hereafter), which includes a laudatory foreword by Bailey and whose chapters are adaptations of many individual papers. See also Baumol's summary (1982), Bailey and Baumol's review of cases (1984), and Kessides's empirical paper (1982). To take a few examples of the self-praise to be found in this literature, contestability is termed "a new theory of industrial organization," which "will transform the field and render it far more applicable to the real world" and be "extraordinarily helpful in the design of public policy" (BPW 1982, xii, xxii). The invisible hand "seems to rule almost everywhere" that ultra-free entry exists (Baumol 1982). And "we hope to provide a unifying framework for a pure theory of industrial organization where none was available before" because the pieces of the previous literature "are generally disconnected" (BPW 1982, 3). The aim of the theory is "ambitious" and the contributions are "fundamental" (BPW 1982, vii, 1).

The odd assumptions of ultra-free entry had, however, been part of the "sustainability" notion offered by the Baumol group several years earlier. For a critique of that notion, and its assumptions, see Shepherd (1982b) and section I of this chapter.

2. My reservations about it are offered in Shepherd (1984). See also Weitzman (1983), Schwartz and Reynolds (1983), Scherer (1983), and Brock (1983). Recent criticisms include Tye (1984a, 1984b), Schwartz and Reynolds (1984), and Helwege and Hendricks (1984a, 1984b).

In general, some theorists find the ultra-free entry, inert markets approach attractive as an analytic treatment for simplifying the study of complex markets. Among others, especially the experienced specialists in industrial organization, the reaction ranges from puzzlement to derision.

3. See Bailey and Baumol (1984) and Bailey, Graham, and Kaplan (1983) for laudatory arguments. Baumol (1984) has also insisted that railroad markets have ultra-free entry, so that the Santa Fe–Southern Pacific railroad merger could not create any market power in the southwestern United States (see section two for a discussion of that case).

The Baumol group discussions include citations of many young theorists who have developed dissertations or essays on specific subissues (see Baumol 1982, and BPW 1982, for references). Currently many dissertations are being devoted to finer points of the model; the theory is easy to understand, and it requires little knowledge of real markets or of the field of industrial organization.

4. On the mainstreams in the field see Shepherd (1984; 1979, chap. 2), Kahn (1971), Blair (1972), and Scherer (1980).

5. I am assured by Professor Baumol that *contestability* has no special linguistic basis, nor did it result from any major effort to discover the most precise possible term. Rather, it just occurred to him.

My alternative wording—"ultra-free entry" and "inert markets"—represents an attempt to reflect exactly what the Baumol group notion is about. Perhaps some other term will eventually be attached to this specific theoretical case.

6. Professor Baumol has suggested that, instead, entrants can offer long-term contracts as a plausible way to obtain total entry before response can occur. Entry occurs, as it were, with a stroke of a pen rather than by the physical creation of the entrant's capacity. Indeed, the contract itself could apparently become a tradeable item with a market value equal to the incumbent's possible rents.

But this suggestion is too easy. It merely transfers the action to contracting wars, and it assumes that incumbents are unable to wield any advantages in offering their own long-term contracts. The same contradictory assumptions still apply, but now in a slightly different setting. Indeed, the incumbent could set standing offers to beat all credible offers by entrants, thereby rendering them not credible and therefore weightless.

7. My discussion here draws on Shepherd (1982b), but the issues are much wider than what I cover here, and the reader is encouraged to consult the whole paper.

8. "Ramsey" was Frank Ramsey, whose 1927 note on taxation provided a simple rule for minimizing the impact of taxes. The BBWP analysis has adapted this rule for the declining cost, inevitable deficit case of a public utility.

9. The Baumol group does try a "dynamic" model in their "sustainability" discussion of the fragile multiproduct regulated monopolist. But its assumptions are as bizarre as those of the one-period analysis: it covers only a two-period comparison, not a process or sequence; and its conclusions bear little relation to any real market (see Shepherd 1982b). The Baumol group theory remains a short-run, static theory, confined to deductions about consumer surplus.

10. The anti-Schumpeterian direction of the Baumol group theory is explored perceptively by Helwege and Hendricks (1984c).

11. For an interesting similar analysis, in more detail (focusing on curves *B* and *C* only), see Schwartz and Reynolds (1984).

12. The seventy-two industries are illustrative; they are the industries in which the 1982 large firms of my large-firm data set are located. This panel is the one whose patterns are reported in table 12–5. The panel is closely similar to those used in Shepherd (1972, 1975, 1979).

13. The Bailey-Baumol survey paper (1984) offers only four possible cases: railroads, airlines, trucking, and telephone service. But their discussion is now only tentative and ambivalent; contestability ideas are only "suggestive" and provide "some framework for discussion." Yet, as I will note in discussing all four cases, Professor Baumol is still making sweeping claims for definitive conclusions (Baumol 1984).

14. Those shares are from my study of the trend of competition in the U.S. economy (Shepherd 1982a).

15. This emerges from their recent discussion (Bailey and Baumol 1984) in which they concede that the behavioral assumptions have not held in the short run. Since their theory is a short-run theory, the admission is a major one.

16. The quotations are from pp. 17–18 and 20–21 of his Verified Statement (Baumol 1984).

References

Bailey, Elizabeth E., and William J. Baumol. 1984. "Deregulation and the Theory of Contestable Markets." *Yale Journal on Regulation* 111–13.

Bailey, Elizabeth E., David R. Graham, and Daniel P. Kaplan. 1983. *Deregulating the Airlines: An Economic Analysis*. Washington, D.C.: Civil Aeronautics Board.

Bain, Joe S. 1956. *Barriers to New Competition*. 1956. Cambridge: Harvard University Press.

———. 1968. *Industrial Organization,* rev. ed. New York: John Wiley.

Baumol, William J. 1982. "Contestable Markets: An Uprising in the Theory of Industry Structure." *American Economic Review* 72:1–15.

———. 1984. "Verified Statement." ICC Finance Docket 30300, April 2.

Baumol, William J., Elizabeth E. Bailey, and Robert D. Willig. 1977. "Weak Invisible Hand Theorems on the Sustainability of Prices in a Multiproduct Natural Monopoly." *American Economic Review* 67:360–65.

Baumol, William J., John C. Panzar, and Robert D. Willig. 1982. *Contestable Markets and the Theory of Industry Structure*. San Diego: Harcourt Brace Jovanovich.

Blair, John M. 1972. *Industrial Concentration*. New York: Harcourt Brace Jovanovich.

Bork, Robert H. 1978. *The Antitrust Paradox*. New York: Basic Books.

Brannman, Lance, Douglas Klein, and Leonard W. Weiss. 1983. "Winning Bids in Five Types of Auctions: Concentration Matters." Paper presented at the EPO Tenth Anniversary Seminar on Economics and Antitrust, EPO 83–13, Antitrust Division, October.

Brock, William A. 1983. "Contestable Markets and the Theory of Industry Structure: A Review Article." *Journal of Political Economy* 91:1055–66.

Caves, Richard E., and Michael E. Porter. 1976. "Barriers to Exit." In *Essays in Industrial Organization in Honor of Joe S. Bain,* ed. Robert T. Masson and P. David Qualls. Cambridge: Ballinger.

———. 1977. "From Entry Barriers to Mobility Barriers." *Quarterly Journal of Economics* 91:241–61.

Chamberlin, Edward H. 1962. *The Theory of Monopolistic Competition*. 8th ed. Cambridge: Harvard University Press.

Clark, John Bates. 1907. *Essentials of Economic Theory*. New York: MacMillan.

Clark, John Maurice. 1923. *Studies in the Economics of Overhead Costs*. Chicago: University of Chicago Press.

Comanor, William S., and Thomas A. Wilson. 1979. "The Effects of Advertising on Competition: A Survey." *Journal of Economic Literature* 17:453–76.

Graham, David R., Daniel P. Kaplan, and David S. Sibley. 1983. "Efficiency and Competition in the Airline Industry." *Bell Journal of Economics* 14:118–38.

Helwege, Ann, and Ann Hendricks. 1984a. "Contestability and Creative Destruction: Two Approaches to Monopoly." Discussion paper, Tufts University, July 1984.

———. 1984b. "Dynamic Considerations in the Regulation of Contestable Markets." Discussion paper, Tufts University, September 1984.

Heywood, John S. 1982. "Empirical Studies of Entry Barriers." University of Michigan. Manuscript.

Kahn, Alfred E. 1971. *The Economics of Regulation.* 2 vols. New York: John Wiley.

Keeler, Theodore E. 1981. "The Revolution in Airline Regulation." In *Case Studies in Regulation,* ed. Leonard W. Weiss and Michael W. Klass. Boston: Little, Brown.

Kessides, Ioannes. 1982. "Toward a Testable Model of Entry: A Study of the U.S. Manufacturing Industries." Princeton University. Manuscript.

Kwoka, John E. 1979. "The Effect of Market Share Distribution on Industry Performance." *Review of Economics and Statistics* 61:101–9.

Landes, William S., and Richard A. Posner. 1981. "Market Power in Antitrust Cases." *Harvard Law Review* 937–96.

Marshall, Alfred. 1920. *Principles of Economics.* 8th ed. London: Macmillan.

Martin, Stephen. 1983. *Market, Firm, and Economic Performance.* Monograph Series in Economics and Finance, New York University.

Neumann, John von, and Oskar Morgenstern. 1944. *Theory of Games and Economic Behavior.* Princeton: Princeton University Press.

Peltzman, Sam. 1977. "The Gains and Losses from Industrial Concentration." *Journal of Law and Economics* 20:229–63.

Posner, Richard A. 1979. "The Chicago School of Economic Analysis." *University of Pennsylvania Law Review* 127:925–48.

Ravenscraft, David J. 1983. "Structure-Profit Relationships at the Line of Business and Industry Level." *Review of Economics and Statistics* 65:22–31.

Robinson, Joan. 1933. *The Economics of Imperfect Competition.* London: Macmillan.

Scherer, Frederic M. 1980. *Industrial Market Structure and Economic Performance.* 2d. ed. Boston: Houghton Mifflin.

———. 1982. Open review letter on "Industry Structure Analysis and Public Policy." Northwestern University, June 15, 5 pp.

Schmalansee, Richard. 1982. "Another Look at Market Power." *Harvard Law Review* 95:1789–1816.

Schwartz, Marius, and Robert J. Reynolds. 1983. "Contestable Markets: An Uprising in the Theory of Industry Structure: Comment." *American Economic Review* 73:488–90.

———. 1984. "On the Limited Relevance of Contestability Theory." Economic Policy Office Discussion Paper, EPO 84–10, Antitrust Division, September.

Shepherd, William G. 1970. *Market Power and Economic Welfare.* New York: Random House.

———. 1972. "The Elements of Market Structure." *Review of Economics and Statistics* 54:25–37.

———. 1975. *The Treatment of Market Power.* New York: Columbia University Press.

———. 1979. *The Economics of Industrial Organization.* Englewood Cliffs, N.J.: Prentice-Hall.

———. 1982a. "Causes of Increased Competition in the U.S. Economy, 1939–1980." *Review of Economics and Statistics* 64:613–26.

———. 1982b. "Competition and Sustainability." In *Deregulation: Appraisal Before the Fact.* ed. Thomas G. Gies and Werner Sichel. Ann Arbor: University of Michigan Business School.

————. 1982c. "Monopoly Profits and Economies of Scale." In *Industrial Organization, Antitrust, and Public Policy,* ed. John Craven. Boston: Kluwer Nijhoff.

————. 1984. "'Contestability' vs. Competition." *American Economic Review* 74: 572–87.

Spence, A. Michael. 1977. "Entry, Capacity, Investment, and Oligopolistic Pricing." *Bell Journal of Economics* 8:534–44.

————. 1983. "Contestable Markets and the Theory of Industry Structure: A Review Article." *Journal of Economic Literature* 21:981–90.

Stigler, George J. 1968. *The Organization of Industry.* Homewood, Ill.: Irwin.

Tye, William B. 1984. "Contestability vs. Competitiion: Comment." Cambridge: Mass. Manuscript.

Weitzman, Martin L. 1983. "Contestable Markets: An Uprising in the Theory of Industry Structure: Comment." *American Economic Review* 73:486–87.

13
Vertical Industry Structure: An Analytical Scheme

Fred M. Westfield

T his chapter presents a novel diagrammatical analysis, using production duality relationships, to compare input-output equilibrium configurations for alternative vertical industry structures. The framework is used to illuminate two problems that have been widely studied. One is vertical integration, the other is rate of return regulation of monopoly. Various other applications suggest themselves.

The Model

The quantity of product sold to final consumers is designated by q. Input quantities required are x and y, and the production function for final product is assumed linear-homogeneous

$$q = f(x, y), \tag{13.1}$$

so that the unit-isoquant is given by

$$1 = f(x/q, y/q) = f(a, b) \tag{13.2}$$

Prices for the inputs are assumed parameters for the purchaser. Consequently, given the price w for x and s for y, cost minimization by producers of the final product, together with the homogeneity assumption, determines input coefficients:

$$a = a(s/w), b = b(s/w), \tag{13.3}$$

as functions of relative input prices.

$$a' \geq 0, b' \leq 0 \tag{13.4}$$

because of convex-to-the-origin isoquants. The equalities of (13.4) hold when increased relative prices of inputs do not alter input coefficients at isoquant corners.

Vertical Integration

Suppose that the input y is an intermediate good that can be produced at constant unit cost. Without vertical integration, the producers of the final product q cannot enter the industry producing y. Instead, they purchase y at price s from a monopolist who produces it at cost r, $s \geq r$. With vertical integration, the cost of y to the combined firm is r. In effect, $s = r$. In either case input x is sold to producers of q at constant price w. This problem has been studied in Westfield (1981) and elsewhere.

Two Market Structures

Consider two alternative market structures. In the nonintegrated case, final product is sold at a *competitive* price p by firms purchasing input x at a competitive marginal cost-price w, and input y at price s, determined by monopoly. This input monopoly sells its entire production to the firms competing in the final product market. The marginal production cost of the intermediate product y is the constant $r \leq s$.

Under these circumstances total profit, φ, for the upstream monopoly is

$$\phi = (s - r)b(s/w)q, \tag{13.5}$$

and unit cost for firms producing final product is
$$c = wa(s/w) + sb(s/w) = c(s,w). \tag{13.6}$$

Given consumer demand

$$q = D(p), D'(p) < 0, \tag{13.7}$$

for final product, we obtain the downstream competitive equilibrium output

$$q = D[c(s,w)] \tag{13.8}$$

Upstream input prices w, s determine downstream competitive product price p and quantity q. Solving (13.8) for s, one obtains

$$s = F(q;w). \tag{13.9}$$

That is, given w, downstream product quantity q specifies price s charged by upstream monopoly.

Accordingly, for this market structure, the input coefficients $a = a(s/w) = a(F(q;w)/w)$, $b = b(s/w) = b(F(q;w)/w)$ are, given w, determined by the competitive market-clearing quantity. Furthermore, we obtain

$$wa[F(q;w)/w] = A(q;w) \qquad (13.10)$$

and

$$F(q;w)b(F(q;w)/w) = B(q;w) \qquad (13.11)$$

such that

$$A(q;w) + B(q;w) = p(q) \qquad (13.12)$$

as the zero-profit condition for competitive equilibrium in the final product market. Here $p(q)$ is the average revenue function—the inverse of $q = D(p)$.

Note that this last equation is an identity. It must hold for every market-clearing quantity q determined by s and, accordingly, p.

To determine which q (and which p and s), we determine q that maximizes upstream monopoly profit (13.5). That is,

$$\max_q \phi = \max_q (F(q;w) - r)b(F(q;w)/w)q \qquad (13.13)$$

$$= \max_q [B(q;w) - rb(F(q;w)/w)]q$$

$$= \max_q \rho(q;w) - \gamma(q;w,r)$$

The first and second order conditions are, respectively,

$$\rho' - \gamma' = 0 \qquad (13.14)$$

$$\rho'' - \gamma'' < 0, \qquad (13.15)$$

where primes represent differentiation with respect to q, and w, r are parameters.

We designate by subscript 1 values of all variables associated with this upstream-monopoly, downstream-competition equilibrium.

The second market structure is integrated monopoly. The integrated firm produces the quantity y at marginal cost r. But price p and quantity q of the final product are determined monopolistically, rather than competitively.

The integrated firm maximizes profit π

$$\max \pi = p(q)q - c(r, w)q \qquad (13.16)$$

$$= R(q) - cq.$$

The first order condition is the familiar marginal revenue–marginal cost equality

$$R'(q) = c(r, w), \qquad (13.17)$$

and the second-order condition is $R''(q) < 0$: marginal revenue with negative slope.

Subscript 2 will designate values of variables corresponding to the integrated monopoly equilibrium.

Diagrammatical Analysis

The two equilibrium configurations can be compared with the help of a diagram. Figure 13–1 consists of four interrelated graphs. Without loss of generality, we set $w = r = 1$ so that the input requirements per unit of final product $a = a(s), b = b(s)$ are expressed in terms of dollars' worth (at prices w, r).

In the northeast quadrant is the unit-cost frontier $c = c(s)$ of downstream product as a function of upstream price s. Immediately below, in the southeast quadrant, is the function $b(s)$ showing the input requirement of y per unit of final downstream product as a function of its price charged by the upstream supplier. From Shepherd's Lemma, we have $dc / ds = b(s)$, so that $b(s)$ is constructed as a curve "marginal" to the "total" curve in the upper quadrant. It is the demand curve, per unit of final product, for input y.

The downward-sloping curve at the top in the northwest quadrant is the demand function for the final product, $D(p)$, or its inverse, the average revenue, $p = p(q)$ for the final product. The dashed $R'(q)$ is the usual marginal revenue function for monopoly. The heavy horizontal lines labeled $c(s)$ are average and marginal cost curves for downstream output. They are horizontal because of assumed constant returns to scale. Their positions are determined by price s charged by the upstream supplier of y and the least unit cost specified by the cost frontier in the northeast quadrant. The position and

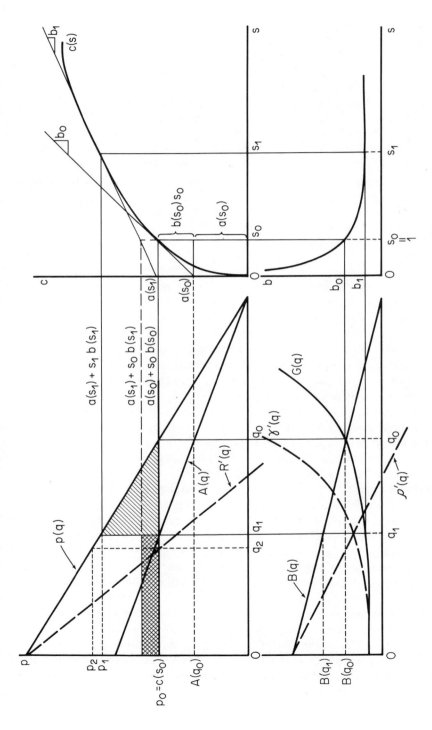

Figure 13–1. Non-Integrated and Integrated Monopoly Equilibria

shape of the frontier, of course, embodies all of the information of the production function (duality).

The curve $A(q)$ in the nortwest quadrant shows the payment A required for the amount of input x needed per unit of final output, if downstream *competitive* equilibrium output is q. For example, consider the output q_0. Under what circumstances is this the competitive equilibrium output? The answer: when the competitive equilibrium price for the final output is p_0. And under what circumstances is the competitive equilibrium price p_0? Answer: when average cost is at the level c_0. And under what circumstances is average cost c_0? The cost frontier shows that this occurs if price for input y is s_0. And s_0 determines $wa(s_0) \geq A(q_0)$, plotted in the northwest quadrant at the output point q_0.

The shape of $A(q)$ is, of course, dictated by properties of the demand and production functions. It is, in fact, given by

$$A(q) = \alpha(q)p(q), \qquad\qquad (13.18)$$

where $\alpha(q)$ is the "relative share" $wa/p = a/p$, paid for x by the competitive downstream industry, producing equilibrium output q at equilibrium prices p and s. $A(q)$ is readily constructed for any demand function in the northwest quadrant and cost frontier (production function) in the northeast quadrant. For any q, say q_0, in the northwest quadrant, determine p_0. For $p_0 = c_0$ one obtains a point s_0, c_0 in the northeast quadrant on the cost frontier. The slope of the tangent $c'(s_0)$ gives $b(s_0)$, and the intercept of the tangent with the c-axis gives the point $c(s_0) - s_0 b(s_0) = a(s_0) = A(q_0)$ in the northwest quadrant on the $A(q)$ curve. In the example sketched in figure 13–1, I have used a linear inverse demand curve $p = p(q)$ and a Cobb-Douglas production function with cost frontier $c = ke^{1-\alpha}$. As relative share α for the Cobb-Douglas is constant, $A(q)$ in this special case becomes the linear function, $\alpha p(q)$, which has been sketched.

Take the vertical difference $p(q) - A(q)$ in the northwest quadrant and obtain $B(q)$ in the southwest quadrant (see equation [13.12]). Note: this curve shows the amount that the downstream industry, selling output q at price p, and paying A per unit of output for input x, will in zero-profit competitive equilibrium pay, per unit of output, for input y. Thus, $B(q)$ is the residual revenue per unit of downstream output, an "average revenue," which the seller of y receives in a competitive downstream equilibrium at alternative prices s.

The corresponding "average cost" curve, in the southwest quadrant, is $G(q) = b(F(q))$. (Remember, $w = r = 1$.) It is constructed as follows: For each q, for example q_0, the amount of input y and its cost to the supplier are given by $c'(s_0) = rb(s_0) = b(s_0)$, the slope of the cost frontier. Thus, the curve marginal to $c(s)$ of the northeast quadrant, that is, its first derivative, gives b in the southeast quadrant on the vertical. Evaluated at s_0, one obtains $b(s_0)$, which, where paired with q_0 in the southwest quadrant gives cost $G(q_0)$, per unit of final output, for the producer of the input y charging s_0.

One may now easily verify that the illustrative output q_0, product price p_0, input prices s_0, where $y_0 = b_0 q_0$, is a very special downstream competitive equilibrium configuration. It is the configuration that results when the upstream price s_0 of y is set at the (constant) marginal and average cost $r = 1$ of y, for which the "average revenue curve" $B(q)$, intersects "average cost curve" $b(F(q)) = G(q)$. Consequently, profit ϕ_0 for the supplier of y, namely $[B(q_0) - G(q_0)]q_0 = 0$. With upstream price s_0 equal to marginal cost $r = 1$ and zero upstream profit, we have the downstream competitive equilibrium configuration that would result if input y were supplied under pure competition.

We now utilize figure 13–1 to determine the equilibrium configuration that results from the maximization of profit ϕ by the supplier of y. Geometrically, upstream total profit ϕ for any competitive downstream equilibrium quantity q is given in the southwest quadrant by the difference in areas of the rectangles $B(q)q = \rho(q)$ and $G(q)q = \gamma(q)$. And this occurs where the dashed "marginal revenue" curve, $\rho'(q)$, associated with the "average revenue" curve $B(q)$, is intersected by the dashed "marginal cost" curve, $\gamma'(q)$, associated with the "average cost" curve $G(q)$, from below. (Compare the first and second order conditions for the maximum, (13.14) and (13.15), given above.) The equilibrium configuration is designated by subscript 1.

Deadweight Loss Analysis

The deadweight losses for various equilibrium positions can be calculated in the northwest quadrant if one accepts the critical assumption that conventional "consumer surplus triangles" can be correctly estimated from the market demand curve $D(p)$. With all other prices in the economy at marginal cost and with the absence of externalities, distorting taxes, and so on, the upstream-downstream competitive equilibrium (subscript 0) is, of course, an equilibrium at which deadweight losses are absence by definition.

The welfare loss from upstream-monopoly, downstream-competition (subscript 1) consists of two parts. First is the loss that would be incurred as a result of a reduction in output from q_0 to q_1 without any alteration in the efficient input proportions that are associated with input marginal cost prices $w = 1, r = 1$. This is also the loss that would result from a specific tax $T_1 = P_1 - P_0$ on downstream product with pure competition in input and output markets. (It is the same welfare loss that would result from integrated monopoly, producing y at marginal cost $r = 1$ and choosing to produce q_1 at price p_1.) For linear demand, the deadweight loss would be

$$\tfrac{1}{2}(q_0 - q_1)(p_1 - p_0). \tag{13.19}$$

For nonlinear demand this is an approximation. The loss is represented by the shaded triangle in the northwest quadrant of figure 13–1. This analysis of course neglects all of the important distributional considerations.

The second part of the deadweight loss stems from inefficient input combination by the downstream industry in response to the input price wedge. If output q_1 is sold at price p_1 by a competitive industry that purchases input y_1 at price $s_1 > r = 1$, set by upstream profit-maximizing monopoly, then the downstream competitive industry determines least-cost input proportions based on price $s_1 > r = 1$, $w = 1$ which will differ from the efficient combinations selected for $s_0 = r = 1$, $w = 1$, provided substitution along an isoquant is feasible and cost effective. A portion of the rectangular area $(p(q_1) - c(s_0))q_1 = \pi_1$ in the northwest quadrant (which for integrated monopoly would represent profit or for a tax would represent transfer payment) is added deadweight loss. This added deadweight loss equals

$$\pi_1 - \phi_1 \equiv \{[c(s_1) - c(s_0)] - [s_1 b(s_1) - s_0 b(s_1)]\} q_1 \tag{13.20}$$

$$\equiv \{[wa(s_1) + s_0 b(s_1)] - [wa(s_0) + s_0 b(s_0)]\} q_1.$$

Here $w = r = s_0 = 1$. This is the shaded rectangle in the northwest quadrant. It is also the difference in the areas

$$[A(q_1) - A(q_0)]q_1 - [B(q_0) - G(q_1)]q_1$$

of rectangles in the northwest and southwest quadrants, respectively.

For integrated monopoly, the equilibrium (subscript 2) is determined in the northwest quadrant by the intersection of marginal revenue $R'(q)$ and $c(s_0)$. This determines p_2, q_2, and so on. The deadweight loss is the triangular area

$$\tfrac{1}{2}(q_0 - q_2)(p_2 - p_0).$$

For this case there are, of course, no added deadweight losses from production inefficiency. The internal price for y is its marginal costs $= r = 1$.

As was shown in Westfield (1981), depending on characteristics of the production function or its cost dual, $c(s)$, $q_1 \gtreqless q_2$. In terms of the diagram, the intersection of ρ' with γ' in the southwest quadrant, which determines q_1, may occur to the right (as in our illustration) of the intersection of R' with $c(s_0)$, which determines q_2, or to its left.

The diagram sketched in figure 13–1 is for a Cobb-Douglas production function and linear demand for final product. As has been proved (1981,

344) and as the geometry confirms, for Cobb-Douglas production functions $q_1 > q_2$.

To allow analysis of the solutions for the general case, we observe that

$$A' = dA/dq = a'F' = a'p'/b.$$

Therefore, the elasticity of $A(q)$ is given

$$dlnq/dlnA = (bwa)/(a'p'q) \tag{13.21}$$

$$= (wa/p)(p/p'q)(b/a')$$

$$= -\alpha Eb/a',$$

where $\alpha = wa/p$ is the relative share of x, and E the price elasticity of demand for final output expressed as a positive number. However, because of cost minimization by downstream firms,

$$a' = b's/w.$$

Thus,

$$dlnq/dlnA = \frac{\alpha E}{(s/w)(b'/b)} = -\alpha E/e, \tag{13.22}$$

where e is the elasticity of output-constant demand for y of the curve $b(s)$ in the southeast quadrant. As $e = \alpha\sigma$, where σ is the elasticity of substitution,

$$dlnq/dlnA = -E/\sigma. \tag{13.23}$$

For each q, the elasticity of $A(q)$ is the ratio of the price elasticity of demand for final product to the elasticity of substitution. (For the Cobb-Douglas production function, $\sigma = 1$, and $p(q)$ and $A(q)$ have, as is shown in figure 13–1, the same elasticity for each q.)

From the identity (13.12)

$$dB(q)/dq = p' - A', \tag{13.24}$$

and setting $\beta = 1 - \alpha$, the relative share for y, we obtain the elasticity of the $B(q)$-curve.

$$dlnq/dlnB = \beta E/(\alpha\sigma - 1). \tag{13.25}$$

Thus $B(q)$ in the southwest quadrant must have positive slope for $\alpha\sigma = e > 1$, with $\rho'(q) > B(q)$. Of course, for Cobb-Douglas $\sigma = 1$; and $dlnq/dlnB = E$, as sketched in figure 13–1.

Similarly, for the function $G(q)$:

$$dlnq/dlnG = \beta E/\alpha\sigma. \tag{13.26}$$

Consequently,

$$\rho'(q) = dqB(q)/dq = B(q)(\alpha\sigma + \beta E - 1)/\beta E \tag{13.27}$$

and

$$\gamma'(q) = dqG(q)/dq = G(q)(\alpha\sigma + \beta E)/\beta E. \tag{13.28}$$

As $\alpha\sigma + \beta E$ will be recognized as the Hicksian price elasticity (Hicks 1968, 244) of derived demand (under conditions of perfectly elastic supply for x and y) for input y sold to a competitive industry, the $\rho' = \gamma'$ condition (13.14) for maximum profit can be interpreted as the marginal cost-marginal revenue equality

$$r = s[1 - 1/(\alpha\sigma + \beta E)] \tag{13.29}$$

for the monopoly producer of y whose marginal cost is r and marginal revenue is the term on the right.

Deadweight loss for nonintegrated monopoly is unambiguously greater than deadweight loss from integrated monopoly when $q_2 > q_1$. This may occur for $0 < \sigma(q_2) < E(q_2)$; that is, for $dlnq/dlnA < -1$, when evaluated at q_2.

The deadweight loss for nonintegrated monopoly and integrated monopoly is equal in the fixed production coefficient case. If $A(q_0) = A(q_2)$ then (as is well known), $q_2 = q_1$, and $dlnq/dlnA = -\infty$. Input monopoly cannot induce downstream substitution among inputs. That is $\pi_2 = \phi_1$, and there is neither private nor social gain from the change in vertical industry structure.

For $\sigma(q_2) > E(q_2)$, that is, for $dlnq/dlnA > -1$, $q_1 > q_2$. In this case, increased deadweight loss from reduced output and higher product price under vertical integration may or may not offset the gain in production efficiency resulting from a partial correction of input proportions. Given the production and demand functions, the analytical framework presented here allows calculation of q_1, p_1 and q_2, p_2 and calculation of deadweight losses associated with each of the equilibria.

Rate of Return Regulation

Now consider input y to be the stock of capital of a regulated monopoly, expressed in dollar's worth. As before, r is the cost of input y, here expressed as an interest rate, and w is the cost of input x. This is the problem first formulated by Averch and Johnson (1962). It has also been used in Westfield [1965).

The regulatory constraint can be written, because of constant returns to scale, as

$$p(q) - wa(\theta/w) - ub(\theta/w) \leq 0,$$

where u is the allowed rate of return determined by the regulatory authority, and θ is the shadow price (interest rate) of capital.

With $R'(q) > 0$ $(E > 1)$, the profit maximum, subject to constraint is given by the solution of

$$p(q) - wa(\theta/w) - ub(\theta/w) = 0. \tag{13.30}$$

$$R'f_y = \theta < r \tag{13.31}$$

$$R'f_x = w, \tag{13.32}$$

where $\theta < r < u$ implies that the regulatory constraint is binding and that $q > 0$.

Because of the assumed linear homogeneous production function (Euler's theorem), one obtains

$$R'(q) = wa(\theta/w) + \theta b(\theta/w) \equiv c(\theta,w). \tag{13.33}$$

Call the output that satisfies these equations q^* and the corresponding product price p^*. They are the Averch-Johnson equilibrium quantity and price. Since

$$R'(q^*) = c(\theta,w) < c(r,w) = p_0 = R'(q_2) < wa(\theta/w) + rb(\theta,w) < p^*, \tag{13.34}$$

where subscript 0 refers to a competitive equilibrium position, and subscript 2 to an unregulated (integrated) monopoly, as in the previous sections of the chapter, we observe the well-known results[1] that $q_0 > q^* > q_2$ and $p_0 < p^* < p_2$.

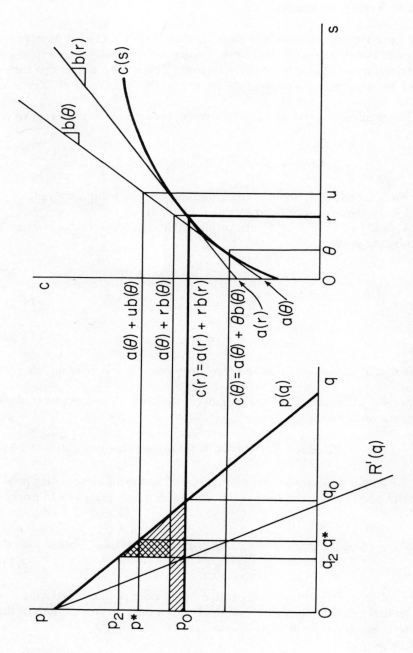

Figure 13–2. Unregulated and Regulated Monopoly Equilibria

Diagrammatical Analysis

In figure 13–2 we again set $w = 1$ without loss of generality.

Unregulated monopoly equilibrium at a market rate of interest r is output q_2 at price p_2. The unit cost frontier in the right panel evaluated at interest rate r, gives marginal cost $c(r)$. Intersection of marginal revenue curve $R'(q)$ with $c(r)$ in the left panel gives q_2. The slope of the unit cost frontier at r gives $b(r)$; the intercept of the tangent at r gives $a(r)$.

Rate of return regulation at the allowed rate $u > r$ leads to a shadow cost of capital $\theta < r$. The unit cost frontier determines $c(\theta)$, and the intersection with $R'(q)$ with $c(\theta)$, equation (13.33), determines q^* and p^* in the left panel. The tangent to the unit cost frontier at θ has slope $b(\theta)$ and interpret $a(\theta)$. Strict concavity of $c(s)$ insures $b(\theta) > b(r)$, $a(\theta) < a(r)$, the A-J effect. The allowed rate of return u that corresponds to shadow price θ for capital is determined by $p^* = a(\theta) + ub(\theta)$, equation (13.30), the equation of the straight line, tangent to the cost frontier at θ, and evaluated at point u, p^* in the right panel. The regulated monopolist's unit costs are given by this tangent line evaluated at r, c^*. Note the wedge $c^* - c_0$ in figure 13–2. This is the excess unit cost induced by $\theta < r < u$ and the resulting excessive use of capital by the regulated firm.

Deadweight loss from regulated monopoly is seen again in the left panel by the shaded areas

$$\tfrac{1}{2}(q_0 - q^*)(p^* - p_0) + q^*(c^* - p_0).$$

This may be compared with deadweight loss from unregulated monopoly

$$\tfrac{1}{2}(q_0 - q_2)(p_2 - p_0).$$

Evidently, rate of return regulation reduces the area of the unregulated monopoly triangle if the allowed rate of return constraint is binding. But as the allowed rate of return u is lowered, shadow price θ falls and the area of the inefficiency rectangle $q^*(c^* - p_0)$ is enlarged as both length and width are increased. Given demand and cost functions, there is clearly a configuration that minimizes deadweight loss from rate of return regulation. (See Klevorick [1971] and Westfield [1971].)

Note

1. The possibility that regulation is counterproductive in the sense $q_0 > q_2 > q^*$, $p_0 < p_2 < p^*$ is ruled out by linear homogeneous production technology that does not allow inferior factors of production. Compare Westfield (1965, 430).

References

Averch, H., and L.L. Johnson. 1962. "Behavior of the Firm Under Regulatory Constraint." *American Economic Review* 52:1052–69.

Hicks, J.R. 1968. *The Theory of Wages*. New York: St. Martin's Press.

Klevorick, A.K. 1971. "The 'Optimal' Fair Rate of Return." *Bell Journal of Economics and Management Science* 2:122–53.

Westfield, F.M. 1965. "Regulation and Conspiracy." *American Economic Review* 55: 424–43.

———. 1971. "Methodology of Evaluating Economic Regulation." *American Economic Review* 61:211–17.

———. 1981. "Vertical Integration: Does Product Price Rise or Fall." *American Economic Review* 71:334–46. (This article lists references to the relevant literature.)

Index

Italic page numbers refer to reference entries.

About the Contributors

Bruce L. Benson, an associate professor of economics at Montana State University, received his Ph.D. from Texas A&M in 1978. He conducts research in regulatory policy analysis, public sector decision making, law and economics, and spatial price theory, publishing in the *American Economic Review, International Journal of Industrial Organization, Journal of Industrial Economics, Journal of Legal Studies,* and *Journal of Urban Economics,* among others.

Richard E. Caves is professor of economics at Harvard University and formerly taught at the University of California, Berkeley. His principal research interests lie in industrial organization, especially in its international and comparative aspects. He is the author of *Multinational Enterprise and Economic Analysis* and *Competition in the Open Economy,* as well as numerous other books and articles.

Donald Dewey is professor of economics at Columbia University. He received his B.A. (1943) at the University of Chicago and his graduate training at Iowa, Cambridge (England), the London School of Economics, and the University of Chicago. He previously taught at Duke University. Researching and publishing predominently in the problems of industrial organization and policy, his works include *Monopoly and the Law* and *The Economics of Imperfect Competition: A Radical Reconstruction.*

Joseph Farrell (born 1954) took his B.A. (1975) and M.Sc. (1976) in mathematics at Oxford University in England. He then studied economics, obtaining the M.Phil. (1979) and D.Phil. (1981) degrees. He was a consultant at Bell Labs and an instructor (1979) and an assistant professor at M.I.T. He is now a senior member of the technical staff at GTE Labs. His research centers on industrial organization and game theory.

Robert C. Goldberg is affiliated with the firm of Schoenberg, Fisher & Newman, Ltd., Chicago, Illinois. He publishes in the areas of trade regulation, distribution channels, contract relations, and complex litigation. He served as an assistant attorney general for the State of Illinois and on the staff of the Federal Trade Commission. He has been chairman of the Illinois Franchise Advisory Board, a member of the Board of the Chicago Chapter of the Federal Bar Association and a member of the American and Chicago Bar Association's Antitrust Committees; and is a member of the Chicago Board of Trade.

Melvin L. Greenhut is Alumni Distinguished Professor of Economics at Texas A&M University. He received his Ph.D. (1951) at Washington University. He is the author of many articles and books. His field of specialization is spatial economics. He has held visiting professorships at the University of Karlsruhe, the University of Cape Town, the University of Mannheim, the University of Pittsburgh, and Michigan State University; he has lectured at the University of Münster, Aoyama Gakuin University (Tokyo), and the Cheng Chi National and Soochow Universities (Taiwan). He previously taught at Florida State and Auburn Universities, among others.

Craig S. Hakkio, a native of Ohio, earned an A.B. from Kenyon College and a Ph.D. (1979) in economics at the University of Chicago. He was formerly an assistant professor of economics at Northwestern University, and a visiting scholar at the Federal Reserve Bank of Kansas City; he is currently a senior economist at the Kansas City Bank. His research and publications are in monetary policy and international macroeconomics.

Austin Kelly is a Ph.D. student in economics at the University of Chicago.

Ronald Krumm is an assistant professor of economics in the Committee on Public Policy Studies and is associate director for research at the Center for Urban Studies at the University of Chicago. He received his Ph.D. in economics in 1981 from the University of Chicago.

Leon N. Moses was born in 1924 in New York City. He graduated from Erasmus Hall High School, 1942. He earned a B.A. with Highest Distinction from Ohio State University in 1947, and a Ph.D. from Harvard University in 1951. He has been professor of economics and management at Northwestern University since 1957. His current research deals with the spatial and temporal decisions of firms and the influence of changes in the regulatory environment on those choices.

Richard F. Muth is Fuller E. Callaway Professor and chairman of the department of economics at Emory University. He received his Ph.D. from the University of Chicago and subsequently taught there in the Graduate School of Business. He has also taught in the departments of economics at Johns Hopkins, Vanderbilt, Washington, and Stanford Universities, and been associated with Resources for the Future and the Institute for Defense Analyses. He has served on presidential task forces on Urban Renewal, Housing, and Urban Affairs, and was a member of the President's Commission on Housing.

Roger G. Noll is professor of economics at Stanford University. He previously taught at the California Institute of Technology, and served on the staffs of the Brookings Institution and the Council of Economic Advisers. He is a former Guggenheim Fellow and Fellow at the Center for Advanced Studies in the Behavioral Sciences, and was a member of the President's Commission for a National Agenda for the Eighties. His most recent books are *The Political Economy of Deregulation,* with coauthor Bruce Owen, and *Regulatory Policy and the Social Sciences,* for which he was a contributor and editor.

Janusz A. Ordover received his doctoral degree from Columbia University. He is now professor and director of graduate studies in the economics department at New York University and an adjunct professor of law at Columbia University Law School. His research and publications have concentrated on the economics of antitrust law and policy. He has served as a consultant to the Federal Trade Commission, American Bar Association, and law firms and corporations. His current research interests center on antitrust and industrial policy in open economies and on the linkages between firm structure and economic welfare.

Robert S. Pindyck received the Ph.D. in economics from M.I.T. in 1971, and is now professor of applied economics in the Sloan School of Management at M.I.T. His areas of research and journal publication in microeconomics and in industrial organization have included natural resources, energy, and regulatory and antitrust policy. He is also the author of *Optimal Planning for Economic Stabilization* and *The Structure of World Energy Demand;* coauthor of *The Economics of the Natural Gas Shortage: 1960–1980, Price Controls and the Natural Gas Shortage,* and *Econometric Models and Economic Forecasts;* and editor of *Advances in the Economics of Energy and Resources.*

William G. Shepherd is professor of economics at the University of Michigan, and is visiting professor of economics, University of Massachusetts, during 1984–85. His Ph.D. is from Yale University, 1963. He is author of *The Economics of Industrial Organization, The Treatment of Market Power, Market Power and Economic Welfare, Public Policies Toward Business, Economics,* and other books and articles on industrial economics. His research covers basic concepts and empirical relationships in the nature of competition, market power, scale economies, efficiency, antitrust, regulation, and public enterprise.

Nirvikar Singh is an assistant professor of economics at the University of California, Santa Cruz. He received his B.S. and M.S. at the London School of Economics, and his Ph.D. at the University of California, Berkeley. The areas of his research and publications include the economics of information and incentives, the strategic behavior of firms, regulation, and public economics.

George S. Tolley is professor of economics at the University of Chicago. He received the B.A. from American University in 1947 and the Ph.D. from the University of Chicago in 1955. He is director of the Center for Urban Studies at the University of Chicago and served as deputy assistant secretary and director of the Office of Tax Analysis of the United States Department of the Treasury.

Fred M. Westfield is professor of economics at Vanderbilt University. He holds a Ph.D. from M.I.T. His research and publications are in microeconomic theory and its applications. As an expert on the economics of public utilities, he has served as consultant to various governmental agencies here and abroad. He has held a Ford Foundation Faculty Fellowship, has been a vice president of the Southern Economic Association, and has served on the editorial board of the *Southern Economic Journal.*

Robert D. Willig is professor of economics and public affairs at Princeton University, and was formerly supervisor in the Economics Research Department of Bell Laboratories. He received his Ph.D. in economics from Stanford University in 1973. He has written, lectured, and consulted on the subjects of industrial organization, the government regulation of business, public interest pricing, and normative microeconomics. He is a former editor of the *American Economic Review,* a fellow of the Econometric Society, a member of the Research Advisory Council of the American Enterprise Institute, an editor of the *Journal of Industrial Economics,* and coeditor of the *Handbook of Industrial Organization.*

About the Editor

Ronald E. Grieson is professor of economics at the University of California, Santa Cruz. Previously he taught in the Departments of Economics at M.I.T., Columbia University, and Princeton University, after receiving the Ph.D. at the University of Rochester (1972). His research and publications are in various areas of applied microeconomics. His previous books include *Public and Urban Economics* and *The Urban Economy and Housing*. He was the director of the M.I.T. Special Program in Public and Urban Economics and currently serves as an editor of the *Journal of Urban Economics*.